Founding a Global Human Rights Culture for Trade Marks

ELGAR INTELLECTUAL PROPERTY AND GLOBAL DEVELOPMENT

Series Editor: Peter K. Yu, *Professor of Law and Co-Director of the Center for Law and Intellectual Property at Texas A&M University School of Law, USA.*

Rapid global economic integration and the increasing importance of technology and information goods have created the need for a broader, deeper and more critical understanding of intellectual property laws and policies. This uniquely designed book series provides an interdisciplinary forum for advancing the debate on the global intellectual property system and related issues that intersect with transnational politics, international governance, and global economic, social, cultural and technological development. The series features the works of established experts and emerging voices in the academy as well as those practising on the front lines. The series' high-quality, informed and accessible volumes include a wide range of materials such as historical narratives, theoretical explanations, substantive discussions, critical evaluations, empirical analyses, comparative studies, and formulations of practical solutions and best practices. The series will appeal to academics, policy makers, judges, practitioners, transnational lawyers and civil society groups as well as students of law, politics, culture, political economy, international relations and development studies.

Titles in the series include:

Intellectual Property and Sustainable Markets
Edited by Ole-Andreas Rognstad and Inger B. Ørstavik

The Interface Between Intellectual Property and Investment Law
An Intertextual Analysis
Emmanuel Kolawole Oke

Climate Change, Sustainable Development and Cleantech
A Pathway for Developing Countries
Joy Y. Xiang

Intellectual Property Objectives in International Investment Agreements
Pratyush Nath Upreti

Intellectual Property Law in South East Asia
Edited by Christoph Antons and Michael Blakeney

Founding a Global Human Rights Culture for Trade Marks
Genevieve Wilkinson

Founding a Global Human Rights Culture for Trade Marks

Genevieve Wilkinson

Senior Lecturer, Faculty of Law, University of Technology Sydney, Australia

ELGAR INTELLECTUAL PROPERTY AND GLOBAL DEVELOPMENT

Edward Elgar
PUBLISHING

Cheltenham, UK • Northampton, MA, USA

Published by
Edward Elgar Publishing Limited
The Lypiatts
15 Lansdown Road
Cheltenham
Glos GL50 2JA
UK

Edward Elgar Publishing, Inc.
William Pratt House
9 Dewey Court
Northampton
Massachusetts 01060
USA

A catalogue record for this book
is available from the British Library

Library of Congress Control Number: 2023939690

This book is available electronically in the **Elgar**online
Law subject collection
http://dx.doi.org/10.4337/9781800889804

ISBN 978 1 80088 979 8 (cased)
ISBN 978 1 80088 980 4 (eBook)

For the centres of my universe, Ben, Bridget and Amelie.

Contents

Abbreviations

AAAQ	Availability, Accessibility, Acceptability and Quality
ACA	Anti-Counterfeit Act (Kenya)
ACR	Anti-Counterfeit Regulations (Kenya)
ACTA	Anti-Counterfeiting Trade Agreement
AHRC	Australian Human Rights Commission
CERD	Convention for the Elimination of All Forms of Racial Discrimination
CESCR	Committee on Economic, Social and Cultural Rights
COMRC	Committee on the Rights of the Child
COP	Conference of Parties
CPTPP	Comprehensive and Progressive Trans-Pacific Partnership
DSU	Dispute Settlement Understanding
EAC	East African Community
ECHR	European Court of Human Rights
ECJ	European Court of Justice
ECR	European Union Charter of Fundamental Rights
EFTA	European Free Trade Association
EUIPO	European Union Intellectual Property Office
FCGP	Framework Convention on Goods Provenance
FCTC	Framework Convention on Tobacco Control
HRATM	Human Rights Assessment for Trade Marks
HRC	Human Rights Committee
ICCPR	International Covenant on Civil and Political Rights
ICESCR	International Covenant on Economic, Social and Cultural Rights
PPE	Personal Protective Equipment
SSFM	Substandard and Falsified Medicines
SUT	Uruguayan Tobacco Control Society

TBT	WTO Agreement on Technical Barriers to Trade
TGA	Therapeutic Goods Administration
TRIPS	Agreement on Trade-Related Aspects of Intellectual Property
UDHR	Universal Declaration of Human Rights
UN	United Nations
UNODC	United Nations Office on Drugs and Crime
USPTO	United States Patent and Trade Mark Office
VCLT	Vienna Convention on the Law of Treaties
WCO	World Customs Organization
WHO	World Health Organization
WIPO	World Intellectual Property Organization
WTO	World Trade Organization

Acknowledgements

I am extremely grateful for the generous help and insightful feedback on draft chapters of this book from Evana Wright, Harry Hobbs, Lisa Ramsey, Gbenga Olatunji and Vicki Huang.

This book has been strengthened by thoughtful and constructive comments on earlier research from Sam Ricketson and Peter Yu, and my mentors during this research, Natalie Stoianoff, Beth Goldblatt and Jill McKeough. I'm very appreciative of the wonderful support from UTS colleagues during the research and writing of this book, including David Lindsay, Anita Stuhmcke, Tracey Booth and Isabella Alexander.

Several people have been integral to finishing this project and I owe many thanks to Olivia Rawlings-Way, Marg Barlow, Elaine Wylie and Harry Hobbs. Evana Wright, you have been part of this project since its inception in 2015 and I could not have reached DA status without you, nor chosen a better support on this journey.

I am incredibly blessed by amazing family and friends who love me, support me and believe in me. Without my brilliant medical parents, I may not have recognised the importance of this project, and without inspiration from my amazing nan, I don't think I would have had the tenacity to finish this book. Thank you friends and family for supporting me. I am very grateful for all of the strong women and men in my life.

The biggest support has been from my beautiful Ben, Bridget and Amelie. Thank you for your patience and love.

PART I

EXISTING CONCEPTIONS OF TRADE MARKS AND HUMAN RIGHTS AND A FRAMEWORK FOR CHANGE

1 The need for increased awareness of human rights implications for trade marks

1 INTRODUCTION

Human rights norms matter for trade mark law. As a form of commercial expression that communicates information about a product, granting trade mark protection can restrict freedom of expression to protect the rights of trade mark owners and consumers. Yet, too often, trade mark law focuses on owner rights and fails to recognise the impact of trade mark protection on human rights. The three case studies in this book demonstrate the impact of trade marks on diverse human rights, expanding analysis beyond the usual focus on the relationship between trade marks and freedom of expression and providing guidance for states to realise human rights obligations. Trade mark laws that are consistent with human rights principles can function to protect human rights to health and life. Ignoring human rights norms in trade mark law can restrict freedom of expression, limit rights to cultural participation and facilitate hate speech. Recent interpretations of the *Agreement on Trade-Related Aspects of Intellectual Property* ('*TRIPS*') by the World Trade Organization ('WTO') Dispute Settlement Bodies present promising opportunities for states to recognise societal interests that are consistent with human rights obligations when they implement multilateral intellectual property agreements into domestic law.[1] However, states are still not obliged by international intellectual property agreements to ensure that trade mark laws are consistent with human rights, despite independent legal and normative obligations to do so.

---

[1] See Panel Report, Australia – Certain Measures Concerning Trademarks, Geographical Indications and Other Plain Packaging Requirements Applicable to Tobacco Products and Packaging, WTO Doc WT/DS435/R, WT/DS441/R, WT/DS458/R, WT/DS467/R (28 June 2018) [7.2406], [7.2588] ('Australia – Tobacco Plain Packaging'). See also Panel Report, Turkey – Certain Measures Concerning the Production, Importation and Marketing of Pharmaceutical Products, WT/DS583/12 (28 April 2022) (affirmed in Turkey – Pharmaceutical Products, WTO Doc WT/DS583/ARB25 (25 July 2022) (Award of the Arbitrators)) ('Turkey – Pharmaceutical Products').

Meanwhile, ensuring compliance is increasingly difficult. Trade marks benefit social welfare by functioning to identify goods and reduce consumer search costs. These benefits are less certain as illicit trade increases, sophisticated reproductions of counterfeit goods proliferate, and substandard goods bearing false trade marks pose threats to human rights to life and health.

Part I of this book explores the existing relationship between trade marks and human rights in international law and theoretical conceptualisations of this relationship. It proposes an analytical framework that will support a human rights culture for trade marks focused on comprehensive and integrated protection of all human rights using a rights-based approach. This introductory chapter identifies systemic fragmentation between the fields of intellectual property law and human rights law. It explores the doctrinal and normative reasons justifying increased consideration of the human rights implications of trade mark law. Enforcement mechanisms that support international agreements underpinning protection for intellectual property rights include provisions that are stronger than the consensus-based approach used by human rights institutions. A concern of this book is that the international legal order is moving towards an emphasis on order, associated with intellectual property agreements, and away from concerns of justice, associated with human rights protection.[2] This encourages a trend towards primacy of intellectual property law over human rights law, which is not justified by normative considerations of justice. Consequently, a more positive culture to support and promote human rights in trade mark law is needed.

Creating a positive human rights culture requires appropriate analytical tools for identifying existing and potential conflicts between intellectual property obligations and human rights. Such analysis forms part of a more comprehensive roadmap for promoting and fostering human rights culture in trade mark law. Chapter 2 of this book explores how existing scholarship on the relationship between human rights and intellectual property recognises that trade mark laws engage human rights, and it develops a Human Rights Assessment for Trade Marks ('HRATM') framework, drawing on the development of human rights frameworks for public health. Existing conceptual models of intellectual property and human rights stop short of holistic and effective protection. Laurence Helfer and Graeme Austin's proposed model recognises the ultimate importance of human rights protection in intellectual property regulation but only recommends limited protection for economic, social and cultural rights.[3]

---

2 Samuel Murumba, 'Foxes and Hedgehogs at the Intersection of Human Rights and Intellectual Property' (2012) 38(1) *Monash University Law Review* 119, 134.

3 Laurence R Helfer and Graeme Austin (eds), *Human Rights and Intellectual Property: Mapping the Global Interface* (Cambridge University Press, 2011) 517.

Christophe Geiger recommends broader protection for some economic, social and cultural rights but does not address limitations in protection for other rights, such as the right to health, in the European fundamental rights system.[4] Peter Yu acknowledges the importance of economic, social and cultural rights and progressive realisation but does not apply this approach to concrete examples of domestic intellectual property law.[5] Nonetheless, analytical approaches from existing scholarship are a valuable part of a human rights culture for trade marks, assisting states to assess the human rights compatibility of trade mark laws, depending on the local conditions in that state.

Applying the HRATM framework to three case studies in Part II of the book improves our understanding of the relationship between trade marks and human rights and the way local conditions in different jurisdictions can influence this relationship. The framework guides comprehensive analysis of the relationship between trade marks and the full breadth of internationally recognised human rights – civil, political, economic, social and cultural rights. Existing literature often focuses on the right to freedom of expression.[6] Even in this area of scholarship, the appropriate relationship between trade marks and freedom of expression remains contested. Comparing recent American and European decisions reveals significant differences in the protection of freedom of expression in relation to registration of contrary trade marks that have implications for prohibitions on hate speech and the human right to participate in culture. However, there is little consideration of the way that internationally significant trade mark issues – including tobacco plain packaging, contrary marks and anti-counterfeiting – engage complex human rights considerations, including rights to health, a fair trial, cultural participation, and moral and material interests for authors. A human rights analysis of these issues demonstrates that it is critically important to found a human rights culture for trade marks and advocate for greater awareness of those issues amongst policymakers so that they can comply with their human rights obligations.

The plain packaging case study analyses the human rights implications of restrictions on the exercise of trade mark rights on tobacco packaging in Australia. Although the human rights impact of restricting the use of trade

---

[4] Christophe Geiger, 'Implementing Intellectual Property Provisions in Human Rights Instruments: Towards a New Social Contract for the Protection of Intangibles' in Christophe Geiger (ed), *Research Handbook on Human Rights and Intellectual Property* (Edward Elgar Publishing, 2015) 661.

[5] Peter K Yu, 'Reconceptualizing Intellectual Property Interests in a Human Rights Framework' (2006) 40(3) *University of California Davis Law Review* 1039. See also Peter K Yu, 'The Anatomy of the Human Rights Framework for Intellectual Property' (2016) 69(1) *SMU Law Review* 37.

[6] See, for example, Helfer and Austin (n 3).

marks on packaging is beneficial, the disputes surrounding Australian plain packaging legislation and comparator legislation in Uruguay show that important human rights implications of plain packaging remain underexplored. This is particularly significant because these disputes chilled introduction of plain packaging legislation in other countries, delaying the human rights benefits of restricting the advertising function of tobacco trade marks. However, the disputes also suggest promising opportunities for greater systemic integration between intellectual property and human rights, which will be aided by the use of the HRATM framework.

The contrary marks case study identifies human rights concerns following two United States Supreme Court decisions that suspended the power of the United States Patent and Trademark Office to refuse registration of disparaging, scandalous and offensive marks.[7] Although these decisions were justified by reference to the applicants' free speech rights, the cultural significance of these marks means that their registration can unnecessarily impair freedom of expression rights of third parties who may wish to use them, restricting their right to participate in culture. Perceptions that trade mark registration suggests government endorsement of the use of these marks can also impact human rights to effective protection from discrimination and hate speech. The comparator European legislation regarding contrary marks recognises human rights differently, consistent with international intellectual property standards.[8] This indicates that, although it reflects the local approach to human rights implementation, the United States approach is problematic for a human rights culture and attempts to use bilateral and plurilateral mechanisms to require other states to implement it need to be discouraged.

The anti-counterfeiting case study also identifies serious human rights concerns posed by counterfeit medical products in Kenya and Sub-Saharan Africa during the Covid-19 pandemic. Although Kenyan legislation largely reflects *TRIPS* minimum standards for enforcement and enshrines further *TRIPS*-plus standards,[9] the case study suggests that widespread distribution of counterfeit goods in Kenya poses serious concerns for protection of the right to health and life, as these goods are more likely to be of substandard quality. The resource-intensive nature of effective cross-border trade mark enforcement, as well as the increasing sophistication of product imitations, seriously impair detection and deterrence of counterfeit goods. The Australian comparator sug-

---

[7] *Matal v Tam*, 137 S Ct 1744, 1747 (2017); *Iancu v Brunetti,* 139 S Ct 2294, 2297 (2019).

[8] Directive (EU) 2015/2436 of the European Parliament and of the Council of 16 December 2015 to Approximate the Laws of the Member States relating to Trade Marks [2015] OJ L 336/1.

[9] *Anti-Counterfeit Act* No 13 of 2008 (Kenya).

gests that this problem is not limited to less economically developed countries. Moreover, economically developed countries have specific human rights obligations to address problems through international assistance and cooperation.

This book uses the case studies of tobacco plain packaging, contrary marks and anti-counterfeiting measures to explore the human rights implications of the exercise, registration and enforcement of trade mark rights. Each primary case study is accompanied by a comparison of regulation of the subject matter in another jurisdiction. Comparison highlights the impact of differences in local conditions, such as mechanisms for domestic recognition of human rights and economic conditions, on the protection of human rights. Specific local conditions influence the application of models designed to harmonise the relationship between human rights and intellectual property protection. Together, the case studies establish that diverse human rights concerns can be engaged by the exercise, registration and enforcement of trade marks, often influenced by the scope of protection available to trade mark owners. The case studies also provide insight into ways to monitor and address fundamental human rights obligations in international law. The resulting lessons are often relevant across diverse jurisdictions, indicating that multilateral reform is needed. For example, Chapter 6 of the book argues that the threats to the right to health identified in the anti-counterfeiting case study necessitate changes to the entire multilateral system.

The HRATM framework also supports rights-based reform to address the serious threats to human rights protection that currently exist due to the gap between human rights and intellectual property obligations in trade mark enforcement worldwide. Part III of the book uses the findings from the case studies to propose an alternative approach to trade mark enforcement that harnesses the value of technology and rights-based principles, including international cooperation, through a Framework Convention for Goods Provenance ('FCGP'). It identifies a series of approaches that are useful for understanding the relationship between trade marks and human rights and can guide the establishment of a human rights culture for trade marks. Methods proposed for ensuring that the operation of trade mark law is consistent with human rights recognise as fully as possible the functions of intellectual property that are consistent with human rights. This recognition permits intellectual property to contribute to broader social welfare objectives that are consistent with the realisation of economic, social and cultural rights.

A human rights culture for trade marks enables states to ensure that trade mark protection regimes function consistently with international obligations to respect, protect and fulfil human rights. A human rights culture for trade marks supports the protection of trade mark rights in a manner that is consistent with human rights obligations. Human rights culture can surround, underpin or influence the development of trade marks protection. Resulting changes may not be appealing for all stakeholders: in many states, reform to existing institutions is required to ensure that trade marks are consistent with human rights.[10] There are complex human rights issues engaged by trade marks, but systematic analysis permits these issues to be understood and balanced against each other so that states can comply with their human rights obligations while implementing multilateral intellectual property standards.

The next section of this chapter introduces important features of the fragmented fields of human rights law and international intellectual property law. The third section explains the normative significance of ensuring that primacy is not given to trade mark obligations over human rights obligations.

2 FRAGMENTATION BETWEEN INTELLECTUAL PROPERTY AND HUMAN RIGHTS

Differences between the fields of intellectual property and human rights strongly influence the legal relationship between human rights and intellectual property. Separation between different fields of international law has resulted in fragmentation: an international legal system that is not cohesive.[11] A lack of cohesion is apparent in the failure to address and recognise relevant human rights in international intellectual property agreements. This can make it difficult for states to balance different obligations in international law.

The broader international context cannot be ignored in attempting to develop a human rights culture for trade marks. Increasingly, the world is recognising the critical impact that intellectual property can play in human rights protection, particularly the right to health. Adjustments to the *TRIPS* agreement following the *Doha Declaration on Public Health*,[12] which responded to the impact of intellectual property on access to medicines in the HIV/AIDS pandemic, have not created a system that can respond quickly to urgent health crises, where intellectual property-protected pharmaceuticals and diagnostic

---

[10] Zehra F Kabasakal Arat, 'Forging A Global Culture of Human Rights: Origins and Prospects of the International Bill of Rights' (2006) 28(2) *Human Rights Quarterly* 416, 424.

[11] See International Law Commission, Fragmentation of International Law: Difficulties Arising from the Diversification and Expansion of International Law. Report of the Study Group of the International Law Commission, Finalized by the Chairman, Martti Koskenniemi, UN GAOR, 58th sess, UN Doc A/CN.4/L.682, A/CN.4/L.682/Add.1, A/CN.4/L.682/Corr.1 (13 April 2006) ('ILC Study Group Report').

[12] *Doha Declaration on the TRIPS Agreement and Public Health*, WTO Doc WT/MIN(01)/DEC/2 (20 November 2001, adopted 14 November 2001) (Ministerial Declaration).

tools are necessary for effective responses.[13] The limited waiver for patent protection for Covid-19 vaccines in 2022 only came after lengthy negotiations, deferring a further decision on protection for diagnostics and therapeutics.[14] The narrow waiver fails to recognise the integrated nature of intellectual property. Even where the information needed to work an invention is contained in a patent, new technology can require know-how that is protected separately as a trade secret.[15] Critical technology transfer that could lessen the impact of this has not occurred.[16] Trade marks are also relevant: access to medicine is negatively impacted if trade marks do not function effectively to prevent dissemination of substandard counterfeit goods.[17]

This book explores cases where fragmentation impacts the development and operation of domestic trade mark legislation. The recent WTO decision in *Australia – Tobacco Plain Packaging*, analysed in the plain packaging case study in Chapter 3, suggests that international intellectual property agreements could be interpreted so that intellectual property and human rights coexist in domestic law.[18] However, there is still no clear roadmap for reconciling competing interests between the two bodies of law and their governing institutions. The institutions that drive the development and enforcement of the two fields are distinct and the approach that they take differs considerably.

2.1 Intellectual Property Institutions and Enforcement

TRIPS entrenched intellectual property into the international trade regime overseen by the WTO.[19] *TRIPS* has subsequently become the focus of international intellectual property law standard-setting and enforcement.[20] The WTO dispute settlement mechanism is structured so that parties in breach may be

---

[13] See Siva Thambisetti et al, 'Addressing Vaccine Inequity During the Covid-19 Pandemic: The TRIPS Intellectual Property Waiver Proposal and Beyond' (2022) 81(2) *Cambridge Law Journal* 384.

[14] *TRIPS Non-Violation And Situation Complaints*, WTO Docs WT/MIN(22)/26 and WT/L/1137 (22 June 2022, adopted on 17 June 2022) (Ministerial Decision).

[15] Thambisetti et al (n 13) 398–399.

[16] Ibid 385–388.

[17] Cf Duncan Matthews, 'Counterfeiting and Public Health' in Christophe Geiger (ed), *Criminal Enforcement of Intellectual Property: A Handbook of Contemporary Research* (Edward Elgar Publishing, 2011) 42.

[18] See Australia – Tobacco Plain Packaging (n 1).

[19] Marrakesh Agreement Establishing the World Trade Organization, opened for signature 15 April 1994, 1867 UNTS 3 (entered into force 1 January 1995) annex 1C ('Agreement on Trade-Related Aspects of Intellectual Property Rights') ('TRIPS').

[20] Christophe Geiger and Luc Desaunettes-Barbero, 'The Revitalisation of the Object and Purpose of the TRIPS Agreement: The *Plain Packaging Reports* and the Awakening of the TRIPS Flexibility Clauses' in Jonathan Griffiths and Tuomas Mylly

subject to economic sanction and these have been applied in some disputes.[21] The multilateral trade mark standards agreed by parties to the *Paris Convention for the Protection of Industrial Property* ('*Paris Convention*')[22] have been incorporated into *TRIPS* and the agreement has expanded certain rights for trade mark owners, including rights for owners of well-known marks.[23] It has also created a system of cross-border enforcement, which requires states to provide mechanisms for detection and enforcement of trade mark owner rights in relation to imported goods bearing counterfeit trade marks.[24]

The WTO is the most important multilateral institution driving the development of international intellectual property norms. Within the WTO, the TRIPS Council oversees *TRIPS* and is composed of representatives of all WTO Member States. It addresses important issues raised by states regarding implementation of the agreements and it can amend *TRIPS* through agreement. The World Intellectual Property Organization ('WIPO') remains important as the institution responsible for intellectual property in the United Nations ('UN') system.[25] WIPO continues to administer the longest-standing international agreement addressing trade marks, the *Paris Convention*, and other international agreements concerning trade mark law. WIPO does not have a permanent observer role on the TRIPS Council, but the two bodies cooperate on some activities. There is limited direct engagement between the TRIPS Council and human rights institutions.[26]

The key *TRIPS* provisions about the protection of trade mark rights are those specified in Part II, Section 2 of *TRIPS* in relation to trade marks, and in Part III relating to enforcement. *TRIPS* incorporated *Paris Convention* standards and further developed substantive trade mark standards.[27] Key obligations

---

(eds), *Global Intellectual Property Protection and New Constitutionalism: Hedging Exclusive Rights* (Oxford University Press, 2021) 267.

21 Matthew Kennedy, *WTO Dispute Settlement and the TRIPS Agreement* (Cambridge University Press, 2016) 298–300.

22 *Paris Convention for the Protection of Industrial Property*, opened for signature 20 March 1883, 828 UNTS 305 (entered into force 6 July 1884, revised at Stockholm 14 July 1967, amended 28 September 1979).

23 *TRIPS* (n 19) pt II.

24 Ibid pt III.

25 Ibid art 2; Daniel J Gervais, *The TRIPS Agreement: Drafting History and Analysis* (Sweet & Maxwell, 4th ed, 2012) 10–11, 187–188.

26 See Klaus D Beiter, 'Establishing Conformity Between TRIPS and Human Rights: Hierarchy in International Law, Human Rights Obligations of the WTO and Extraterritorial State Obligations Under the International Covenant on Economic, Social and Cultural Rights' in Hanns Ullrich et al (eds), *TRIPS Plus 20: From Trade Rules to Market Principles* (Springer, 2016) 445.

27 *TRIPS* (n 19) art 2(1). The *Agreement* also incorporated the relevant provisions of the *Paris Convention*.

that extended *Paris Convention* protection included expansion of the definition of a trade mark;[28] the introduction of the presumption of registrability;[29] protection for well-known service marks; and protection for distinctiveness acquired through use.[30] Requirements that Member States provide mechanisms to address counterfeiting confer additional cross-border protection for trade marks and copyright owners.[31] The anti-counterfeiting protection regime provides rights that strongly benefit owners of trade marks who engage in international trade.[32] Prevention of counterfeit activities focuses on border control and the provisions of *TRIPS* establish mechanisms to effect this.[33] Part III of *TRIPS* addresses general obligations for enforcement procedures in Section 1[34] and specific requirements in Section 2.[35] Specific requirements include that civil judicial procedures be fair and equitable;[36] and that Member States provide judicial authority to make orders regarding production of evidence,[37] injunctions,[38] compensatory damages and indemnification of legal fees,[39] as well as other remedies to deter infringement.[40] There are further special requirements related to border measures regarding the importation of counterfeit trade marks or pirated copyright goods that permit seizure of these goods in certain circumstances.[41] Article 1.1 retains some provision for WTO Members to determine appropriate implementation methods.[42] It can permit flexibility within the scope of the prescribed standards.[43] Flexibility is relevant to the ability of

---

[28] Sam Ricketson, The Paris Convention for the Protection of Industrial Property: A Commentary (Oxford University Press, 2015) 645.

[29] Working Party to Review the Trade Marks Legislation, *Recommended Changes to the Australian Trade Marks Legislation* (Australian Government Publishing Service, 1992) 41–42.

[30] Christopher J Arup, 'The Prospective GATT Agreement for Intellectual Property Protection' (1993) 4 *Australian Intellectual Property Journal* 181, 189–191.

[31] *TRIPS* (n 19) pt III.

[32] Peter K Yu, 'The Comparative Economics of International Intellectual Property Agreements' in Theodore Eisenberg and Giovanni B Ramello (eds), *Comparative Law and Economics* (Edward Elgar Publishing, 2016) 282, 282–283.

[33] *TRIPS* (n 19) pt III.

[34] Ibid art 41.

[35] Ibid art 49 extends the principles of section 2 to cases where a civil remedy is ordered as a result of administrative procedures on the merits of a case.

[36] Ibid art 42.

[37] Ibid art 43.

[38] Ibid art 44.

[39] Ibid art 45.

[40] Ibid art 46.

[41] Ibid pt III s 4.

[42] Ibid art 1(1).

[43] Kennedy (n 21) 123.

states to exercise domestic regulatory autonomy consistent with the object and purpose of the agreement found in Articles 7 and 8.

Enforcement of *TRIPS* is governed by the *WTO Dispute Settlement Understanding* ('*DSU*').[44] The *DSU* provides a range of remedies in cases where a party successfully complains that another party is non-compliant with *TRIPS*, including retaliatory trade sanctions.[45] However, only a small number of proceedings that interpret *TRIPS* have been finally decided by Dispute Settlement Bodies applying the *DSU*.[46] A number of other disputes have been initiated but resolved through negotiation.[47] This small number of decisions means guidance for the implementation of *TRIPS* is limited for WTO Member States.[48] This can contribute to a chilling regulatory environment where states are unwilling to test whether policy can be shaped to use the flexibility mechanisms of *TRIPS* to privilege justifiable domestic interests.[49] States may either be unable or unwilling to legislate in a manner that uses *TRIPS* flexibility mechanisms or emphasises national interests. This may limit the willingness of states to use *TRIPS* flexibility mechanisms to meet their human rights obligations. However, the recent *Australia – Tobacco Plain Packaging* decision indicates that the flexibility mechanisms embedded into *TRIPS* can support restrictions on intellectual property rights.

2.2 Human Rights Institutions and Enforcement

As human rights derive from 'the dignity and worth inherent in the human person', the human person is the central subject and principal beneficiary of human rights.[50] Human rights are universal, inalienable and indivisible. The *Charter of the United Nations* ('*UN Charter*') establishes that states have

---

[44] *Marrakesh Agreement Establishing the World Trade Organization*, opened for signature 15 April 1994, 1867 UNTS 3 (entered into force 1 January 1995) annex 2 ('*DSU*').

[45] See Kennedy (n 21) 4–8, 28.

[46] Peter K Yu, 'TRIPS and its Achilles Heel' (2011) 18(2) *Journal of Intellectual Property Law* 479, 508–511.

[47] See Kennedy (n 21), xxxiv–xxxvi.

[48] Antony Taubman, 'Australia's Interests under TRIPS Dispute Settlement: Trade Negotiations by Other Means, Multilateral Defense of Domestic Policy Choice, or Safeguarding Market Access' (2008) 9(1) *Melbourne Journal of International Law* 217, 234.

[49] See Lukasz Gruszczynski, 'Australian Plain Packaging Law, International Litigation and Regulatory Chilling Effect' (2014) 5(2) *European Journal of Risk Regulation* 242.

[50] Vienna Declaration and Programme of Action: Adopted by the World Conference on Human Rights, UN GAOR, UN Doc A/CONF.157/23 (25 June 1993) Preamble para 2 ('Vienna').

obligations to recognise and protect human rights and should cooperate and assist in the global realisation of human rights.[51] Subsequently, states have established key human rights treaties that define the scope of human rights protection and guide our understanding of individual human rights entitlements. This book uses human rights standards found in key human rights instruments, particularly the *Universal Declaration of Human Rights* ('*UDHR*'),[52] the *International Covenant on Civil and Political Rights* ('*ICCPR*'),[53] the *International Covenant on Economic, Social and Cultural Rights* ('*ICESCR*')[54] and the *Convention on the Rights of the Child* ('*CRC*').[55]

Within the UN, human rights issues are the focus of UN charter-based bodies such as the Human Rights Council, which monitors human rights issues and state compliance with human rights, and treaty-making bodies, which implement specific human rights treaties, such as *ICESCR*, by monitoring compliance and guiding implementation of state parties.[56] Human rights treaties are often interpreted by treaty-making bodies of appointed experts in general comments regarding the interpretation of each treaty following consultation.[57] This permits dynamic interpretation of the law as comments can be reissued.

Human rights law is often described as lacking teeth.[58] Although all UN Members are bound by the *UN Charter* and the *UDHR* can be characterised as an authoritative interpretation of the references to human rights, not all UN Members belong to all human rights treaties that transform the *UDHR* into binding and enforceable obligations. States that are parties may also make reservations when they sign the treaty. The nature of enforcement mechanisms available for implementation of human rights is criticised as contributing to widespread failure to implement many human rights.[59] This perception of

---

[51] Charter of the United Nations arts 55, 56.

[52] *Universal Declaration of Human Rights*, GA Res 217A (III), UN GAOR, UN Doc A/810 (10 December 1948) ('*UDHR*').

[53] *International Covenant on Civil and Political Rights*, opened for signature 16 December 1966, 999 UNTS 171 (entered into force 23 March 1976) ('*ICCPR*').

[54] *International Covenant on Economic, Social and Cultural Rights*, opened for signature 16 December 1966, 993 UNTS 3 (entered into force 3 January 1976) ('*ICESCR*').

[55] *Convention on the Rights of the Child*, opened for signature 20 November 1989, 1577 UNTS 3 (entered into force 2 September 1990).

[56] Oliver De Schutter, *International Human Rights Law: Cases, Materials, Commentary* (Cambridge University Press, 3rd ed, 2019) 943–944, 869–872.

[57] Ibid 872.

[58] Rhona K M Smith, *Textbook on International Human Rights Law* (Oxford University Press, 7th ed, 2016) 51.

[59] ILC Study Group Report (n 11) 51.

toothlessness is relevant to understanding the relationship between intellectual property and human rights, which may influence states that are required to choose between competing obligations in international human rights law and international intellectual property law. WTO enforcement mechanisms available for *TRIPS* breaches include powerful deterrents.[60] These remain stronger deterrents than the consensus-based mechanisms available for human rights institutions.[61] Progressive realisation of economic, social and cultural rights can make it more difficult to demonstrate how compliance with trade laws compels breaches of human rights, such as the right to health.[62]

The continuing distinction made between economic, social and cultural rights and civil and political rights is also relevant to enforcement and the status of the respective obligations, in comparison with other systems of law such as international intellectual property law obligations. Historically, civil and political rights have been perceived to be of higher status and more enforceable than economic, social and cultural rights.[63] There is less interpretation of how economic, social and cultural rights should protect individuals because of the relatively recent entry into force in 2013 of the *Optional Protocol to the International Covenant on Economic, Social and Cultural Rights*, which established complaint and inquiry mechanisms pursuant to *ICESCR*.[64] In contrast, the *First Optional Protocol to the International Covenant on Civil and Political Rights*, permitting individuals to make complaints against states regarding compliance with the *ICCPR*, entered into force on 23 March 1976.[65] Although the majority of states are party to both the *ICESCR* and the *ICCPR*,

---

[60] Kennedy (n 21) 288.

[61] See Murumba (n 2) 135–136.

[62] Laurence R Helfer, 'Mapping the Interface between Human Rights and Intellectual Property' in Christophe Geiger (ed), *Research Handbook on Human Rights and Intellectual Property* (Edward Elgar Publishing, 2015) 6, 11–12.

[63] This distinction is and should be questioned: see, for example, Andrew Byrnes, 'The Protection and Enjoyment of Economic Social and Cultural Rights' in Paula Gerber and Melissa Castan (eds), *Contemporary Perspectives on Human Rights Law in Australia* (Thomson Reuters, 2012) 125, 130–131; Peggy Ducoulombier, 'Interaction between Human Rights: Are All Human Rights Equal?' in Christophe Geiger (ed), *Research Handbook on Human Rights and Intellectual Property* (Edward Elgar Publishing, 2015).

[64] *Optional Protocol to the International Covenant on Economic, Social and Cultural Rights*, adopted 10 December 2009, 869 UNTS 34 (entered into force 5 May 2013). Byrnes identifies lack of justiciability of economic, social and cultural human rights as one of the bases for according them less status than civil and political rights: Byrnes (n 63) 130–131.

[65] *Optional Protocol to the International Covenant on Civil and Political Rights*, opened for signature 16 December 1966, 999 UNTS 302 (entered into force 23 March 1976).

in domestic jurisdictions civil and political rights are often accorded higher status than economic, social and cultural rights.[66]

The differences in structure between the two agreements regarding derogation can also influence the value accorded to them.[67] While the *ICCPR* provides states with clearer standards to guide compliance, the *ICESCR* approach is more dynamic and facilitates continuous improvement of economic, social and cultural rights standards within states. The *ICESCR* recognises that economic, social and cultural rights are dependent on resources and should be progressively realised.[68] Interpretation of the *ICESCR* provides guidance on core obligations for specific rights and prohibits retrogression once standards are realised.[69] The *ICCPR* provides less flexibility. States can derogate from civil and political rights in times of public emergency but they need to notify the UN Secretary-General of the details.[70] Certain rights, such as the right to freedom from torture, cannot be derogated from. These non-derogable provisions are more likely to align with *jus cogens* norms.[71] These norms have primacy over other international laws.[72] *Jus cogens* norms can be used to justify the primacy of human rights over intellectual property and are relevant to hierarchy between international laws. However, determining which human rights can be considered peremptory is not settled in international law and the application of *jus cogens* arguments to support primacy remains unclear.[73]

2.3 Seeking Common Ground

Fragmentation is problematic when standards within separate fields of law appear to operate inconsistently with each other and states need to reconcile competing obligations internally and in their dealings with other states. When these perceived inconsistencies result in disputes between states, fragmenta-

---

66 See Andrew Byrnes, 'Second-Class Rights Yet Again? Economic, Social and Cultural Rights in the Report of the National Human Rights Consultation' (2010) 33(1) *UNSW Law Journal* 193.

67 See Philip Alston and Ryan Goodman, *International Human Rights* (Oxford University Press, 2013) 394. See also Philip Alston and Gerard Quinn, 'The Nature and Scope of States Parties' Obligations under the International Covenant on Economic, Social and Cultural Rights' (1987) 9(2) *Human Rights Quarterly* 156, 216–219.

68 *ICESCR* (n 54) art 2.

69 Committee on Economic, Social and Cultural Rights, *General Comment No 3: The Nature of States Parties' Obligations (Art 2, Para 1 of the Covenant)*, UN ESCOR, 5th sess, UN Doc E/1991/23 (14 December 1990) [9].

70 *ICCPR* (n 53) art 4.

71 See examples in De Schutter (n 56) 85.

72 Ibid.

73 Ibid.

tion creates difficulty in finding appropriate mechanisms for the interpretation of issues that engage multiple specialised bodies of international law.[74]

In the absence of a cohesive mechanism for dispute settlement, the approach taken within public international law to competing systems emphasises interpretation guided by the rules of treaty interpretation found in the *Vienna Convention on the Law of Treaties* ('*VCLT*').[75] However, finding an appropriate forum to resolve conflicts between intellectual property and human rights is more complex. Although the International Court of Justice could address inter-systemic conflicts involving human rights agreements and the *Paris Convention*, it does not have binding jurisdiction over WTO agreements and disputes. Decision-makers within institutions that are focused on one field of law will have a greater understanding of that field of law and may exhibit systemic bias.[76] Ruse-Khan proposes a 'conflict-rule of integration'.[77] This approach applies to potentially conflicting systems, such as human rights and intellectual property. Where there are 'two or more valid and applicable rules which point to an incompatible decision' and one approach needs to be selected, 'the underlying rule system which is more able to integrate the other system's rules applies'.[78] This values the ability of a rule system 'to integrate the objectives and interests represented by other rules as a connecting factor', which can be linked to 'the public international law principle of integration'.[79]

Approaches to both human rights and intellectual property dispute resolution systems respectively have limitations for this type of systemic integration. Treaty-making bodies, including the Human Rights Committee and the Committee on Economic, Social and Cultural Rights ('CESCR') , receive complaints of human rights breaches from individuals and focus consideration on breaches of human rights rather than resolving conflicts between competing legal systems.[80] The main human rights treaties include mechanisms for the resolution of disputes between state parties over a state's fulfilment of its obligations under the treaty. These are very rarely used, although individual compliance is addressed by the treaty-making bodies through state reporting and

---

74 See Henning Grosse Ruse-Khan, 'A Conflict-of-Laws Approach to Competing Rationalities in International Law: The Case of Plain Packaging between Intellectual Property, Trade, Investment and Health' (2013) 9(2) *Journal of Private International Law* 308.

75 Ibid 310–311; *Vienna* (n 50); *ILC Study Group Report* (n 11) 207 [412].

76 Ruse-Khan (n 74) 335–337.

77 Ibid 331.

78 Ibid.

79 Ibid.

80 Committee on Economic, Social and Cultural Rights, *Views: Communication No. 1/2013*, 57th sess, UN Doc E/C.12/57/D/1/2013 (20 April 2016, adopted 4 March 2016) ('*López Rodríguez v Spain*').

the mechanisms of the Human Rights Council. Human rights treaties prescribe limited permissible exceptions or limitations that may accommodate some interests related to intellectual property protection, such as the restrictions that trade mark protection can pose on commercial freedom of expression.[81]

The WTO provides a clear approach to dispute resolution binding on WTO Members. The *Paris Convention* permits resolution of disputes through the International Court of Justice, but intellectual property disputes have not been addressed in this forum.[82] There is no reference to human rights in *TRIPS*, yet the flexibility mechanisms of the agreement could permit consideration of human rights in settlement of disputes surrounding *TRIPS* statutes.[83] Interpretations of relevant provisions that could permit greater domestic regulatory autonomy, including Articles 7 and 8, are limited.[84] Article 8 of *TRIPS* privileges policy protecting public health, which is relevant to the human right to health.[85] Yet Article 8 provides no clear provision for the right to freedom of expression, although the exercise of trade mark rights can restrict commercial expression.[86] In WTO disputes about *TRIPS* compliance, human rights arguments have not yet been addressed. The WTO Appellate Body has acknowledged that the agreement should not be read in isolation from public international law.[87] The reference to public international law by WTO dispute settlement mechanisms is limited in practice.[88] The decision in *Australia – Tobacco Plain Packaging* confirms a trend towards recognition of national interests supported by those flexibilities and shows that agreements like the *Framework Convention on*

---

81 See *ICCPR* (n 53) art 19(3).

82 Ricketson (n 28) 323.

83 See, for example, Sub-Commission on the Promotion and Protection of Human Rights, Economic, Social and Cultural Rights: The Impact of the Agreement on Trade-Related Aspects of Intellectual Property Rights on Human Rights – Report of the High Commissioner, UN ESCOR, 52nd sess, Agenda Item 4, UN Doc E/CN.4/Sub.2/2001/13 (27 June 2001) [65]–[67].

84 Taubman (n 48). But see '*Australia – Tobacco Plain Packaging*' (n 1) [7.2429].

85 Genevieve Wilkinson, 'The Human Rights (Parliamentary Security) Act 2011 (Cth) and the Increasingly Visible Intersections between the Human Right to Health and Intellectual Property in Australia' (2016) 105 *Intellectual Property Forum* 46.

86 See Andreas Rahmatian, 'Trade Marks and Human Rights' in Paul Torremans (ed), *Intellectual Property and Human Rights: Enhanced Edition of Copyright and Human Rights* (Kluwer Law International, 2nd ed, 2008) 335, 347–356. See also Jonathan Griffiths, 'Is There a Right to an Immoral Trademark?' in Paul Torremans (ed), *Intellectual Property Law and Human Rights* (Kluwer Law International, 3rd ed, 2015) 425.

87 Appellate Body Report, *United States – Standards for Reformulated and Conventional Gasoline*, WTO Doc WT/DS2/AB/R, AB-1996-1 (20 May 1996) 17.

88 Gabrielle Marceau, 'WTO Dispute Settlement and Human Rights' (2002) 13(4) *European Journal of International Law* 753, 766–767.

Tobacco Control can influence disputes.[89] However, the interpretation of the scope of rights protected by *TRIPS* Article 20 also suggests that this provision can provide owners with broad trade mark protection.[90] The scope of protection offered by Article 20 for trade mark use in the course of trade[91] was 'not limited to the use of a trademark for the specific purpose of distinguishing the goods and services of one undertaking from those of other undertakings' and includes 'a wider range of commercial, advertising and promotion activities'.[92]

Even where there has been greater consideration of *TRIPS* flexibilities, the WTO dispute settlement bodies have not placed great emphasis on human rights. This may reflect failures by the disputants to emphasise human rights-based arguments, disinterest in human rights or the limited number of disputes. However, this may be slowly changing: a WTO Dispute Settlement Body recently recognised the relevance of the right to health to a claim contesting the inconsistency of requirements on foreign pharmaceutical suppliers with national treatment protection, provided in a WTO covered agreement, General Agreement on Tariffs and Trade 1994 ('GATT 1994').[93]

2.4 Further Fragmentation

Forum-shifting of intellectual property standard-setting to bilateral and plurilateral trade and investment agreements has further fragmented the international landscape. Some bilateral and plurilateral trade and investment agreements seek to expand protection for trade mark owners beyond minimum standards found in *TRIPS* and the *Paris Convention*. Ong identifies two areas where the United States has used bilateral free trade agreements to export domestic trade mark obligations.[94] First, agreements require strong protection for non-visually perceptible marks, such as sound marks.[95] The second, more controversial, area is additional protection for well-known marks, including protection

---

89 See Australia – Tobacco Plain Packaging (n 1) [7.2604].

90 Genevieve Wilkinson, 'Packaging Domestic Interests into Intellectual Property Law: Lessons from Tobacco Plain Packaging Disputes' 47(2) *Monash University Law Review* 142, 156–158.

91 Australia – Tobacco Plain Packaging (n 1) [7.2260].

92 Ibid [7.2285–7.2286].

93 See Turkey – Pharmaceutical Products (n 1).

94 Burton Ong, 'The Trademark Law Provisions of Bilateral Free Trade Agreements' in Graeme B Dinwoodie and Marc D Janis (eds), *Trademark Law and Theory: A Handbook of Contemporary Research* (Edward Elgar Publishing, 2008) 229, 240–242.

95 Ibid. See *Australia-United States Free Trade Agreement*, signed 18 May 2004, [2005] ATS 1 (entered into force 1 January 2005) art 17.2.2 ('*Australia-United States Free Trade Agreement*').

against tarnishment, dilution and misappropriation of associated goodwill.[96] Ong suggests that this expands the protection provided for well-known marks in *TRIPS* to include the first six articles of the 'Joint Recommendation Concerning Provision of the Protection of Well-Known Marks', adopted by the General Assembly of WIPO and the Assembly of the Paris Union in 1999.[97] This recommendation encouraged states to protect well-known marks beyond protection later enshrined in *TRIPS*. Ong argues that the *US–Jordan Free Trade Agreement* and the *US–Singapore Free Trade Agreement* oblige the signatory states to give effect to these *TRIPS*-plus recommendations.[98]

The impact of increasing protection for trade mark owners of well-known marks has been most evident in the United States,[99] but such protection has also increased in other jurisdictions, including Europe.[100] The link between trade mark protection and brand protection is used to justify expansion of rights domestically but has also been criticised. Decisions of the European Court of Justice have generated debates questioning increasing protection for well-known marks in Europe.[101] Gangjee and Burrell argue that even where the essential function of the mark as 'a guarantee of origin and thus consistent quality' is not harmed, the European Court of Justice is prepared to protect the image of a mark from free riders.[102] This guarantee of origin rationale originally balanced concerns that trade marks impede the free movement of trade.[103] Davis argues that the European Court of Justice should maintain the distinction between trade marks and branding.[104] It should not be influenced by the 'need to protect brand values at all costs', in part because brand valuation should be treated with caution.[105]

The high value attributed to branding and trade marks has given trade mark owners strong incentives to seek expansive protection.[106] These interests can

---

96 Ong (n 94) 242–248.

97 Ibid 242.

98 Ibid.

99 *Trademark Dilution Revision Act*, 15 USC § 1125(c) (2006); Michael Handler, 'What Can Harm the Reputation of a Trademark? A Critical Re-Evaluation of Dilution by Tarnishment' (2016) 106(3) *Trade Mark Reporter* 639.

100 See Dev Gangjee and Robert Burrell, 'Because You're Worth It: L'Oreal and the Prohibition on Free Riding' (2010) 73(2) *Modern Law Review* 282; Handler (n 99).

101 Gangjee and Burrell (n 100).

102 Ibid 294–295.

103 Ibid.

104 Jennifer Davis, 'The Value of Trade Marks: Economic Assets and Cultural Icons' in Ysolde Gendreau (ed), *Intellectual Property: Bridging Aesthetics and Economics – Propriété Intellectuelle: Entre L'Art et L'Argent* (Editions Themis, 2006).

105 Ibid 122.

106 Jennifer Files Beerline, 'Anti-Dilution Law, New and Improved: The Trademark Dilution Revision Act of 2006' (2008) 23(1) *Berkeley Technology Law Journal* 511, 514.

influence legislative development that responds to well-resourced lobbying.[107] Courts can respond to this by interpreting legislation narrowly, although this can also prompt corrective legislation that entrenches broad trade mark monopolies.[108]

For net exporters of intellectual property and net importers with strong export markets, it is advantageous for expanded protection to operate in other jurisdictions.[109] When strong exporters enter bilateral or plurilateral agreements, they can negotiate for these to include expanded intellectual property protection.[110] The impact of these agreements is amplified by international obligations of national treatment and most favoured nation requirements for intellectual property.[111]

The *Paris Convention* enshrined principles of national treatment: each state party was required to protect the covered intellectual property rights of nationals of other Members of the agreement with standards equivalent to protection provided to its own nationals.[112] The national treatment requirements were retained and extended to all areas of intellectual property covered by *TRIPS*.[113] Most favoured nation obligations are characteristic of other trade agreements covered by the WTO regime.[114] This restricts discrimination between trading partners by requiring the benefits agreed between WTO Members and other countries to be extended by those Members to all other WTO Members.[115] Consequently, benefits agreed between any WTO Members that are relevant to the areas of intellectual property covered by the agreement are extended to

---

[107] Ibid 523–524; John Braithwaite and Peter Drahos, *Global Business Regulation* (Cambridge University Press, 2000) 61–63.

[108] Beerline (n 106) 521–522.

[109] Susan K Sell, 'TRIPS Was Never Enough: Vertical Forum Shifting, FTAs, ACTA and TPP' (2011) 18(2) *Journal of Intellectual Property Law* 447, 452–455. For recent statistics about major exporters and importers of charges for the use of intellectual property, see World Trade Organization, *World Trade Statistical Review 2017* (World Trade Organization, 2017) 135 https://www.wto.org/english/res_e/statis_e/wts2017_e/wts17_toc_e.htm.

[110] Sell (n 109) 452–455.

[111] *TRIPS* (n 19) arts 3, 4. The combination of national treatment and most favoured nation principles in *TRIPS* with explicit standards has meant that intellectual property standards have increased for many states. See Osei Tutu, who argues that this combination is more restrictive than other WTO agreements: J Janewa Osei Tutu, 'Value Divergence in Global Intellectual Property Law' (2012) 87(4) *Indiana Law Journal* 1640, 1654–1656.

[112] Ricketson (n 28) 336–339.

[113] *TRIPS* (n 19) art 3.

[114] Kennedy (n 21) 207–212.

[115] Gervais (n 25) 209–211.

all Members.[116] There are certain exceptions, such as agreements made prior to the conclusion of *TRIPS*.[117] However, states that agree to expand intellectual property protection through subsequent bilateral and plurilateral trade agreements must offer the same protection to all *TRIPS* Members.[118] Including these standards in future trade agreements with other parties becomes advantageous: it increases foreign protection for their own nationals, which *TRIPS* requires them to provide to all nationals of WTO Member States.[119]

The incorporation of intellectual property provisions into trade agreements between developing countries and developed countries has frequently increased standards as a result of the operation of national treatment and most favoured nation principles in *TRIPS*.[120] This contributes to an expansion of intellectual property rights. These expanded protections are problematic if they restrict the ability of states to meet their international human rights obligations. There is limited evidence available of systematic human rights analysis of these often secretly negotiated trade agreements, so conflicts are foreseeable.

A human rights culture is designed to limit the impact of systemic fragmentation. Dispute resolution mechanisms that can accommodate both systems are valuable but are only one part of that culture. The HRATM framework for analysis developed in Chapter 2 is designed so that states can proactively address conflicts between intellectual property and human rights and monitor their ongoing compliance with human rights obligations. This is increasingly important because of expanding global protection for trade mark monopolies. It is problematic that there are no clear mechanisms for addressing the human rights implications of the increasing protection of trade mark owner rights found in plurilateral and bilateral trade and investment agreements and endorsed in *Australia – Tobacco Plain Packaging* for protection of owners beyond the traditional source identification of trade marks. Like the WTO agreements, trade and investment agreements include enforcement mechanisms that are stronger than the consensus-based approach used by human rights institutions. However, the protection of intellectual property rights as assets, through investor–state dispute mechanisms that protect foreign investors, is now a common feature of trade and investment agreements between

---

[116] *TRIPS* (n 19) art 4.

[117] Ibid art 4(d).

[118] Anselm Kamperman Sanders and Dalindyebo Shabalala, 'Intellectual Property Treaties and Development' in Daniel J Gervais (ed), *Intellectual Property, Trade and Development: Strategies to Optimize Economic Development in a TRIPS-Plus Era* (Oxford University Press, 2nd ed, 2014) 41, 68.

[119] *TRIPS* (n 19) arts 3, 4. Kamperman Sanders and Shabalala argue that many developing countries have resisted this: Kamperman Sanders and Shabalala (n 118) 68.

[120] Kamperman Sanders and Shabalala (n 118) 68.

states.[121] This strengthens protection for trade mark owners. The next section explores how both normative and positivist considerations support increased consideration of the human rights implications of trade mark law.

3 NORMATIVISM, POSITIVISM AND THE RELATIONSHIP BETWEEN INTELLECTUAL PROPERTY AND HUMAN RIGHTS

Both human rights law and intellectual property law have normative and positivist dimensions. A deliberative or positivist conception of human rights law is much closer to the instrumentalist approach taken in international intellectual property law than a natural law conception.[122] However, normative legitimacy means that it is also important to understand what law ought to be, and human rights law remains much more closely linked to normative considerations of justice.[123] This section identifies normative justifications for both human rights and trade marks, and recognises the problems of a legal order where intellectual property rights that expand beyond normative justifications for their protection have increasing primacy over human rights and considerations of justice that are a feature of natural law.

3.1 Justifications for Human Rights Protection

Human rights are an articulation of rights inherent to all human beings. A natural rights approach posits that human rights are derived from a transcendental source, such as human reason or a religious basis.[124] Murumba characterises natural rights as the forerunner of the modern doctrine of human rights, and argues that natural rights privileged entitlement in natural law's universe of duty during the Enlightenment period and the 17th- and 18th-century European and American revolutions.[125] Natural rights justifications support the primary interest in human rights law: the protection of the inalienable human rights of individuals. The binding nature of both human rights and intellectual

---

[121] Rochelle C Dreyfuss and Susy Frankel, 'From Incentive to Commodity to Asset: How International Law is Reconceptualizing Intellectual Property' (2015) 36(4) *Michigan Journal of International Law* 557, 566–575.

[122] Murumba (n 2) 133–134.

[123] Ibid.

[124] Marie-Bénédicte Dembour, 'What are Human Rights? Four Schools of Thought' (2010) 32(1) *Human Rights Quarterly* 1, 2–3.

[125] Murumba (n 2) 132. See Leo Strauss, *Studies in Platonic Political Philosophy* (University of Chicago Press, 1983) 141–146.

property obligations also means that positivist justifications can support them as a system of authoritative rules.

The connection between law and morality is contested by positivism, which developed in reaction to natural law to emphasise the importance of rules and authority to law.[126] Austin argued that law is command backed by sanction.[127] Hart developed positivist theory, arguing that law constitutes a system of rules that are given authority and meaning by social practices and conventions.[128] This contrasts to Strauss's argument, derived from Plato and Aristotle, that natural law provides validity for all positive law.[129] Positive law is invalid if it contradicts natural law.[130] The positivist separability theory, that there is 'no necessary connection between law and morality', should be questioned on the basis that facts cannot be completely separated from values but are grounded in a fact–value complex encompassing extremities of legal order and justice.[131] Law is partly rooted in justice so concerns of justice cannot be ignored, but law also depends on order as it necessarily responds to the 'demands of justice in a systematic and orderly manner'.[132] The emphasis we place on certain facts reflects our values.[133] The tension between facts and values corresponds to the tension identified between legal positivism and traditional natural law.[134] If we conceive of '[l]aw as a fact-value complex', we find a place for synthesis of legal positivism and moral concerns.[135] Murumba links 'facticity' to intellectual property law and 'normativity' to human rights law, but argues that it is a distortion to equate the fields to a dichotomy of positivism and normativism and contends that the fields lie on a spectrum between the dichotomies.[136]

This book establishes the need for a more proactive culture to support and promote human rights in trade mark law. In current practice, Murumba suggests that global intellectual property law is a regression towards command–sanction legal positivism, and human rights as a corrective has only been directly successful as a last resort.[137] Confining the role of human rights to

---

126 Murumba (n 2) 131–132.

127 Ibid 132, citing John Austin, *The Province of Jurisprudence Determined* (John Murray Publishers, 1832).

128 Murumba (n 2) 132–133.

129 Strauss (n 125) 141.

130 Ibid.

131 Murumba (n 2) 139.

132 Ibid 141.

133 Ibid 139.

134 Ibid 140–141.

135 Ibid 140.

136 Ibid 141.

137 Ibid; Noah Novogrodsky, 'After AIDS' (2013) 14(2) *Melbourne University Law Review* 643.

a last resort to balance unjust intellectual property laws is problematic for building a harmonising relationship between human rights and intellectual property. Prescriptive models addressing the relationship between human rights and intellectual property need to comprehensively consider these legal trends. Murumba uses the nature of legality to show that normative concerns still have an important role in the international legal framework.[138] The dichotomy between positivism and natural law should be minimised by recognising an inclusive spectrum when assessing conflicts between the fields and the legitimacy of competing rights.[139]

Positivism is a very useful tool for resolving political, philosophical and religious disagreements between states that are parties to human rights agreements.[140] However, human rights justifications remain tied to normative origins in natural law that emphasise the inherent dignity of the individual and the universal and inalienable nature of individual rights. These principles influence the HRATM framework developed in Chapter 2. Justice links natural law, natural rights and human rights. However, they have each evolved differently.[141] For Locke, law moved away from justice and developed to serve the individual and 'his desire expressed through free will'.[142] The doctrines of both Locke and Rousseau derive not from a hierarchic order of man's natural ends, but the lowest of those ends – self-preservation.[143] Locke ties self-preservation to the right to property and develops his theory from this point.[144] Locke's emphasis on property rights arguably justifies intellectual property rights. Importantly, egalitarian social concerns in the 19th century balanced the strong individual and libertarian influence of the 18th century, and synthesis between these movements can be found in the modern human rights regime.[145]

Human rights standards used in this research are rights that have been agreed on and derive from societal agreement in key human rights instruments.[146] Where relevant, customary international law is considered. A significant advantage of a positivist approach is the way it permits states with diverse

---

[138] Murumba (n 2).

[139] Ibid 140–141.

[140] See Jennifer Prah Ruger, 'Toward a Theory of a Right to Health: Capability and Incompletely Theorized Agreements' (2006) 18(2) *Yale Journal of Law & the Humanities* 273, 304–305.

[141] Costas Douzinas, *The End of Human Rights* (Hart Publishing, 2000) 84.

[142] Ibid.

[143] Strauss (n 125) 143–144.

[144] Ibid 145.

[145] Murumba (n 2) 130, citing Louis Henkin, *The Age of Rights* (Columbia University Press, 1990).

[146] Dembour (n 124) 3.

philosophical and religious backgrounds to agree, despite these differences.[147] However, these laws should be consistent with normative underpinnings of justice.[148]

3.2 Justifications for Intellectual Property Protection

Theoretical justifications can be used to contest laws that are inconsistent with them.[149] Theoretical justifications also assist in the understanding of the beneficial aspects of intellectual property laws and the different stakeholders, whose interests should be considered in assessing the function and value of trade mark law. For trade mark protection, Loughlan identifies three potentially competing interests: owner interests in protecting goodwill and property, consumer interests in recognising trade marks as a badge of origin and not being deceived or confused, and public interests in competition and open communication.[150] Protection of these interests shapes the development of domestic intellectual property legislation, which is a focus of the case studies in this book. Fisher identifies four main theoretical approaches to intellectual property: the utilitarian approach, the Lockean approach, personality theory and social planning theory.[151] Each theory can be blended in intellectual property legislation, explanatory materials and decisions.[152] The relevance of each justification to trade mark law, discussed in the paragraphs below, supports assessment of the normative basis for specific types of trade mark protection and how closely they align with considerations of justice.

In economic theory, trade mark law benefits social welfare by reducing search costs, protecting consumers and providing an incentive for maintaining consistent quality.[153] The function of trade marks strongly influences the underlying rationale and theoretical justifications for trade mark law.[154] Trade

---

147 See Ruger (n 140) 304–305.

148 Murumba (n 2) 140–141.

149 William Fisher, 'Theories of Intellectual Property' in Stephen R Munzer (ed), *New Essays in the Legal and Political Theory of Property* (Cambridge University Press, 2001) 168, 194–199.

150 Patricia Loughlan explains that these interests are often in contest in Australian trade mark law: Patricia Loughlan, 'The Campomar Model of Competing Interests' (2005) 27(8) *European Intellectual Property Review* 289, 292.

151 Fisher (n 149) 169–173.

152 See ibid 175, 194–199.

153 William M Landes and Richard A Posner, The Economic Structure of Intellectual Property Law (Harvard University Press, 2003) 173 ('The Economic Structure of Intellectual Property Law').

154 *JT International SA v Commonwealth of Australia; British American Tobacco Australasia Ltd v Commonwealth of Australia* (2012) 250 CLR 1, 27–28 (French CJ).

marks convey information that permits consumers to distinguish goods and services from other goods and services in trade.[155] Trade marks can also have a semiotic value by increasing the number of words that efficiently describe things, reducing communication and information costs.[156] They can contribute to the development of generic words, as well as culturally significant terms that enrich language with their 'intrinsic pleasingness'.[157] The strength of the model relies on the efficiency of trade marks as a naming function of things, provided that it is quicker to use trade marks and the products that are named by those trade marks are of consistent quality.[158]

Economic theory justifying trade marks corresponds to utilitarian justifications for intellectual property.[159] Trade mark rights reward investment and the production of quality products and are justifiable in economic theory where their role in increasing market efficiency improves social welfare.[160] Trade marks function to permit variety by ensuring that products from different sources can be efficiently and effectively identified, reducing search costs.[161] Trade marks also constitute an incentive for consistent quality: a lack of consistent quality can impair goodwill associated with a product.[162] By protecting distinguishing signs, trade mark laws can be linked to justice as they incentivise consistent quality and the development of goodwill by protecting against freeriding. However, trade marks are increasingly valued by trade mark owners for the information they convey about brands, which functions to advertise trade marked goods.[163]

---

155 Trade Marks Act 1995 (Cth) s 17.

156 Landes and Posner, The Economic Structure of Intellectual Property Law (n 153) 167–168.

157 William M Landes and Richard A Posner, 'Trademark Law: An Economic Perspective' (1987) 30(2) *Journal of Law and Economics* 265, 271 ('Trademark Law: An Economic Perspective'); Landes and Posner, *The Economic Structure of Intellectual Property Law* (n 153) 168–169. See also Thomas D Drescher, 'The Transformation and Evolution of Trademarks: From Signals to Symbols to Myth' (1992) 82(3) *Trademark Reporter* 301, 339.

158 Fisher (n 149) 167–168.

159 Ibid 169.

160 Lionel Bently and Brad Sherman, *Intellectual Property Law* (Oxford University Press, 4th ed, 2014) 816; Stacey L Dogan and Mark A Lemley, 'A Search-Costs Theory of Limiting Doctrines in Trademark Law' (2007) 97(6) *Trademark Reporter* 1223.

161 Landes and Posner, The Economic Structure of Intellectual Property Law (n 153) 173.

162 Elmer William Hanak, III, 'The Quality Assurance Function of Trademarks' (1974) 43(3) *Fordham Law Review* 301, 363–364, citing Frank I Schechter, 'The Rational Basis of Trademark Protection' (1927) 40(6) *Harvard Law Review* 813, 818.

163 See Davis (n 104).

Natural rights support grants of intellectual property where there is sufficient labour exerted in the creation of intellectual products and granting rights to the labourer does not unjustifiably deplete the public domain or commons.[164] However, characterising trade marks as creations in their own right can be problematic as this ignores the role of consumers and the public in the associations between a mark and a source of goodwill.[165] The owner (often not the creator) also exerts labour in establishing reputation in the mark.[166]

Personality theory characterises intellectual creations as an extension of a person and their protection as a means of recognising their significance to personhood, justifying grants of attribution and integrity as a vehicle for the actualisation of the individual.[167] However, the explicit protection that Article 15(1)(c) of the *ICESCR* provides for the moral interests of authors of artistic or literary creations is rarely legally recognised for the authors of trade marks, who frequently create trade marks and assign their interests in those marks to corporations (through specific contract or employment contract).[168]

Social planning theory recognises the role of intellectual property in achieving 'a just and attractive culture'.[169] A trade mark system structured to achieve a just and attractive culture balances the rights of trade mark owners, other traders and competitors, 'stressing the cultural and expressive rights of the public in trade marks'.[170] These arguments support limiting expansive rights for trade mark owners as there is a public interest in being able to use culturally significant marks in communication.[171]

Narrow legislative recognition for creators of trade marks in registration systems suggests that natural law and personality theory justifications have limited modern relevance. Social planning theory indicates more recently recognised public interests, which are arguably more consistent with human rights. The 20th-century dominance of economic theory persists, but the extent to which it can be used to justify expansion of the rights of owners is con-

---

164 Fisher identifies several problems with the application of Lockean theory to intellectual property generally: (n 149) 170, 184–189.

165 Bently and Sherman (n 160) 815.

166 See Steven Wilf, 'Who Authors Trademarks?' (1999) 17(1) *Cardozo Art and Entertainment Law Journal* 1, 2.

167 Fisher (n 149) 171–172.

168 Genevieve Wilkinson, 'Exploring Moral Interests in the Intellectual Creations underlying Trade Marks' in Ysolde Gendreau (ed), *Research Handbook on Intellectual Property and Moral Rights* (Edward Elgar Publishing, forthcoming).

169 Fisher (n 149) 172–173.

170 Mohammad Amin Naser, 'Re-Examining the Functions of Trademark Law' (2008) 8(1) *Chicago Kent Law Review* 99, 102.

171 Cf Megan Richardson, 'Trade Marks and Language' (2004) 26(2) *Sydney Law Review* 193, 216–220.

troversial.[172] The increased economic value of trade marks and branding has encouraged trade mark owners to protect their property interests assertively.[173] Trade mark interests have increasingly moved away from traditional normative justifications for protection of intangible property towards a property-based justification.

Criticisms of expansion of trade mark rights beyond search costs justifications are often linked to expansion of trade mark protection rights that protect owners against dilution and tarnishment[174] who increasingly place value on branding and trade marks.[175] Dilution of a mark is alleged to occur if use on unrelated goods or services negatively impacts on the reputation and distinctiveness of the mark.[176] Tarnishment occurs when a mark is associated with another, usually unrelated, good or service in a manner that invites negative associations with the original brand and negatively impacts on the reputation of the mark.[177]

Griffiths argues that a law and economics approach (founded largely in the work of Landes and Posner) is primarily based on the essential function of a trade mark as a guarantee of a specific origin, so that it can simultaneously reduce search costs for consumers and become a focal point for goodwill that can increase economic benefits associated with reputation.[178] An economic argument can be made that blurring or tarnishment protects the communicative function of a trade mark. However, these broader rights should be limited to cases where the expanded protection is a necessary incentive for production, which would improve social welfare sufficiently that it outweighed costs associated with adverse impacts on competition.[179] Griffiths notes that patent and copyright laws focus on balancing incentives against adverse impact, and suggests that overall contribution to social impact and trade mark law should be similarly balanced.[180] Even if trade mark rights are likened to tangible property, the economic justification for extending legal protection would be limited to ensuring 'their effectiveness and reliability as trade marks unless the

---

172 See Andrew Griffiths, 'A Law-and-Economics Perspective on Trade Marks' in Lionel Bently, Jennifer Davis and Jane C Ginsburg (eds), *Trade Marks and Brands: An Interdisciplinary Critique* (Cambridge University Press, 2008) 241; Bently and Sherman (n 160) 816–818.

173 See Davis (n 104) 97.

174 Dogan and Lemley (n 160) 1238; Handler (n 99).

175 Beerline (n 106) 514.

176 Handler (n 99) 639–640.

177 Ibid 640.

178 Griffiths (n 172) 245–255.

179 Ibid 264.

180 Ibid.

resulting benefits would outweigh the costs'.[181] Problematically, the costs of these monopolies can expand if owners use letters of demand to make spurious claims against individuals with limited resources and legal knowledge who do not have the capacity to defend themselves, even though their expressive uses of marks are completely defensible.[182]

The utilitarian emphasis of intellectual property on net social welfare encourages the identification of a common goal of human welfare between intellectual property and human rights, which can be linked to justice.[183] Rights that move beyond utilitarian justifications do not necessarily embody social welfare objectives. This is relevant to the legitimacy of such expansion, particularly if it is inconsistent with human rights protection.[184] Broader rights for trade mark owners may also be inconsistent with the underlying rationales for trade mark protection.[185] Expansion of trade mark law in some jurisdictions can influence attempts to enlarge these rights at a multilateral level by forum-shifting and including them in plurilateral and bilateral agreements.[186] A strong approach to protecting trade mark rights should be scrutinised. It is only appropriate for certain economic conditions.[187] International obligations that are not sensitive to these local conditions and restrict domestic regulatory autonomy can have a significant impact on a broad range of interests and concerns, including but not limited to sustainable development and human rights.[188]

Expansion of trade mark protection is also significant because of their functional role. While other intellectual property rights stimulate the production of commodities, trade marks are signs that attach to the product themselves.[189] Intellectual property theory emphasises this stimulation function. Machlup and Penrose identify rationales for patents underpinning a utilitarian approach that emphasises the benefits for society of innovation, which becomes public but is

---

[181] Ibid 266.

[182] This will be explored in Chapter 4.

[183] See Estelle Derclaye, 'Intellectual Property and Human Rights: Coinciding and Cooperating' in Paul Torremans (ed), *Intellectual Property and Human Rights: Enhanced Edition of Copyright and Human Rights* (Kluwer Law International, 2nd ed, 2008) 133.

[184] See J Janewa Osei Tutu, 'Humanizing Intellectual Property: Moving Beyond the Natural Rights Property Focus' (2017) 20(1) *Vanderbilt Journal of Entertainment and Technology Law* 207.

[185] Fisher (n 149) 194–199.

[186] Ong (n 94) 240–248.

[187] Beerline describes amendments to the *Trademark Dilution Revision Act* as a compromise between interests in the United States: Beerline (n 106) 523–524.

[188] Kamperman Sanders and Shabalala (n 118).

[189] Ibid.

temporarily protected by patents.[190] Inventors are rewarded for their innovation with a limited patent monopoly; patents provide a monopoly, which enables inventors to profit from their work; or patents are granted in exchange for the disclosure of secrets.[191] Copyright protection similarly encourages creators to share their cultural contributions through publication of work by protecting creators against copying.[192]

Trade marks can support other intellectual property rights by continuing to protect the associated products after the rights expire, but overlapping protection should be carefully scrutinised.[193] The auxiliary function of trade marks can beneficially protect innovative contributions to science and culture that may not easily obtain protection using the mechanisms of copyright and patent protection. However, the auxiliary role of trade marks in expanding the material interests of creators can potentially interfere with a balance of interests provided by other regimes, such as copyright and patent law.[194] Trade mark protection for copyright works that have entered the public domain can undermine user interests by extending restrictions over the relevant material.[195] Trade marks can entrench higher prices for originator pharmaceutical brands after the expiration of patent protection, which arguably interferes with the bargain inherent in the patent monopoly that the public will benefit from the innovation once the monopoly expires.[196] As this bargain often justifies the conferral of intellectual property monopolies, it is an important concern.[197]

---

[190] Fritz Machlup and Edith Penrose, 'The Patent Controversy in the Nineteenth Century' (1950) 10(1) *Journal of Economic History* 1, 10.

[191] Ibid.

[192] Fisher (n 149) 169, citing William M Landes and Richard A Posner, 'An Economic Analysis of Copyright Law' (1989) 18(2) *Journal of Legal Studies* 325.

[193] Catherine Colston, *Principles of Intellectual Property Law* (Cavendish Publishing, 1999) 31.

[194] In relation to patents and trade marks, see Peter Drahos, 'Negotiating Intellectual Property Rights: Between Coercion and Knowledge' in Peter Drahos and Ruth Mayne (eds), *Global Intellectual Property Rights: Knowledge, Access and Development* (Palgrave Macmillan, 2002) 161, 174–175, citing Joe Staten Bain, *Barriers to New Competition: Their Character and Consequences in Manufacturing Industries* (Harvard University Press, 1956). For a pertinent discussion of the impact of trade marking materials previously protected by copyright, see Martin Senftleben, 'Vigeland and the Status of Cultural Concerns in Trade Mark Law – The EFTA Court Develops More Effective Tools for the Preservation of the Public Domain' 48(6) *IIC – International Review of Intellectual Property and Competition Law* 683.

[195] See Sentfleben (n 194).

[196] Drahos (n 194) 174–175, citing Bain (n 194).

[197] For example, in relation to patents, see Machlup and Penrose (n 190) 27.

4 CONCLUSION

International intellectual property law is expanding, but the fragmentation between intellectual property and human rights and the inadequacy of existing dispute mechanisms to support systemic integration makes it difficult to ensure that the expansion reflects normative concerns important to both human rights and intellectual property. The HRATM framework used in this book to ensure recognition for economic, social and cultural rights as well as civil and political rights[198] is developed in Chapter 2 and is designed to be used with existing models to found a global human rights culture for trade marks. This pluralistic, flexible approach is an important foundation for a human rights culture for trade marks that can effectively harmonise the two fields.

Rather than proposing a single harmonising framework, the book expands the literature by assessing the applicability of mechanisms recommended by existing conceptual models to domestic legislation. States should place greater emphasis on recognising economic, social and cultural rights, but should also consider the valuable analytical approaches recommended by existing models conceptualising the relationship between intellectual property and human rights and adapt their use so it is appropriate to their own local conditions. Policymakers need guidance on balancing economic, social and cultural rights with protection of intellectual property rights. The HRATM framework is a significant contribution to recognising the importance of economic, social and cultural rights in their relationship to trade marks, but it is only part of the solution. Applying the framework in three case studies demonstrates why protecting, respecting and promoting human rights is critical in domestic trade mark law and in international agreements that protect intellectual property.

This book will assist states to recognise why protecting, respecting and promoting human rights is critical in domestic trade mark law and in international agreements that protect intellectual property. Monitoring serious human rights concerns accompanying domestic implementation of international intellectual property obligations is a necessary step towards founding a globally relevant human rights culture for trade marks and a necessary foundation for transformation of trade mark protection to address associated human rights concerns. The HRATM framework also embeds rights-based principles to support adjustments to trade mark law necessary to realise human rights. This supports proposals for transformation through multilateral agreement and rethinking approaches to negotiating trade agreements in the final part of the book. A human rights culture for trade marks must be dynamic, but the foundations

[198] See Ruth Okediji, 'Does Intellectual Property Need Human Rights?' (2018) 50(1) *New York University Journal of International Law and Politics* 1.

explored in this book provide a valuable roadmap for realigning order with justice in domestic protection for trade marks.

2 Conceptualising trade marks and human rights: the case for recognising all human rights

1 INTRODUCTION

A human rights culture for trade marks should include a rights-based framework for understanding and addressing human rights obligations, recognising that changes to trade mark laws are effected through domestic laws implementing international intellectual property law agreements and trade agreements. Local conditions are critical to understanding the relationship between intellectual property and human rights.[1] Realising economic, social and cultural rights when intellectual property protection operates requires recognition that international cooperation and assistance may be needed to support domestic approaches that recognise human rights obligations. This chapter explores important concepts underpinning a human rights culture for trade marks.

Models for understanding the relationship between human rights and intellectual property provide a conceptual framework for the analysis of the relationship between the two fields. Originally, the relationship between human rights and intellectual property was conceptualised as either in conflict or in coexistence.[2] As the interactions between the regimes increased and were more deeply analysed, a series of prescriptive models that recognised some conflict between intellectual property and human rights proposed approaches to harmonising the fields to manage that conflict.[3] Prescriptive, harmonising models are particularly useful for identifying adjustments necessary to found a human

[1] See Ruth Okediji, 'Does Intellectual Property Need Human Rights?' (2018) 50(1) *New York University Journal of International Law and Politics* 1, 67.

[2] Laurence R Helfer, 'Human Rights and Intellectual Property: Conflict or Coexistence' (2003) 5(1) Minnesota Intellectual Property Review 47 ('Human Rights and Intellectual Property: Conflict or Coexistence').

[3] Laurence R Helfer and Graeme Austin (eds), *Human Rights and Intellectual Property: Mapping the Global Interface* (Cambridge University Press, 2011).

rights culture for trade marks. However, the focus of most of the models is not on trade mark protection but on copyright and patents. This chapter addresses this and explores the human rights implications of trade mark protection in relation to these models.

The following section of this chapter identifies the legal obligations underlying models conceptualising human rights and intellectual property. The third section then identifies key examples of these models and considers how trade marks are addressed in prescriptive, harmonising frameworks. The fourth section explores the ongoing development of a human rights culture for health, which embeds transformative rights-based principles underpinning economic, social and cultural rights into public health paradigms. This precedent influences the Human Rights Assessment for Trade Marks ('HRATM') framework proposed in the fifth section of the chapter. The HRATM framework guides states to assess how domestic trade mark protection complies with integrated human rights obligations and rights-based principles. This analysis and insights from other prescriptive frameworks support adjustments of trade mark protection where it is needed to support realisation of domestic human rights obligations. The findings from the case studies help develop a clearer picture of the proposed human rights culture for trade marks.

2 LEGAL FRAMEWORK UNDERPINNING MODELS FOR HUMAN RIGHTS AND INTELLECTUAL PROPERTY

Economic paradigms have dominated trade mark law for decades[4] and there is minimal reference to human rights in intellectual property agreements.[5] Yet understanding whether trade marks protection engages human rights considerations is critical. Trade marks function to both protect and restrict human rights. Human rights are a necessary concern for the overwhelming majority of states, as United Nations ('UN') Members. States are obliged to protect human rights in Article 55 of the *Charter of the United Nations* ('*UN Charter*'). Article 56 further obliges them to cooperate to protect human rights. The *Universal Declaration of Human Rights* ('*UDHR*') then recognises individual entitlements to realisation of economic, social and cultural rights 'through

[4] See William Fisher, 'Theories of Intellectual Property' in Stephen R Munzer (ed), *New Essays in the Legal and Political Theory of Property* (Cambridge University Press, 2001) 168, 169; William M Landes and Richard A Posner, *The Economic Structure of Intellectual Property Law* (Harvard University Press, 2003) 173.

[5] Peter K Yu 'Intellectual Property and Human Rights 2.0' (2019) 53 *University of Richmond Law Review* 1375, 1393–1394.

national effort and international cooperation'.[6] The *UDHR* provides an authoritative interpretation of human rights that is supported by binding obligations found in key human rights agreements,[7] including the *International Covenant on Civil and Political Rights* ('*ICCPR*')[8] and the *International Covenant on Economic, Social and Cultural Rights* ('*ICESCR*').[9] The charter obligations are particularly powerful because the *UN Charter* prevails to the extent that it conflicts with other international laws.[10]

Considering the *UDHR* drafting history, Plomer suggests that there is 'little support for the view that IP rights are fundamental human rights, although the modalities of national and international IP and patent laws may certainly, and indeed, should be deployed in the service of human rights'.[11] *UDHR* Article 27 provides:

> 1. Everyone has the right freely to participate in the cultural life of the community, to enjoy the arts and to share in scientific advancement and its benefits.
> 2. Everyone has the right to the protection of the moral and material interests resulting from any scientific, literary or artistic production of which he is the author.[12]

Shaver argues that the framers of Article 27 were primarily concerned with 'ensuring universal access to the fruits of science and technology as well as to the realm of cultural and artistic life, broadly understood'.[13] History suggests that the interests protected are limited to the creator's right to obtain a decent standard of living from their work and to preserve their moral rights of attribution and integrity.[14] This approach emphasises social welfare and the need to benefit from science, fostering and defending human dignity and the

---

[6] *Universal Declaration of Human Rights*, GA Res 217A (III), UN GAOR, UN Doc A/810 (10 December 1948) art 22 ('*UDHR*').

[7] *Vienna Declaration and Programme of Action: Adopted by the World Conference on Human Rights*, UN GAOR, UN Doc A/CONF.157/23 (25 June 1993) ('*VDPA*').

[8] *International Covenant on Civil and Political Rights*, opened for signature 16 December 1966, 999 UNTS 171 (entered into force 23 March 1976) ('*ICCPR*').

[9] *International Covenant on Economic, Social and Cultural Rights*, opened for signature 16 December 1966, 993 UNTS 3 (entered into force 3 January 1976) ('*ICESCR*').

[10] *Charter of the United Nations* art 103 ('*UN Charter*').

[11] Aurora Plomer, 'The Human Rights Paradox: Intellectual Property Rights and Rights of Access to Science.' *Human Rights Quarterly* (2013): 143, 175.

[12] *UDHR* (n 6) art 27; *ICESCR* (n 9) art 15.

[13] Lea Shaver, 'The Right to Science and Culture' (2010) 1 *Wisconsin Law Review* 121, 134.

[14] Ibid, 150.

common good and, to this end, limiting the protection provided for creators and authors.[15]

ICESCR Article 15 translates *UDHR* Article 27 into a more detailed obligation. Article 15 provides that:

> (1) The States Parties to the present Covenant recognize the right of everyone:
> (a) To take part in cultural life;
> (b) To enjoy the benefits of scientific progress and its applications;
> (c) To benefit from the protection of the moral and material interests resulting from any scientific, literary or artistic production of which he is the author.
> (2) The steps to be taken by the States Parties to the present Covenant to achieve the full realization of this right shall include those necessary for the conservation, the development and the diffusion of science and culture.
> (3) The States Parties to the present Covenant undertake to respect the freedom indispensable for scientific research and creative activity.
> (4) The States Parties to the present Covenant recognize the benefits to be derived from the encouragement and development of international contacts and co-operation in the scientific and cultural fields.

Human rights bodies have characterised intellectual property protection as a social product in their evolving interpretation of *ICESCR* Article 15.[16] This characterisation emphasises intellectual property's functional nature but shows that the objectives of human rights and intellectual property can overlap. Many human rights frameworks for intellectual property identify Article 15(1)(c) as a human right that intellectual property can function to protect, although other parts of Article 15 can limit the scope of that protection.[17] Shaver develops previous interpretations by Chapman, emphasising an integrated approach to a functioning intellectual property system that emphasises all of the elements

---

[15] Ibid.

[16] The Committee on Economic Social and Cultural Rights ('CESCR') considered Article 15(1)(c) in 2006, Article 15(1)(a) in 2009 and Article 15(1)(b) in 2020. Committee on Economic, Social and Cultural Rights, *General Comment No. 17: The Right of Everyone to Benefit from the Protection of the Moral and Material Interests Resulting from Any Scientific, Literary or Artistic Production of Which He or She Is the Author (Art 15, Para 1(c) of the Covenant)*, UN ESCOR, 35th sess, UN Doc E/C.12/GC/17 (12 January 2006) [35] ('*General Comment 17*'); Committee on Economic, Social and Cultural Rights, *General Comment No. 21: Right of Everyone to Take Part in Cultural Life (art. 15, para. 1a of the Covenant on Economic, Social and Cultural Rights)*, 43rd sess, UN Doc E/C.12/GC/21 (21 December 2009) ('*General Comment 21*'); Committee on Economic, Social and Cultural Rights, *General Comment No. 25 (2020) on Science and Economic, Social and Cultural Rights (article 15(1)(b), (2), (3) and (4) of the International Covenant on Economic, Social and Cultural Rights)*, 67th sess, UN Doc E/C.12/GC/25 (30 April 2020) [62] ('*General Comment 25*').

[17] Shaver (n 13) 150.

of Article 15.[18] This book uses the term 'right to benefit from science and culture' to describe the integrated right, reflecting that authors benefit from recognition of their moral and material interests, just as individuals benefit from participation in culture and access to the benefits of science.

Another right that can link intellectual property to human rights protection is the right to property. *UDHR* Article 17 provides that '[e]veryone has the right to own property alone as well as in association with others' and 'no one shall be arbitrarily deprived of their property.' This protection was not translated into the *ICCPR* nor the *ICESCR* but many domestic and regional human rights frameworks protect the right to property, which can aid interpretation of what the right confers. Human rights protection should be significantly narrower than the general property rights protection that underpins capitalist economies.[19] The underlying human right can be interpreted to restrict interference with enjoyment of personal property, such as expropriation by states. Although states are permitted a wide margin of appreciation,[20] European courts recently found that a state's failure to enforce copyright protection could also engage individual protection for the right to property.[21]

The next section considers three different approaches to understanding the relationship between intellectual property and human rights: conflict, coexistence and prescriptive harmonisation models. Varying weight is given to *ICESCR* Article 15 and right to property protection in these models.

3 MODELS CONCEPTUALISING THE RELATIONSHIP BETWEEN HUMAN RIGHTS AND INTELLECTUAL PROPERTY

3.1 Conflict Models

Conflict models focus on the difficulties that the intellectual property regime imposed by *TRIPS* presents for a number of different human rights, such as the right to health, the right to education and the right to food, particularly in

---

[18] Ibid. See also Audrey R Chapman, 'Towards an Understanding of the Right to Enjoy the Benefits of Scientific Progress and its Applications' (2009) 8(1) *Journal of Human Rights* 1.

[19] See Peter K Yu, 'The Anatomy of the Human Rights Framework for Intellectual Property' (2016) 69(1) *SMU Law Review* 37, 92–95 ('The Anatomy of the Human Rights Framework for Intellectual Property').

[20] *Anheuser-Busch Inc v Portugal (Merits)* (2007) I Eur Court HR 39 ('*Anheuser-Busch v Portugal*').

[21] *Safarov v Azerbaijan* (European Court of Human Rights, Chamber, Application no. 885/12, 1 September 2022).

developing countries. Conflict models draw largely on the output of human rights institutions in the 2000s,[22] in which actual and potential conflicts between *TRIPS* and numerous human rights are identified in non-binding reports and resolutions describing the conflict, often focusing on restrictions that patent protection pose for access to medicines.[23] The approach to resolving the conflict was to assert the primacy of human rights over international trade law.[24] The protection for human rights (and health) provided for in Article 55 of the *UN Charter*, and the obligation on states to cooperate to protect human rights further provided in Articles 55 and 56, supported primacy. However, in practice, human rights laws are rarely used to overrule conflicting intellectual property laws.[25]

A large body of obligations in intellectual property agreements and trade agreements bind most states. Interpretative tools in international law could be used to address conflicts between intellectual property and human rights, but the structure of the international legal framework means that this is practically difficult because there is no clear mechanism for conflict resolution between the fragmented fields of law.[26] Dispute resolution mechanisms could address fragmentation of this nature, yet no institutional mechanisms currently operate effectively to adjudicate considerations of human rights law and intellectual property law.[27] Even if a dispute resolution forum could adjudicate between the two fields, and human rights primacy was accepted using interpretative rules of hierarchy, because of the operation of the *UN Charter* (or the operation of *jus cogens* principles), the adjudication would only apply to an individual conflict. Expecting states to recognise the importance of human rights requires more than successful doctrinal argument in specific disputes; it requires a transformative understanding that intellectual property obligations can pose serious human rights concerns that may require domestic, regional and global institutional change.

---

22 See David Weissbrodt and Kell Schott, 'Human Rights Approach to Intellectual Property Protection: The Genesis and Application of Sub-Commission Resolution 2000/7' (2003) 5(1) *Minnesota Intellectual Property Review* 1.

23 Helfer and Austin (n 3) 53–56.

24 Ibid 65–71.

25 See Okediji (n 1).

26 See Henning Grosse Ruse-Khan, 'A Conflict-of-Laws Approach to Competing Rationalities in International Law: The Case of Plain Packaging between Intellectual Property, Trade, Investment and Health' (2013) 9(2) *Journal of Private International Law* 308.

27 Ibid.

3.2 Coexistence Models

An alternative approach to a conflict model is a coexistence model. The coexistence model asserts that there is little or no conflict between international intellectual property law and international human rights law.[28] According to this model, the two fields can operate harmoniously. This is because both fields fundamentally question the balance between private individual rights to receive limited monopolies as an incentive to create and innovate, on one hand, and public rights to access and consume the results of creation and innovation, on the other.[29] This emphasises the flexibilities provided by Articles 7 and 8 of *TRIPS*, as it situates the tension between the fields in the balance between incentives to innovate and access to innovation.[30] Minero argues that *TRIPS* provides the framework to resolve that tension.[31]

One tenet of the coexistence model is the similarity of the underlying objectives for each of the fields.[32] Despite both fields utilising the concept of a balancing of interests and rights, this exercise is influenced by normative principles that differ in critical ways.[33] Human rights law balances competing human rights, focusing on the interests of the individual and the obligations of states to individuals and each other, although collective human rights are increasingly recognised as human rights law evolves.[34] While intellectual property traditionally balances the need to incentivise innovation and reward

---

[28] Laurence R Helfer, 'Human Rights and Intellectual Property: Mapping an Evolving and Contested Relationship' in Rochelle C Dreyfuss and Justine Pila (eds), *The Oxford Handbook of Intellectual Property Law* (Oxford University Press, 2018) 117, 130 ('Human Rights and Intellectual Property: Mapping an Evolving and Contested Relationship').

[29] Helfer and Austin (n 3) 73; *General Comment 17* (n 16) [2].

[30] Helfer and Austin (n 3) 73; Helfer, 'Human Rights and Intellectual Property: Conflict or Coexistence' (n 2) 48–49.

[31] See Gemma Minero, 'Intellectual Property and Human Rights: Coinciding and Cooperating' in Paul Torremans (ed), *Intellectual Property and Human Rights: Enhanced Edition of Copyright and Human Rights* (Kluwer Law International, 4th ed, 2020) 169, 172. See also Rochelle Cooper Dreyfuss, 'Patents and Human Rights: The Paradox Reexamined' in Christophe Geiger (ed), *Intellectual Property and Access to Science and Culture: Convergence or Conflict?* (Global Perspectives for the Intellectual Property System, CEIPI-ICTSD, Issue 3, 2016) 54.

[32] Estelle Derclaye, 'Intellectual Property and Human Rights: Coinciding and Cooperating' in Paul Torremans (ed), *Intellectual Property and Human Rights: Enhanced Edition of Copyright and Human Rights* (Kluwer Law International, 2nd ed, 2008) 133.

[33] Plomer (n 11) 150.

[34] See, for example, *The Human Right to a Clean, Healthy and Sustainable Environment*, GA Res 76/300, UN Doc A/RES/76/300 (1 August 2022, adopted 28 July 2022).

private innovators against the social welfare concerns of the public, there is an increasing trend towards the protection of property interests in intellectual property.[35] Gervais argues that calibration of domestic intellectual property policy is possible through the flexibilities available in the *TRIPS* agreement that enable different domestic implementation of the international standards.[36] However, international intellectual property structures at bilateral, regional and multilateral levels can restrict domestic regulatory autonomy to recognise obligations to implement policies that support the realisation of human rights, including the right to health.[37] This expanded protection for trade mark owners is not consistent with economic theory, which is the dominant utilitarian theory justifying the protection of trade mark rights, or with property-based justifications using Lockean principles to support the grant of intellectual property rights for individuals.[38] It further moves away from the focus on the rights of the individual towards the protection of assets and investments primarily owned by corporations.[39] This highlights differences in the objectives of the two fields, suggesting that coexistence between them should not be uncritically accepted on the grounds of normative similarity.

Coexistence remains important as a goal. The instrumental objectives of socially beneficial intellectual property are valuable if they are consistent with realisation of human rights, particularly economic, social and cultural rights.[40] If not, adjustment is needed.

3.3 Prescriptive Models

Prescriptive models recognise the potential for conflicts between the fields of human rights and intellectual property, but also identify strategies for harmonisation or integration between the two fields, designed to facilitate coexistence. A prescriptive approach can propose strategies that recognise the potential

---

[35] Rochelle C Dreyfuss and Susy Frankel, 'From Incentive to Commodity to Asset: How International Law is Reconceptualizing Intellectual Property' (2015) 36(4) *Michigan Journal of International Law* 557, 570–571.

[36] Daniel J Gervais, 'IP Calibration' in Daniel J Gervais (ed), *Intellectual Property, Trade and Development: Strategies to Optimize Economic Development in a TRIPS-Plus Era* (Oxford University Press, 2nd ed, 2014) 86.

[37] Dreyfuss and Frankel (n 35) 566–575.

[38] See Fisher (n 4) 169–173.

[39] Christophe Geiger, 'Implementing Intellectual Property Provisions in Human Rights Instruments: Towards a New Social Contract for the Protection of Intangibles' in Christophe Geiger (ed), *Research Handbook on Human Rights and Intellectual Property* (Edward Elgar Publishing, 2015) 661, 662–664; Dreyfuss and Frankel (n 35) 566–575.

[40] See *General Comment 25* (n 16).

social welfare benefits of intellectual property protection while valuing human rights. Harmonising models incorporate prescriptive approaches to dealing with the conflict, often recognising the relevance of human rights in the *UDHR*, *ICCPR* and *ICESCR* that may be protected through intellectual property rights. They are more nuanced than simply asserting human rights primacy or asserting that the present utilisation of flexibility mechanisms in *TRIPS* sufficiently addresses conflicts between intellectual property and human rights. There are many prescriptive models. This chapter considers how three models developed by leading scholars that propose valuable harmonisation approaches address trade marks.

3.3.1 Yu's model

Peter Yu's model of protection emphasises human rights primacy and values the objectives of intellectual property law by asserting that resolving conflicts between intellectual property and human rights involves recognising human rights protection for some patent rights and some copyrights.[41] Yu identifies organising principles for understanding the relationship between intellectual property and Article 15(1)(c):

1. Intellectual property rights and human rights that can be used to protect some rights associated with intangible property are not the same things.[42]
2. The moral and material interests protected by human rights law are not interchangeable, so protecting one interest will not usually satisfy protection of the other.[43]
3. Human rights law requires minimum essential protection for intangible property, and extra protection found in intellectual property law should not harm other human rights.[44]
4. Different types of productions may require different forms of intellectual property. Yu suggests that this might involve trade mark protection in the case of scientific productions.[45]
5. Article 15(1)(c) provides sufficient flexibility to permit each state to protect the minimum requirements in a way that is locally appropriate.[46]

---

[41] Yu, 'The Anatomy of the Human Rights Framework for Intellectual Property' (n 19) 54–55.
[42] Ibid 54–55.
[43] Ibid 55–56.
[44] Ibid 57–60.
[45] Ibid 60.
[46] Ibid 61–62.

6. There is a wide range of protections that can satisfy the requirements of Article 15(1)(c) that do not necessarily originate in the intellectual property regime.[47]
7. Different types of intellectual property protection can satisfy the requirements of Article 15(1)(c).[48]

These principles underpin Yu's structural approach to understanding Article 15(1)(c). This approach first considers what scientific, literary or artistic productions can include.[49] Yu considers scientific productions and analyses how Article 15(1)(c) protection can include patent protection. The second layer identifies separate moral and material interests that are relevant to the production, including endogenous limits internalised within the intellectual property system.[50] Yu then considers the nature of protection that can be accorded to scientific productions[51] and, finally, identifies the exogenous limitations on that protection.[52] He concludes that 'some aspects of intellectual property rights (including patent rights) can be recognized as human rights'.[53]

Although Yu acknowledges a potential role for trade marks in the protection of scientific publications,[54] he maintains that the basis for human rights protection of trade marks is questionable.[55] Yu does not consider corporate trade mark rights to have human rights attributes, as corporations cannot possess human rights.[56] He cites Brinkhof's argument that trade marks are 'concerned not so much with the intellectual achievements of individuals, but rather with the regulation of competition through the prevention of confusion arising between participants in a market'.[57] Yu also notes Chapman's argument that there is no 'basis in human rights to justify using intellectual property instruments as a means to protect economic investments'.[58] However, Chapman does

---

47 Ibid 62–63.
48 Ibid 63–64.
49 Ibid 64.
50 Ibid 64–65.
51 Ibid 65.
52 Ibid 65–66.
53 Ibid 95.
54 Ibid 60.
55 Ibid 55.
56 See ibid.
57 Jan Brinkhof, 'On Patents and Human Rights' in Willem Grosheide (ed), *Intellectual Property and Human Rights: A Paradox* (Edward Elgar Publishing, 2010) 140, 140.
58 Yu, 'The Anatomy of the Human Rights Framework for Intellectual Property' (n 19) 55, citing Audrey R Chapman, 'Core Obligations Related to ICESCR Article 15(1)(C)' in Audrey R Chapman and Sage Russell (eds), *Core Obligations: Building a Framework for Economic, Social and Cultural Rights* (Intersentia, 2002) 316–317.

not ignore trade marks and argues that human rights should be incorporated into assessment of trade mark applications.[59]

The analysis mechanism used by Yu can show how some trade marks might qualify for Article 15(1)(c) protection. Different types of trade marks can be identified in the artistic or literary production layer. Utilising a bottom–up approach and examining individual trade marks, they can be understood as positively contributing to culture: they can contain artistic works and imbue certain existing or new words with cultural meaning. Increasingly, certain marks are recognised for their cultural significance.[60] From the perspective of the interest layer, trade mark law can protect the material rights of creators of trade marks that constitute literary or artistic productions where they have some claim to ownership rights and someone else tries to use their work.[61] In current legal practice, moral rights are protected only where trade mark creators qualify for copyright protection. Word trade marks are rarely considered to constitute literary works,[62] although device marks may contain artistic works protectable by copyright.[63] Just as patent monopolies are limited in time, trade mark monopolies are limited by a use requirement.[64] This is an endogenous limitation that may be a problematic difference between trade marks and human rights, which are enduring rights.[65] However, the rights that Article 15(1)(c) confers on creators contemplate specific material remuneration, rather than continuing remuneration.[66] Recognition of moral rights for creators need not always be tied to continuing registration; a historical register might suffice for attribution.[67] Signs that are protected as trade marks can contribute

---

[59] Audrey R Chapman, *Approaching Intellectual Property Rights as a Human Right: Obligations Related to Article 15 (1) (c). Commission on Economic Social and Cultural Rights Discussion* Paper, 24th sess, Agenda Item 3, UN Doc E/C.12/2000/12 (3 October 2000).

[60] Megan Richardson, 'Trade Marks and Language' (2004) 26(2) *Sydney Law Review* 193, 194–197; Helfer and Austin (n 3) 307–309.

[61] In Australia, this can be protected in the grounds of opposition provided in *Trade Marks Act 1995* (Cth) ss 58, 58A, unless ownership is modified by employment or contractual arrangements.

[62] *Exxon Corporation v Exxon Insurance Consultants International Ltd* [1982] Ch 119, 143 (Stephenson LJ).

[63] *Advantage-Rent-A-Car Inc v Advantage Car Rental Pty Ltd* (2001) 52 IPR 24.

[64] See Yu, 'The Anatomy of the Human Rights Framework for Intellectual Property' (n 19) 76.

[65] See Megan M Carpenter, 'Trademarks and Human Rights: Oil and Water? Or Chocolate and Peanut Butter?' (2009) 99(4) *Trademark Reporter* 892, 901.

[66] *General Comment 17* (n 16).

[67] Genevieve Wilkinson, 'Exploring Moral Interests in the Intellectual Creations underlying Trade Marks' in Ysolde Gendreau (ed), *Research Handbook on Intellectual Property and Moral Rights* (Edward Elgar Publishing, forthcoming).

to culture, although to the extent that this engages Article 15(1)(c), they can be protected by a wide range of protections, including unfair competition law and copyright law.[68]

Whether trade marks function to protect human rights is relevant because Yu has developed a further model for resolving conflicts between human rights and intellectual property rights that function to protect Article 15. This model balances the protection provided by these articles for the moral and material rights of creators and authors against other human rights.[69] Yu argues that rather than focusing on whether human rights and intellectual property conflict or coexist, it is better to accept that their overlapping human rights attributes (such as the protection of moral and material interests found in *ICESCR* Article 15) mean that they both conflict and coexist.[70] This perspective will assist consideration of 'how we can alleviate the tension and resolve the conflict between the human rights and the non-human-rights aspects of intellectual property protection'.[71]

Using this approach, Yu divides the conflicts into internal conflicts, which engage Article 15 and can be characterised as disputes between competing human rights, and external conflicts.[72] Once an external conflict is identified, Yu applies the principle of human rights primacy to privilege human rights protection.[73] Where an internal conflict exists, there are three possible resolution approaches: a just remuneration approach that includes compulsory licensing to prevent human rights restrictions; a core minimum approach that provides minimum essential levels of protection to authors and inventors as well as core minimum obligations for other human rights; and a progressive realisation approach that focuses on asking what should be protected, with states using best measures to realise their human rights obligations, commensurate with available resources.[74] These approaches can be complementary, and Yu proposes a systematic method for addressing conflicts between internal rights, beginning with conflicts within the right itself.[75] Ultimately, the approach emphasises the primacy of human rights where there is an external

---

[68] Ibid.

[69] Peter K Yu, 'Reconceptualizing Intellectual Property Interests in a Human Rights Framework' (2006) 40(3) *University of California Davis Law Review* 1039 ('Reconceptualizing Intellectual Property Interests in a Human Rights Framework').

[70] Ibid 1078.

[71] Ibid.

[72] Ibid.

[73] Ibid.

[74] Ibid 1094–1123.

[75] Ibid.

conflict between intellectual property rights that can be protected as human rights and intellectual property rights that human rights does not protect.[76]

This model provides a mechanism for recognising that in some cases intellectual property can function to protect human rights but limits the risk that corporate intellectual property owners can capture human rights discourse by asserting that they have a human rights entitlement to broad intellectual property protection. Where protection for Article 15(1)(c) is detrimental to other human rights, Yu provides multiple tools for ensuring that protection is balanced against other human rights concerns. There is very limited consideration of trade marks in Yu's models because he argues that their protection through Article 15 is questionable.[77] He discounts the existence of a right to property to protect corporate interests, exploring an interpretation of the right that supports common ownership of property in the public domain.[78] However, in some cases there is overlap between trade mark protection and patent protection, and trade marks can protect human rights in this auxiliary role.[79]

3.3.2 Geiger's model

Christophe Geiger's model integrates protection for intellectual property rights, drawing primarily on *UDHR* Article 27, into a domestic or regional human rights framework.[80] Some protection for the right to property is presently available in both the *First Protocol to the European Convention on Human Rights* ('*First Protocol*') and the *European Union Charter of Fundamental Rights* ('*ECR*').[81] He proposes greater emphasis in these instruments on the objectives of intellectual property protection that are highlighted in *UDHR* Article 27,[82] arguing that this can address criticism of the protection of intellectual property, in these systems and more generally.

---

[76] Ibid 1092–1093.

[77] Yu, 'The Anatomy of the Human Rights Framework for Intellectual Property' (n 19) 55.

[78] Ibid 94–95.

[79] Ibid 60.

[80] Geiger does not exclude right to property justified protection: Geiger (n 39) 661–689. Geiger explores a similar model in Christophe Geiger, 'Building an Ethical Framework for Intellectual Property in the EU: Time to Revise the Charter of Fundamental Rights' in Gustavo Ghidini (ed), *Reforming Intellectual Property* (Edward Elgar Publishing, 2022) 77.

[81] Geiger (n 39) 667–672, 678–685. See *Charter of Fundamental Rights of the European Union* [2010] OJ C 83/389 (entered into force 1 December 2009) art 17 ('*ECR*'); *Protocol to the Convention for the Protection of Human Rights and Fundamental Freedoms*, signed 20 March 1952, 213 UNTS 262 (entered into force 18 May 1954) art 1 ('*First Protocol*').

[82] Geiger (n 39) 662–664, 672–673.

In Geiger's model, constitutional courts can determine the extent to which protection for intellectual property provided should be circumscribed by other rights to 'participate in the cultural life of the community, to enjoy the arts and to share in scientific advancement and its benefits'.[83] This integrated inclusion of Article 27 could address concerns that permitting property rights protection for intellectual property may unnecessarily elevate broad protection for intellectual property to the status of fundamental rights.[84] This could exceed the protection that the international human rights instruments provide, and fail to recognise the close connection between protection for intellectual property and protection for the other rights articulated in *UDHR* Article 27 and *ICESCR* Article 15.[85] Globally, Article 27-based constitutional protection is currently underdeveloped, even where the right already exists.[86] However, the human rights protected in Article 27 also need to be recognised in trade agreements: the constitutional protections advocated by Geiger do not comprehensively address these agreements.

Geiger attempts to promote coexistence between intellectual property and human rights law by suggesting three different approaches to protecting certain elements of intellectual property as fundamental rights, through amendment to the *ECR*. He alternatively proposes to integrate protection similar to that provided by *UDHR* Article 27 into either of the fundamental rights to: property; freedom of arts and sciences; or freedom of expression and information.[87] *ECR* Article 17(2) currently provides that 'intellectual property shall be protected'. This has been interpreted to include trade marks.[88] The alternative provisions proposed reference protection for 'scientific, literary or artistic productions'.[89] Geiger does not address how this would apply to trade marks. Trade marks have been included in the scope of protection available under Article 1 of the *First Protocol*.[90] However, Geiger criticises 'unconditionally equating [intellectual property] protection with the constitutionally granted right to property'[91] and

---

83 Ibid 678–680.

84 See John Morijn, 'Conflicts between Fundamental Rights or Conflicting Fundamental Rights Vocabularies? An Analysis of Diverging Uses of "Fundamental Rights" in the Context of International and European Trade Law' in Eva Brems (ed), *Conflicts between Fundamental Rights* (Intersentia, 2008) 591, 616.

85 See Ernst-Ulrich Petersmann, 'Human Rights and International Economic Law' (2012) 4(2) *Trade Law and Development* 283.

86 Geiger (n 39) 667.

87 Ibid 686–688.

88 See ibid 670–672. See also *L'Oréal SA v Bellure NV* (C-487/07) [2009] ECR I-5185.

89 Geiger (n 39) 686–688.

90 Ibid 668–669.

91 Ibid 666.

notes that multiple layers of protection available through intellectual property can be problematic in the way that they contribute to a maximalist approach to rights protection.[92] If the right to property is not amended and the right is integrated into the right to freedom of arts and sciences, or the right to freedom of expression and information, Geiger supports the continued protection of intellectual property as part of the right to property, as long as that protection remains limited to safeguarding the public interest and does not expand.[93]

This approach is directed towards changing perceptions of intellectual property that Geiger views as negative for human rights.[94] Geiger's second proposal for integrating Article 27 into existing protection for freedom of arts and sciences is best designed to recognise the integrated nature of the right. Article 13 of the *ECR* currently provides: 'The arts and scientific research shall be free of constraint. Academic freedom shall be respected.'

The proposed new article would provide:

1. Everyone has the right to benefit from the achievements of scientific progress, to enjoy the arts and to participate in the cultural life of the community.
2. Creators of scientific, literary or artistic production shall have the right to the protection of the moral and material interests resulting from their creative activity. The rights granted are regulated by law in so far as is necessary to guarantee the rights in the preceding paragraph and the general interest.
3. The arts and scientific research shall be free of constraint. Academic freedom shall be respected.[95]

The application of Geiger's approach in Part II of this book focuses on this proposal. Because Geiger integrates his model within domestic or regional constitutional frameworks, the mechanisms for resolving disputes where trade mark protection engages human rights concerns are likely to be guided by the approach taken to resolve conflicts by the relevant constitutional framework. The constitutional framework can also influence what other rights are protected. This may not be consistent with the protections provided in the key international human rights agreements and the interpretation of these protections by the relevant treaty-making body.[96] Problematically, European constitutional frameworks do not give sufficient weight to economic, social and

[92] Ibid 664.
[93] Ibid 668, 672, 680.
[94] Ibid 663–664.
[95] Ibid 687.
[96] Ducoulombier (n 63) 39–41.

cultural rights.[97] Ducoulombier criticises the limited protection of economic, social and cultural rights in the European Court of Human Rights framework, although additional protection is available in the *European Social Charter*.[98] Some economic, social and cultural rights are included in the *ECR*, such as protection for the right to health, which encompasses rights to preventative health care and benefits from medical treatment, but the scope protected by the right can limit meaningful recognition.[99]

3.3.3 Helfer and Austin's model

Helfer and Austin's model proposes an approach to assessing how to balance competing intellectual property and human rights interests, and they argue that intellectual property and human rights have a common objective 'to encourage creativity and innovation that benefits society as a whole'.[100] The approach ultimately privileges human rights protection, yet attempts to preserve the social welfare benefits of the intellectual property system by rejecting wholesale expansions or restrictions of intellectual property rights.[101] Where possible, the use of existing international intellectual property law standards is preserved by incorporating questions that emphasise the social value of intellectual property into human rights assessments:[102]

1. Is intellectual property actually restrictive of the relevant human right or freedom, or are other factors, such as structural limitations, causing the restriction?
2. What is the positive impact of intellectual property?
3. What is the negative impact of intellectual property?
4. What is the relative causal contribution of intellectual property in comparison with other factors?
5. What legal and policy measures can facilitate human rights outcomes?

These welfare preservation considerations are analysed in the case studies.

The model recommends the use of measurement tools such as human rights impact assessments to determine the impact of intellectual property on human rights.[103] If possible, where intellectual property rights are implicated, and

---

[97] See Courtney Jung, Ran Hirschl and Evan Rosevear, 'Economic and Social Rights in National Constitutions' (2014) 62(4) *American Journal of Comparative Law* 1043, 1057.

[98] Ducoulombier (n 63) 39–41.

[99] *ECR* (n 81) art 35.

[100] Helfer and Austin (n 3) 520.

[101] Ibid 516–517.

[102] Ibid 519–520.

[103] Ibid 518–520.

can protect these human rights ends, they should be protected. However, in circumstances where intellectual property rights conflict with human rights, they should be modified or, in some circumstances, discarded to protect human rights.[104] The model incorporates, where possible, international law that regulates trade marks.[105] Helfer and Austin prescribe that where restrictions on these laws are necessary, it is important to recognise intellectual property law's common objective with human rights 'to encourage creativity and innovation that benefits society as a whole'.[106]

Helfer and Austin identify both protective and restrictive human rights standards for intellectual property.[107] The protective element preserves minimum standards of intellectual property protection in relation to Article 15(1)(c) of the *ICESCR*, Article 27 of the *UDHR* and Article 1 of the *First Protocol*.[108] It requires that states 'recognize and respect the rights of individuals and groups to enjoy a modicum of economic and moral benefit from their creative and innovative activities' and 'refrain from bad faith and arbitrary interferences with intellectual property rights that the state itself has previously granted or recognized'.[109] The former is consistent with the guidance provided by the Committee on Economic, Social and Cultural Rights ('CESCR') regarding Article 15 in *General Comment 17*.[110] The latter is consistent with protection in the *First Protocol*[111] and provides human rights protection against state interference with property rights for trade mark owners.[112]

The focus of Helfer and Austin's detailed analysis of the human rights implications of trade mark protection is on freedom of expression.[113] The impact of trade mark protection on expression means that this analysis is valuable, but trade mark protection can also function to significantly impact realisation of economic, social and cultural rights. This relationship between trade mark protection and human rights engages quite different considerations, such as the function of progressive realisation and the impact of resource restrictions,

---

[104] Ibid 1. See also Laurence R Helfer, 'Mapping the Interface between Human Rights and Intellectual Property' in Christophe Geiger (ed), *Research Handbook on Human Rights and Intellectual Property* (Edward Elgar Publishing, 2015) 6, 14 ('Mapping the Interface between Human Rights and Intellectual Property').

[105] Helfer and Austin (n 3) 521.

[106] Ibid 520.

[107] Ibid 513–522.

[108] Ibid 513–516.

[109] Ibid 512.

[110] *General Comment 17* (n 16).

[111] Helfer and Austin (n 3) 515–516, 212–220.

[112] Ibid.

[113] Ibid 283–312. There is also a shorter analysis of the relationship between trade mark protection and Indigenous human rights: 496–502.

which are explored in detail in the plain packaging and anti-counterfeiting case studies. The social welfare benefits of trade marks are also less aligned with encouragement of creativity and innovation other than types of intellectual property such as copyright or patent protection, the core objective of human rights and intellectual property recognised by Helfer and Austin, although they can support this function.

Helfer and Austin's model proposes that the ultimate focus should be the protection of a threshold of human rights, including 'noninterference with civil and political rights and guaranteeing minimum levels of economic and social well-being in areas such as health, food and education', which can be protected by various means.[114] Although a key component of the model proposed by Helfer and Austin is the measurement of 'human rights ends' using the standard of minimum rights, it is not clear exactly how the minimum levels for other economic, social and cultural rights can be measured. In 2007, Helfer used the language of 'core obligations'.[115] This approach is not clearly adopted by Helfer and Austin in 2011, when they articulate what a minimum standard comprises in relation to human rights protection for intellectual property.[116] In subsequent discussion of the model, Helfer argues that the proposed framework requires states to specify the 'minimum entitlements relating to health, food, education, and so forth that international human rights law requires and then [identify] the range of legal and policy mechanisms available to achieve those outcomes'.[117]

3.4 Conceptualising the Relationship Between Human Rights and Trade Marks

The prescriptive, harmonising models analysed do not adequately consider the human rights implications of trade marks or address the economic, social and cultural rights concerns posed by intellectual property. Features of existing models are useful for understanding aspects of the relationship and identifying important human rights implications of the trade mark laws being studied for human rights.

An important feature of Geiger's model is the recognition that the right within *UDHR* Article 27 is an integrated one and human rights protection for intellectual property rights needs to be limited to ensure all aspects of the right

---

[114] Helfer and Austin (n 3) 517.

[115] Laurence R Helfer, 'Towards a Human Rights Framework for Intellectual Property' (2006) 40 *University of California Davis Law Review* 971.

[116] Helfer and Austin (n 3) 513–516.

[117] Helfer, 'Mapping the Interface between Human Rights and Intellectual Property' (n 104) 14.

are valued. However, the applicability of his proposals for a human rights culture is limited in at least two ways. First, they operate within a mature human rights protection system not found in all parts of the world. Second, the European human rights constitutional framework includes rights not found in international human rights law and does not give the same weight to the protection of economic, social and cultural rights as it gives to civil and political rights.[118]

Yu argues that trade marks should not be entitled to human rights protection. However, his model helps to recognise how trade marks can function to protect the human rights of authors of literary, artistic and scientific productions. Trade marks are also relevant to protection of artistic and literary productions. In both cases, the function of trade mark ownership needs to be viewed within an integrated assessment of *ICESCR* Article 15 to ensure that it does not unnecessarily limit access to the benefits of science and participation in culture. However, the model is not tailored to provide an integrated assessment of all relevant human rights implications of trade mark protection, including the application of rights-based principles, which is important for founding a human rights culture. Although they do not propose a specific assessment mechanism, Helfer and Austin recognise the value of human rights impact assessments and propose an approach for recognising the social welfare benefits of intellectual property. The approach can apply to trade marks. However, their model provides limited protection for economic, social and cultural rights. This is problematic as trade marks can function to both restrict and protect economic, social and cultural rights, and this engages different types of rights-based considerations such as progressive realisation and maximum available resources.

Progressive realisation of economic, social and cultural rights means that protection may operate differently between states but the *UN Charter* obliges states to cooperate to reduce this inequality.[119] Okediji identifies the failure of human rights frameworks to address economic, social and cultural rights as highly problematic for justifying using human rights frameworks for intellectual property. She criticises existing human rights frameworks for intellectual property for strengthening private rights, which makes it harder to 'use IP doctrines effectively for promoting human welfare objectives'.[120] The CESCR characterises the contribution of intellectual property rights to social welfare as, generally, of a different nature from human rights which are essential to

[118] Ducoulombier (n 63) 42.
[119] *UN Charter* (n 10) arts 55, 56.
[120] Okediji (n 1) 4.

humanity and human dignity.[121] The object and purpose of economic, social and cultural rights centralises human dignity and welfare for all individuals.[122] As a social product, intellectual property promotes socially beneficial science and culture by providing the incentive to innovate, create and disseminate – as well as, in the case of trade marks, protecting consumers.[123] However, the intellectual property system is not the only means available for incentivising innovation and creation,[124] nor the only means to protect consumers.[125] Accordingly, Part III of this book proposes a novel approach for addressing human rights concerns linked to ineffective trade mark enforcement, using a mechanism separate from existing, multilateral intellectual property protection systems.

4 HOW TO FOUND A CULTURE

Developing a human rights culture for trade marks will require the transformation of existing values in domestic and international law, but this transformation first requires an understanding of the human rights implications of trade mark protection. The first step of the HRATM framework developed in this section assesses the human rights implications of trade marks and the final step balances any competing human rights concerns against each other. The HRATM framework is applied to assess concrete examples of trade mark protection in Part II of this book, and to consider the human rights implications of the registration, exercise, scope and enforcement of trade mark rights. Assessment is the first step to see where transformation is needed[126] and requires state accountability for implementation of international intellectual property obligations while prioritising realisation of economic, social and cultural rights. The HRATM framework also considers rights-based principles relevant to trade marks and human rights, emphasising principles relevant to economic, social and cultural rights as well as civil and political rights. These principles and harmonisation approaches from Yu, Geiger, and Helfer and

---

[121] *General Comment 17* (n 16) [2–4].

[122] Audrey Chapman, *Global Health, Human Rights and the Challenge of Neoliberal Policies* (Cambridge University Press, 2016) 17.

[123] J Janewa Osei Tutu, 'Humanizing Intellectual Property: Moving Beyond the Natural Rights Property Focus' (2017) 20(1) *Vanderbilt Journal of Entertainment and Technology Law* 207, 213–214.

[124] Thomas Pogge, 'Human Rights and Global Health: A Research Program' (2005) 36(1–2) *Metaphilosophy* 182, 184–194. See also Thomas Pogge, 'Access to Medicines' (2008) 1(2) *Public Health Ethics* 73.

[125] Michael D Pendleton, 'Excising Consumer Protection: The Key to Reforming Trade Mark Law' (1992) 3 *Australian Intellectual Property Journal* 110.

[126] Cf Okediji (n 1) 24–25.

Austin support a more transformative approach to the relationship between intellectual property and human rights.[127] The HRATM framework underpins the proposal for redesigning existing approaches to communicating origin and guaranteeing the provenance of goods in Chapter 6 so that transformation supports a human rights culture for trade marks.

Trade mark protection has important human rights implications. Actors within a human rights culture for trade marks need to proactively address the concern that existing human rights approaches to intellectual property systems are insufficient to recognise their impact on economic, social and cultural rights and effect meaningful change. Actors should also use human rights protection as a corrective when expanding protection for trade marks negatively impacts human rights. Analysis of that human rights relationship, using a rights-based framework, underpins these actions. In the jurisdictions studied in this book, the dominant paradigm in trade mark protection is an economic paradigm that focuses on the protection of owner rights as property. The flexibilities provided in the *Paris Convention* and *TRIPS* for the protection of societal interests that could include human rights protection are not mandatory. A human rights culture needs a more deliberate approach. The HRATM framework developed in this chapter to assess the human rights implications of trade mark law builds on analytical frameworks developed to assess economic, social and cultural rights, particularly the right to health. Intentional identification of human rights implications using analytical tools has been a valuable mechanism within a broader movement towards increasing respect, protection and fulfilment of the right to health in the international health system.

4.1 Development of a Health and Human Rights Framework

The development of a human rights culture for health provides valuable insights into how it is possible to strengthen human rights realisation when another paradigm is dominant. There is a dominant economic paradigm in trade mark law. The key international agreements concerning trade marks are within international intellectual property law and trade law – fields that make infrequent direct references to human rights. The dominant paradigm for health law remains public health, but in recent decades a synergistic health and human rights framework has developed. Consequently, the protection of human rights has been more heavily emphasised in public health law. The human rights culture surrounding health increasingly recognises key economic, social and cultural concerns that should be considered and addressed within a transformative human rights culture for trade marks.

---

[127] See ibid 9–10.

The World Health Organization ('WHO') proclaimed the importance of the human right to health and enshrined it in its constitution in 1946.[128] Yet a public health approach emphasising health outcomes has been the dominant paradigm, reflecting geo-political tensions between a Western emphasis on civil and political rights and an Eastern emphasis on economic, social and cultural rights.[129] Health was characterised as a global public good[130] and necessary public health measures became potentially justifiable restrictions on other human rights in certain circumstances.[131] This prioritised population health rather than individual rights to human health.[132] This emphasis on entire populations to understand demography relevant to public health initiatives contrasts with the emphasis on the individual and the dignity of the individual in human rights law, although there is overlap of the concerns in each field as public health systems can be used effectively by states to fulfil the right to health.[133] Epidemiology underpins public health investigations and data is essential to both fields.[134] Public health describes a health-related problem and provides a basis for intervention and promotion.[135] The human right to health guides our assessment of health issues within a context of progressive realisation of economic, social and cultural rights and a broader human rights framework grounded in non-discrimination, participation and accountability.[136] In 2005, the WHO revised its *International Health Regulations* and explicitly required that their implementation be 'with full respect for the dignity, human rights and fundamental freedoms of persons'.[137] This support for a human rights approach to implementation by the WHO is contemporaneous with more detailed defi-

---

[128] World Health Organization, *Preamble to the Constitution, Adopted by the International Health Conference, New York, 1946* (World Health Organization, 1948).

[129] See John Tobin, *The Right to Health in International Law* (Oxford University Press, 2012) 30–32.

[130] Fiona Sim and Martin McKee, *Issues in Public Health* (Open University Press, 2nd ed, 2011) 186.

[131] See, for example, *ICCPR* (n 8) art 19(3).

[132] Sim and McKee (n 130) 186; Brigit Toebes, 'Human Rights and Public Health: Towards a Balanced Relationship' (2015) 19(4) *The International Journal of Human Rights* 488, 488–491.

[133] Chapman (n 122) 37.

[134] Hamed A Adetunji, 'Principles of Epidemiology' in Frances Wilson and Mzwandile Mabhala (eds), *Key Concepts in Public Health* (SAGE, 2009) 36.

[135] See L Kay Bartholomew Eldredge et al, *Planning Health Promotion Programs: An Intervention Mapping Approach* (John Wiley & Sons, 4th ed, 2016) 7–8.

[136] Paul Hunt, 'Interpreting the International Right to Health in a Human Rights-Based Approach to Health' (2016) 18(2) *Health and Human Rights* 109.

[137] World Health Organization, *International Health Regulations (2005)* (World Health Organization, 3rd ed, 2016) art 3.1.

nitions of the right to health in scholarship and policy.[138] Recognition of the foundational importance of health to individuals, communities and nations is important to both public health and the right to health.[139] Recognising a human rights approach is currently important for negotiation of a new WHO treaty to address pandemics.[140]

A human rights approach to health has used the legal and moral legitimacy associated with the fundamental nature of human rights, building on the recognition of the importance of the right to health in the HIV/AIDS epidemic.[141] Although Novogrodsky criticises the failure of the right to health to be used successfully in other contexts[142] and other theorists have identified the use of human rights only as a weapon of last resort,[143] the right is increasingly recognised as relevant to health concerns.[144] There is clear evidence of the consideration of the right to health in the growing use of human rights impact assessments, health impact assessments and right to health impact assessments.[145] Bustreo and Hunt observe an increasing reference by states to the right to health in the World Health Assembly as indicative of 'profound changes in the relationship between health and human rights' in many countries.[146] There is also evidence of the impact of the right to health in relation to

---

[138] Sim and McKee (n 130) 186.

[139] Lawrence O Gostin, *Global Health Law* (Harvard University Press, 2014) 17–31; Committee on Economic, Social and Cultural Rights, *General Comment No 14: The Right to the Highest Attainable Standard of Health (Article 12 of the Covenant)*, UN ESCOR, 22nd sess, UN Doc E/C.12/2000/4 (11 August 2000) [1] ('*General Comment 14*').

[140] See Lawrence O Gostin, Benjamin Mason Meier and Barbara Stocking, 'Developing an Innovative Pandemic Treaty to Advance Global Health Security' (2021) 49 *Journal of Law, Medicine & Ethics* 503.

[141] See Duncan Matthews, 'Intellectual Property Rights, Human Rights and the Right to Health' in Willem Grosheide (ed), *Intellectual Property and Human Rights: A Paradox* (Edward Elgar Publishing, 2010) 136. See also Noah Novogrodsky, 'After AIDS' (2013) 14(2) *Melbourne University Law Review* 643, 650–651.

[142] Novogrodsky (n 141) 657.

[143] Samuel Murumba, 'Foxes and Hedgehogs at the Intersection of Human Rights and Intellectual Property' (2012) 38(1) *Monash University Law Review* 119, 135–136.

[144] Chapman (n 122) 311. See also Laurence R Helfer, Karen J Alter and Florencia Guerzovich, 'Islands of Effective International Adjudication: Constructing an Intellectual Property Rule of Law in the Andean Community' (2009) 103(1) *American Journal of International Law* 1.

[145] See Lisa Forman and Gillian MacNaughton, 'Moving Theory into Practice: Human Rights Impact Assessment of Intellectual Property Rights in Trade Agreements' (2015) 7(1) *Journal of Human Rights Practice* 109, 131–132.

[146] Flavia Bustreo and Paul Hunt, 'The Right to Health Is Coming of Age: Evidence of Impact and the Importance of Leadership' (2013) 34(4) *Journal of Public Health Policy* 574, 575.

policies, laws and interventions in specific countries.[147] The characterisation of human rights as a tool to promote public health is useful because it encourages emphasis on dignity in public health measures, which builds public confidence in those measures and increases their authority, and recognises that there is a fundamental right to live in an environment conducive to the human right to health.[148] The WHO Secretary-General recognised that addressing human rights was critical in the Covid-19 pandemic and a human rights framework provided 'a crucial structure that can strengthen the effectiveness of global efforts to address the pandemic'.[149]

The interactions between the fields of public health and human rights are growing as a human rights culture for health evolves.[150] Taket notes that, increasingly, effective health promotion is linked to empowerment-based approaches and these have strong congruence with human rights approaches.[151] Tobin argues that there is a mutually supportive connection between the idea within public health discourse that the state remains responsible for the protection and promotion of the health of its citizens, and the obligation that is placed on states in human rights law to protect the right to health of individuals.[152] Combined with the developing literature on the human right to health and increased institutional focus on the right, this has contributed to a human rights framework for action in public health.[153] Gruskin and Tarantola argue that this could be 'used to shape specific interventions aimed at reducing the impact of health conditions on the lives of individuals and populations'.[154] Although they have critical differences between them, the two approaches should not be characterised as mutually exclusive but complementary.

---

147 Flavia Bustreo and Paul Hunt, *Women's and Children's Health: Evidence of Impact of Human Rights* (World Health Organization, 2013) 22–24.

148 Sim and McKee (n 130) 186.

149 World Health Organization, *Addressing Human Rights as Key to the COVID-19 Response* (WHO, 21 April 2020) https://www.who.int/publications/i/item/addressing-human-rights-as-key-to-the-covid-19-response.

150 Ann R Taket, *Health Equity, Social Justice and Human Rights* (Routledge, 2012) 1.

151 Ibid.

152 See John Tobin (n 129) 41.

153 See an example of influence of these factors in Orielle Solar and Alec Irwin, 'A Conceptual Framework for Action on the Social Determinants of Health' (Social Determinants of Health Discussion Paper 2, World Health Organization, 2010) 12–16 http://www.who.int/sdhconference/resources/ConceptualframeworkforactiononSDH_eng.pdf.

154 Sofia Gruskin and Daniel Tarantola, 'Health and Human Rights' in Sofia Gruskin et al (eds), *Perspectives on Health and Human Rights* (Routledge, 2005) 3, 43.

4.2 Using Assessment Tools to Build a Human Rights Culture for Health

Frameworks that support a complementary public health and human rights approach continue to evolve, reflecting the dynamic nature of human rights.[155] In 2005, Gruskin and Tarantola developed an approach suggested by Gostin and Mann to frame a series of questions that could be used for assessing policies and programmes using a health and human rights framework.[156] The intention was to use the approach to determine 'whether health policies, programmes and practices [were] valid from both a public health and a human rights perspective'.[157]

Standards found in the human rights-based approach to development have been influential in the evolution of rights-based approaches to health. Pillars of this approach included 'universality and inalienability, indivisibility, interdependence and interrelatedness, non-discrimination and equality, participation and inclusion, accountability and the rule of law'.[158] In 2010, Gruskin, Bogecho and Ferguson proposed operational norms and standards for a rights-based approach to health: availability, accessibility, acceptability and quality ('AAAQ'), participation, non-discrimination, transparency and accountability.[159] In 2015, Hunt, Yamin and Bustreo described a growing integration of human rights into health,[160] despite significant work remaining to achieve a common understanding of a human rights-based approach to health.[161] Hunt, Yamin and Bustreo emphasise that human rights approaches use interdisciplinary approaches, including those from social sciences, medicine and public health, to the measurement of outcomes.[162]

---

[155] See Philip Alston, 'Conjuring Up New Human Rights: A Proposal for Quality Control' (1984) 78(3) *American Journal of International Law* 607.

[156] Gruskin and Tarantola (n 154) 43–45.

[157] Ibid 39.

[158] For an example of an early rights-based approach to development, see: United Nations Development Group, *The Human Rights Based Approach to Development Cooperation: Towards a Common Understanding Among UN Agencies* (United Nations, 2003) 2.

[159] Sofia Gruskin, Dina Bogecho and Laura Ferguson, '"Rights-Based Approaches" to Health Policies and Programs: Articulations, Ambiguities, and Assessment' (2010) 31(2) *Journal of Public Health Policy* 129, 129–145.

[160] Paul Hunt, Alicia Ely Yamin and Flavia Bustreo, 'Making the Case: What Is the Evidence of Impact of Applying Human Rights-Based Approaches to Health?' (2015) 17(2) *Health and Human Rights Journal* 1, 3.

[161] Ibid 8. Taket criticises a lack of awareness of human rights in the public health workforce and public health students: Taket (n 150) 1.

[162] Hunt, Ely Yamin and Bustreo (n 160) 1–2.

In 2016, Hunt reviewed existing frameworks and agreed that AAAQ is closely associated with the right to health, but suggested that Gruskin, Bogecho and Ferguson's 'minimal list' needed to be expanded to address progressive realisation, maximum available resources, and international assistance and cooperation.[163] Hunt focused on operationalising the right and identified important features of human rights-based approaches to health.[164] These included consideration of all relevant human rights including participation, equality and non-discrimination.[165] Hunt's emphasis on progressive realisation, maximum available resources, and international cooperation and assistance is particularly valuable to assess many of the human rights concerns posed by trade mark protection in this book. Hunt argues that both established human rights non-governmental organisations and health professionals need to engage with the health and human rights movement for the right to health to be operationalised.[166] Similarly, a human rights culture for trade marks should be supported by the conscious recognition of the relevance of human rights to intellectual property by legal professionals and civil society actors.

The use of human rights analytical frameworks to assess health measures and laws has strengthened the human rights impact of public health interventions. The HRATM framework described below adapts the frameworks that have emerged to promote realisation of the right to health and develops a mechanism to analyse the human rights implications for trade marks. The framework is designed to strengthen mutually supportive interactions between intellectual property and human rights.

5 THE HUMAN RIGHTS ASSESSMENT FOR TRADE MARKS ('HRATM') FRAMEWORK

This section sets out the human rights-based approach that will be used in the case studies as a standard for measuring compliance with human rights in trade mark legislation. Human rights can also be transformative. Considering a transformative engagement between health and human rights, Yamin advocates the use of broad definitions of economic, social and cultural rights, despite the 'narrow conceptions of rights [that] continue to be reflected in public discourse and underpin neoliberal paradigms of economic development and globaliza-

[163] Hunt (n 136) 115.

[164] Hunt (n 136).

[165] Ibid 115.

[166] Paul Hunt, 'The Health and Human Rights Movement: Progress and Obstacles' (2008) 15(5) *Journal of Law and Medicine* 714, 723.

tion'.[167] The approach that she proposes emphasises the social component of health and argues that all components of a rights-based approach must be tied to society and involve states 'taking suffering seriously',[168] accepting their responsibility to provide international assistance and cooperation to ensure the realisation of economic, social and cultural rights in low-income countries.[169] Okediji also argues that human rights need to play a more transformative role when we conceptualise the relationship between intellectual property and human rights.[170] Trade mark laws need to function to respect, protect and fulfil human rights for this transformation to occur.

Systematic analysis is valuable for identifying where trade marks protection supports or limits human rights. Greater understanding of the human rights implications of health laws and public health systems has influenced a synergistic approach and integration of human rights within the public health paradigm. Tools designed to specifically understand the human rights implications of trade marks will support the development of a human rights culture for trade marks that preserves current features of the dominant economic paradigm, where they support intellectual property to function as a social product that benefits human rights. Impact assessments are useful mechanisms for highlighting the potential and actual human rights impacts of certain pieces of legislation, operations, policies or programmes.[171] There is no single approach to human rights-based analysis. Approaches can be tailored to the subject matter that they analyse, although they build on work done in other fields. Assessment approaches can emphasise different rights-based principles, depending on the focus of the assessment. They are a key aspect of a transformative human rights approach for trade marks.

The HRATM framework used in the case studies tailors existing assessment tools and explores the following questions:

1. What human rights are implicated by the trade mark laws studied and how are they impacted by the operation of the legislation specifically (as opposed to other factors)?

---

[167] Alicia Ely Yamin, 'Will We Take Suffering Seriously? Reflections on What Applying a Human Rights Framework to Health Means and Why We Should Care' (2008) 10(1) *Health and Human Rights* 45, 46. Chapman also critiques the impact of neo-liberalism on realisation of the right to health: Chapman (n 122).

[168] Yamin (n 167) 53.

[169] Ibid 54.

[170] See Okediji (n 1).

[171] Alana Klein, 'So Long as You Have Your Health: Health Care Distribution in Canada and Proceduralist Human Rights' (2012) 30(2) *Windsor Yearbook of Access to Justice* 247, 254–262.

2. What mechanisms for monitoring and accountability are in place to ensure that human rights standards are met?
3. Are principles of participation, empowerment and transparency met in the formulation and operation of the laws?
4. Are principles of international cooperation and assistance relevant to the realisation of human rights in relation to this law?
5. How can rights and interests be balanced against each other? Are any restrictions on human rights or their progressive realisation permissible? If the law restricts certain human rights, is this balanced against benefits for other human rights?

The HRATM framework recognises that states are obliged to implement some core standards of economic, social and cultural rights, despite vastly different available resources. Relevant considerations include progressive realisation, maximum available resources, and international cooperation and assistance. Effectiveness of laws and policies in realising human rights objectives is a critical concern in assessing whether these principles operate.[172]

The HRATM framework values the interdependent and interrelated nature of human rights. This involves assessing the impact of law on different human rights; considering how competing human rights interests can be balanced against each other; and analysing whether rights-based principles are functioning to operationalise human rights.[173] Protection from discrimination is considered within the integrated human rights analysis rather than as a separate rights-based indicator, consistent with its protection in both the *ICESCR* and the *ICCPR*.[174] A significant and important advantage of a human rights approach is that it embeds a framework that requires states to monitor and be accountable for human rights.[175] Even where one right appears to be strongly relevant to trade mark protection, the interdependent nature of human rights also engages assessment of the impact of protection on other relevant human rights.[176] Recognising interdependence assists an integrated human rights anal-

---

172 Committee on Economic, Social and Cultural Rights, *General Comment No 3: The Nature of States Parties' Obligations (Art 2, Para 1 of the Covenant)*, UN ESCOR, 5th sess, UN Doc E/1991/23 (14 December 1990) [9]–[13] ('*General Comment 3*').

173 Hunt (n 136) 116.

174 *ICCPR* (n 8) arts 26, 2.1, 3. *ICESCR* (n 9) arts 2.2, 3.

175 Potts identifies accountability and monitoring as important distinguishing features of the human right to health from public health: Helen Potts, 'The Right to Health in Public Health: Is This a New Approach?' (2008) 15(5) *Journal of Law and Medicine* 725, 741.

176 Jonathan Mann, *Health and Human Rights: A Reader* (Routledge, 1999) 232; Alicia Ely Yamin, 'Will We Take Suffering Seriously? Reflections on What Applying

ysis of intellectual property legislation that balances all relevant rights against each other.

Where there are restrictions on rights, it is necessary to balance rights against each other. The case studies identify potential conflicts between a range of human rights, not limited to those involving human rights to moral and material protection of authors' intellectual creations. Human rights are often difficult to balance against each other because inalienability suggests rights should not be taken away or limited, even by other rights, as human rights are indivisible.[177] The inalienable nature of human rights restricts domestic regulatory autonomy for states in their implementation of human rights agreements, such as the *ICESCR* and the *ICCPR*.[178] The *ICCPR* provides for extremely limited exceptions for implementation of civil and political rights.[179] There is greater scope for domestic regulatory autonomy in relation to economic, social and cultural rights. Recognising the resource-dependent nature of economic, social and cultural rights, the CESCR provides that rights are to be progressively realised, consistent with maximum available resources.[180] However, core minimum rights should not be progressively realised; they should be immediately implemented.[181] In cases where states are not able to meet core minimum obligations, international assistance and cooperation is necessary and this may include adjustments to requirements for meeting international intellectual property obligations.[182] An example of a mechanism that reflects different available resources is the graduated timetable for the implementation of *TRIPS* dependent on stages of economic development. However, these adjustments need to be monitored for effectiveness. Even though developing and least developed states had the opportunity to implement *TRIPS* more slowly, many have already implemented these standards as well as *TRIPS*-plus standards.[183] These protections can deepen a culture in which states are failing to use the flexibility mechanisms that are available to them through *TRIPS*.[184]

---

a Human Rights Framework to Health Means and Why We Should Care' (2008) 10(1) *Health and Human Rights* 45; Hunt (n 136).

177 *VDPA* (n 7) pt 1 para 5.

178 See ibid; *UDHR* (n 6) preamble.

179 *ICCPR* (n 8) art 4.

180 *ICESCR* (n 9) art 2.1.

181 *General Comment 14* (n 139) [43].

182 *General Comment 3* (n 172) [13]–[14].

183 See Carolyn Deere, *The Implementation Game: The TRIPS Agreement and the Global Politics of Intellectual Property Reform in Developing Countries* (Oxford University Press, 2009) 79, 91, 101.

184 See Henning Grosse Ruse-Khan, 'The (Non) Use of Treaty Object and Purpose in Intellectual Property Disputes in the WTO' (Max Planck Institute for Intellectual

The way that human rights should be balanced against each other is complex.[185] Certain human rights have internal balancing mechanisms, such as the right to freedom of expression.[186] The principle of progressive realisation of rights to the maximum of available resources can also guide balancing economic, social and cultural rights against each other.[187] However, it must be acknowledged that the way in which competing human rights can be balanced against each other is not always easily resolved by applying these mechanisms and principles. Addressing conflicts between human rights, Ducoulombier characterises interdependence and indivisibility as 'political and philosophical ideas' rather than practice.[188] The European Court of Human Rights ('ECtHR') treats rights found in the *European Convention on Human Rights* as more important than other human rights, such as excluded economic, social and cultural rights. Her concern is relevant to the feasibility of Geiger's model and the economic, social and cultural rights protection threshold proposed by Helfer and Austin.[189] When balancing rights, an important distinction exists between partial conflicts and total conflicts. Partial conflicts may be addressed through regulation that enables both rights to be recognised.[190] In total conflicts, one right cannot be recognised without alienating the rights of another.[191] Zucca uses cases considered by the ECtHR to support the argument that it may not be possible to use legal reasoning to resolve all conflicts of rights.[192] He argues that it remains important to recognise and understand these conflicts.[193]

Recognition that all conflicts may not be resolved aligns with understanding that different tools from the prescriptive models described in this chapter have different relevance to understanding the concerns identified in the case studies. No single model considered in this chapter can be used by all states to harmo-

---

Property and Competition Law Research Paper No 11–15, 28 September 2011) https://papers.ssrn.com/abstract=1939859.

[185] James W Nickel, 'Rethinking Indivisibility: Towards A Theory of Supporting Relations between Human Rights' (2008) 30(4) *Human Rights Quarterly* 984, 987.

[186] *ICCPR* (n 8) art 19(3). This permits the right to freedom of expression to be limited by states where it is limited by law, proportionately for the objective of being necessary for respect of the rights or reputations of others, for the protection of national security, public order, or public health or morals.

[187] *General Comment 3* (n 172) [9]–[13].

[188] Ducolombier (n 63) 40.

[189] Ibid 42. See also Ida Elisabeth Koch, *Human Rights as Indivisible Rights: The Protection of Socio-Economic Demands Under the European Convention on Human Rights* (Martinus Nijhoff Publishers, 2009) 321–324.

[190] Lorenzo Zucca, 'Conflicts of Fundamental Rights as Constitutional Dilemmas' in Eva Brems (ed), *Conflicts between Fundamental Rights* (Intersentia, 2008) 19, 27.

[191] Ibid.

[192] Ibid.

[193] Ibid 24.

nise human rights and trade marks. A human rights culture for trade marks is flexible so that it can be adapted to the different local conditions within states while guiding them toward improvement and transformation. Different local conditions include economic constraints, geo-political influences and the way that states implement human rights obligations in domestic or regional mechanisms for human rights protection.[194] Jurisdictional comparisons are used in each chapter to better understand what weight should be given to local conditions when drawing broader conclusions about what is needed to build a human rights culture for trade mark.

6 CONCLUSION

The HRATM framework recognises interdependent human rights obligations and special features of economic, social and cultural rights that are important to the relationship between intellectual property and human rights. The analytical approach should be used with other approaches recommended by existing models that conceptualise the relationship between intellectual property and human rights, to build a human rights culture for trade marks that emphasises binding human rights obligations. The approaches considered may be applied differently to understand the relationship between human rights and trade marks in individual states. Using a range of analytical approaches in a manner that recognises different local conditions may provide novel insights in countries where there are problems with the comprehensive implementation of human rights obligations. Further modifications that respond to specific local conditions, such as competing economic constraints, are also important to a global human rights culture for trade mark protection so that all states can promote and foster their binding international human rights obligations.

Intellectual property policy needs to be calibrated with human rights obligations. This chapter proposes a framework for analysis of the human rights implications of domestic trade mark laws. The HRATM framework enables states to identify human rights implications, and its application in the case studies in Part II of this book explores how to deal with identified human rights concerns from specific examples of trade mark law. Insights from these domestic examples support the proposal in Part III for a more proactive, global approach to ensuring that trade mark law permits human rights to be respected, protected and fulfilled.

---

[194] See Okediji (n 1) 6–7.

PART II

GLOBAL CASE STUDIES: ASSESSING HUMAN RIGHTS IMPLICATIONS OF DOMESTIC TRADE MARK LAWS

3 Tobacco plain packaging case study: Australia and Uruguay[1]

1 INTRODUCTION

When Australia introduced comprehensive plain packaging of tobacco products in 2011, the measures were proclaimed as the most restrictive in the world and were strongly opposed by tobacco companies.[2] Among the many rights that tobacco companies argued the measures violated, their claims that their ability to exercise their trade mark and other intellectual property rights was impaired gained significant attention. A constitutional dispute in the High Court of Australia asserted that the legislation was an acquisition of intellectual property rights without compensation on just terms.[3] An investor–state dispute claimed the measures expropriated trade mark assets from a foreign investor protected by the Australia–Hong Kong Bilateral Investment Treaty and was inconsistent with protections guaranteeing fair and equitable treatment.[4] The packaging restrictions were also disputed as inconsistent with World Trade Organization ('WTO') obligations requiring minimum protections for intellectual property and regulating technical barriers to trade. Yet these restrictions on the way that owners could use their trade marks on tobacco packaging were successfully defended by the Australian government.[5] In the only dispute

[1] This chapter reproduces parts of the following, earlier work: Genevieve Wilkinson, 'Tobacco Plain Packaging, Human Rights and the Object and Purpose of International Trade Mark Protection' in Susy Frankel (ed), *The Object and Purpose of Intellectual Property* (Edward Elgar Publishing, 2019).

[2] Mary Scott Kennedy, 'Australia's Tobacco Plain Packaging Act: Convergence of Public Health and Global Trade' (2014) 39(2) *North Carolina Journal of International Law* 591, 612–613.

[3] *JT International SA v Commonwealth of Australia; British American Tobacco Australasia Limited v The Commonwealth* (2012) 250 CLR 1.

[4] *Australia/Hong King Investment Agreement for the Promotion and Protection of Investments (Philip Morris Asia Ltd v Commonwealth of Australia)* (Notice of Arbitration, UNCITRAL PCA, Case No 2012-12, 21 November 2011) ('*PMA Notice of Arbitration*').

[5] Panel Reports, *Australia – Certain Measures Concerning Trademarks, Geographical Indications and Other Plain Packaging Requirements Applicable to Tobacco*

where it was necessary to justify the legislative restrictions that were imposed on tobacco companies, the WTO Disputes, the measures were characterised as long-term measures that would restrict tobacco consumption when existing tobacco decline in Australia had plateaued.[6] Although legislation already required graphic health warnings on tobacco packaging, policymakers viewed the continued use of distinctive trade marks, colour and imagery on packaging as the last available vehicle for advertising in Australia.[7] The WTO Appellate Body confirmed that these interests justified the way that plain packaging measures placed special requirements on the use of tobacco-related trade marks.[8]

Tobacco consumption has long been recognised as a serious concern for global health that has justified extensive restrictions on advertising in countries like Australia. There is evidence of direct links between packet advertising that includes the use of trade marks to create positive brand perceptions and initiation of tobacco consumption.[9] In a highly influential study in 2000, Saffer and Chaloupka emphasised the importance of comprehensive tobacco advertising bans, as a more limited approach would have minimal effect.[10] This recognises a significant causal contribution between package advertising using trade marks and tobacco consumption where there are no other mechanisms for advertising.[11] Accordingly, the use by an owner of a tobacco-related trade mark on product packaging to induce individuals to consume tobacco can directly

---

Products and Packaging, WTO Docs WT/DS435/R, WT/DS441/R, WT/DS458/R and WT/DS467/R (28 June 2018) ('*Australia – Tobacco Plain Packaging*').

6 See Panel Reports, *Australia – Certain Measures Concerning Trademarks, Geographical Indications and Other Plain Packaging Requirements Applicable to Tobacco Products and Packaging: Addendum*, WTO Docs WT/DS435/R/Add.1, WT/DS441/R/Add.1, WT/DS458/R/Add.1 and WT/DS467/R/Add.1 (28 June 2018) 'Integrated Executive Summary of the Arguments of Australia' B-96 [5].

7 Matthew Thomas, *Tobacco Plain Packaging Bill 2011, Bills Digest* (Digest No 35 of 2011–12, 24 August 2011) 5.

8 Appellate Body Reports, *Australia – Certain Measures Concerning Trademarks, Geographical Indications and Other Plain Packaging Requirements Applicable to Tobacco Products and* Packaging, WTO Docs WT/DS435/AB/R and WT/DS441/AB/R (9 June 2020) [6.697] ('*Appellate Body Reports*').

9 National Preventative Health Taskforce, *Australia: Healthiest Country by 2020. Technical Report 2 – Tobacco Control in Australia: Making Smoking History, including Addendum for October 2008 to June 2009* (2009) 20 ('*Technical Report 2 – Tobacco Control in Australia*').

10 Henry Saffer and Frank Chaloupka, 'The Effect of Tobacco Advertising Bans on Tobacco Consumption' (2000) 19(6) *Journal of Health Economics* 1117.

11 Thomas (n 7) 5; Richard Edwards et al, 'Impact of Removing Point-of-Sale Tobacco Displays: Data from a New Zealand Youth Survey' (2017) 26(4) *Tobacco Control* 392.

engage states' obligations to protect individuals in realisation of the right to health.[12] Interpretation of the right to health by the Committee on Economic, Social and Cultural Rights ('CESCR') and the Committee on the Rights of the Child ('COMRC') identifies state obligations to protect individuals from the harmful impact of tobacco.[13] Owners of tobacco-related trade marks have demonstrated systematic disregard for the health and safety of individuals and obstructed access to information about the harmful and addictive impact of smoking.[14]

Tobacco consumption and its regulation raise complex human rights considerations, but disputes about plain packaging in the WTO, international arbitration and domestic courts gave limited weight to human rights protection. This chapter applies the Human Rights Assessment for Trade Marks ('HRATM') framework developed in Chapter 2 to the restrictions on trade mark rights resulting from Australian plain packaging legislation and identifies relevant human rights considerations, assessing the consistency of the legislation with rights-based principles of monitoring and accountability, transparency and participation, international cooperation and assistance, and balancing interdependent rights. Although the outcomes reached in the disputes are largely consistent with human rights protection, the analysis explores ways that explicit consideration of the human rights questions identified by the HRATM framework in policy development and implementation would enhance human rights protection. Carefully considering these questions will not only strengthen the justification that states use to support appropriate restrictions on trade mark rights, but it can improve the ability of the measures to protect human rights effectively. This highlights the limitations of a public health approach to tobacco control for addressing the complex human rights concerns raised by tobacco plain packaging. The legislation also raises questions of children's human rights, creators' rights and rights to freedom of expression, property and development. These human rights obligations have received little explicit attention in policy development and implementation in Australia and other countries that have introduced tobacco plain packaging, including Uruguay. However, the WTO plain packaging decisions provide greater opportunities

---

[12] Committee on Economic, Social and Cultural Rights, *General Comment No 14: The Right to the Highest Attainable Standard of Health (Art 12 of the Covenant)*, 22nd sess, UN Doc E/C.12/2000/4 (11 August 2000) [51] ('*General Comment 14*').

[13] Ibid. *Charter of the United Nations* arts 55, 56; Committee on the Rights of the Child, *CRC General Comment No 4: Adolescent Health and Development in the Context of the Convention on the Rights of the Child*, 33rd sess, UN Doc CRC/GC/2003/4 (1 July 2003) [6], [21]–[22] ('*CRC General Comment 4*').

[14] Brigit Toebes et al, 'A Missing Voice: The Human Rights of Children to a Tobacco-Free Environment' (2018) 27(1) *Tobacco Control* 3, 4 ('A Missing Voice').

for systemic integration between international intellectual property laws and human rights laws. There may also be further opportunities for states to protect human rights when intellectual property laws are challenged in investor–state arbitration.

The second section of this chapter outlines the plain packaging legislation, its justifications and the disputes about its introduction and implementation. The third section conducts a human rights analysis of the legislation. The fourth section applies the analysis to assess the implications of the *Australia – Tobacco Plain Packaging* decision for human rights. The fifth section of the chapter compares the WTO dispute with the investor–state dispute brought against Uruguay by Philip Morris. Finally, the chapter explores the need for change to address the chilling impacts of tobacco litigation and build a more effective human rights culture for trade marks.

2 AUSTRALIAN PLAIN PACKAGING LEGISLATION AND RELATED DISPUTES

2.1 Plain Packaging Legislation

Australia was the first in the world to completely restrict tobacco advertising on packaging when it introduced tobacco plain packaging legislation in 2011. Tobacco advertising on packaging has been established to influence the initiation of tobacco consumption.[15] Tobacco consumption has been characterised as a global health epidemic.[16] Initiation of tobacco consumption is particularly relevant to young smokers: tobacco companies target them as an important market.[17]

Tobacco consumption has significant negative consequences for the right to health. This was recognised multilaterally when states agreed to the World Health Organization ('WHO') *Framework Convention on Tobacco Control* ('*FCTC*').[18] As part of the *FCTC*, Member States participate in the governing body, the Conference of Parties ('COP'). One of the functions of the COP is to adopt guidelines for certain provisions of the agreement.

Article 11 of the *FCTC* requires parties to the treaty to adopt and implement effective packaging and labelling measures within three years of becoming

15 *Technical Report 2 – Tobacco Control in Australia* (n 9) 20.

16 Andrew D Mitchell and Tania Voon, 'Introduction' in Andrew D Mitchell and Tania Voon (eds), *The Global Tobacco Epidemic and the Law* (Edward Elgar Publishing, 2014) 1.

17 Toebes et al, 'A Missing Voice' (n 14) 3–5.

18 *WHO Framework Convention on Tobacco Control*, opened for signature 21 May 2003, 2302 UNTS 166 (entered into force 27 February 2005) preamble ('*FCTC*').

a party, including measures requiring minimum sizing of graphic warnings about the negative health impacts of tobacco on tobacco packaging. The Guidelines to Article 11 were adopted by the COP 2008 to assist states to improve the effectiveness of measures for the packaging and labelling of tobacco-related products in November 2008.[19] Part of the guidelines recommend that parties adopt plain packaging measures.[20] Contemporaneously, plain packaging was identified as a key priority in reducing rates of tobacco consumption in Australia in a 2008 discussion paper released by the Australian Government National Health Taskforce (the 'National Health Taskforce Paper').[21]

Subsequently, the *Tobacco Plain Packaging Act 2011* (Cth), the *Trade Marks (Plain Packaging) Act 2011* (Cth) and supporting regulations (plain packaging legislation) introduced broad requirements for the packaging of tobacco-related products. Plain packaging legislation limits advertising. It limits use of trade marks to their traditional function of indicating badge of origin and associated quality.[22] The most relevant requirements to intellectual property are those that impact on the ability of owners of tobacco-related trade marks to use their marks on packaging.[23] Relevantly, the restrictions permit only use of word marks in prescribed size, font and colour in a designated position on the packet.[24] Graphics or device marks cannot be used.[25] The *Tobacco Plain Packaging Act 2011* articulates the primary policy concerns of plain packaging legislation: the protection of public health and the implementation of the *FCTC*.[26] The legislation is intended to achieve this by regulating the packaging and appearance of tobacco products to reduce their appeal to consumers, increase the effectiveness of health warnings and limit the capacity of packaging to mislead consumers about the 'harmful effects of smoking or using tobacco products'.[27]

What was the impact of this on owners of tobacco-related trade marks? Plain packaging legislation permits word marks to continue to be used by trade mark

---

19 At its third session in November 2008, the Conference of the Parties ('COP') adopted guidelines for implementation of Article 11 of the WHO *FCTC* on 'Packaging and Labelling of Tobacco Products' (Decision FCTC/COP3(10)) ('*Guidelines*').

20 Ibid [46].

21 National Preventative Health Taskforce, *Australia: The Healthiest Country by 2020. Discussion Paper* (2008) 23–24 ('*National Health Taskforce Paper*').

22 *Tobacco Plain Packaging Act 2011* (Cth) s 21.

23 Ibid s 20.

24 Ibid s 21.

25 Ibid.

26 Ibid s 3(1).

27 Ibid s 3(2). See images of examples of plain packaging: *Australia – Tobacco Plain Packaging* (n 5) [2.32].

owners in a restricted way to denote the source of the product.[28] The legislation also permits trade marks to stay on the register, even where they might be susceptible to non-use actions as a result of the legislation, which enabled trade mark owners to continue to exclude others from using the relevant registered marks.[29] Tobacco companies have argued that these restrictions on the use of their trade marks have significant economic consequences.[30] Tobacco-related trade mark owners have claimed breach of their rights in domestic constitutional litigation,[31] investor–state dispute litigation[32] and the dispute settlement mechanisms of the WTO.[33]

2.2 Plain Packaging Disputes

In the High Court of Australia, JT International and British American Tobacco unsuccessfully argued that Australian plain packaging legislation constituted acquisition of their trade mark rights by the government and this was inconsistent with constitutional requirements that the acquisition of property be on 'just terms'.[34] The High Court found that the legislation did not acquire the applicants' intellectual property rights, so the claim could not be established.[35] Separately, Philip Morris Asia commenced an international investment arbitration action against Australia. Philip Morris Asia argued that changes resulting from plain packaging legislation deprived them of the value of their investment as it was enacted subsequent to their acquisition of intellectual property rights to tobacco.[36] This was alleged to be inconsistent with the *Australia-Hong Kong Bilateral Investment Treaty*.[37] However, it was found that these rights had been deliberately acquired so as to exploit the investor–state dispute mechanism.[38] The action ended in interlocutory proceedings that determined that

---

28 *Tobacco Plain Packaging Act 2011* (Cth) s 21.

29 Explanatory Memorandum, Tobacco Plain Packaging Bill 2011 (Cth) 15 ('Tobacco Plain Packaging Bill Explanatory Memorandum').

30 *PMA Notice of Arbitration* (n 4) [8.3].

31 *JT International SA v Commonwealth of Australia*; *British American Tobacco Australasia Limited v The Commonwealth* (n 3).

32 *Philip Morris Asia Limited v The Commonwealth of Australia* (Award on Jurisdiction and Admissibility, UNCITRAL PCA Case No 2012-12, 17 December 2015) [48] ('*PMA Award on Jurisdiction and Admissibility*').

33 *Australia – Tobacco Plain Packaging* (n 5).

34 *JT International SA v Commonwealth of Australia; British American Tobacco Australasia Limited v The Commonwealth* (n 3).

35 Ibid 34–5 (French CJ).

36 *PMA Award on Jurisdiction and Admissibility*' (n 32).

37 *PMA Notice of Arbitration* (n 4) [8.3].

38 *PMA Award on Jurisdiction and Admissibility* (n 32).

the bringing of the claim in these circumstances constituted an abuse of right under international law.[39] Even though legal costs were awarded in Australia's favour, extensive costs were not covered by this order.[40]

The WTO Disputes provided the most detailed examination of the restrictions that plain packaging legislation imposed on tobacco-related intellectual property rights. The WTO Disputes were brought against Australia by Cuba, the Dominican Republic, Honduras and Indonesia, pursuant to the *WTO Dispute Settlement Understanding* ('*DSU*').[41] Ukraine also initiated but then suspended a dispute, which subsequently lapsed.[42] The complaints asserted that Australia's plain packaging legislation breached Article 20 of *TRIPS* as it contained special requirements that unjustifiably encumbered the use of tobacco-related trade marks in the course of trade.[43] A range of other complaints were also made, asserting breaches of *TRIPS* and the WTO Agreement on Technical Barriers to Trade ('TBT'). Australia justified the impugned provisions, citing domestic public health objectives and compliance with the *FCTC*.[44] These complaints were ultimately unsuccessful and the WTO Dispute Settlement Bodies confirmed that TRIPS does not confer a right to use a trade mark on owners.[45]

Importantly, tobacco companies with interests in the promotion and sale of tobacco openly acknowledged that they have funded the WTO actions against Australia.[46] This funding relationship engages human rights obligations for states to perform human rights scrutiny of corporate entities operating in their territories.[47] Permitting tobacco companies to fund actions that assert rights

---

39 Ibid [586]–[588].

40 *Philip Morris Asia Ltd v Australia* (Final Award Regarding Costs, UNCITRAL PCA Case No 2012-12, 8 March 2017).

41 *Marrakesh Agreement Establishing the World Trade Organization*, opened for signature 15 April 1994, 1867 UNTS 3 (entered into force 1 January 1995) annex 2 ('*DSU*').

42 *Australia – Tobacco Plain Packaging* (n 5) [1.51]–[1.54].

43 See, for example, *Australia – Certain Measures Concerning Trademarks and Other Plain Packaging Requirements Applicable to Tobacco Products and Packaging*, WTO Docs WT/DS435/1, IP/D/31, G/TBT/D/40 and G/L/986 (10 April 2014) (Request for Consultations by Honduras).

44 *Australia – Tobacco Plain Packaging* (n 5) [7.2576]–[7.2581]. The Panel upheld this justification: at [7.2586]–[7.2606].

45 *Appellate Body Reports* (n 8) [7.7].

46 Stephanie Nebehay, 'Australia Says Big Tobacco Aiding WTO Challengers', *Reuters* (online, 23 May 2012) http://www.reuters.com/article/trade-tobacco-idUSLE8GMHBW20120522.

47 *General Comment 24* explicitly requires parties to the *ICESCR* to consider measures such as restricting marketing tobacco products to protect public health: Committee on Economic, Social and Cultural Rights, *General Comment No 24: State Obligations*

to market products that are known to be harmful to health can engage human rights obligations to protect individuals from potential infringements of the right to health, which are discussed in the next section.

3 THE HUMAN RIGHTS IMPLICATIONS OF PLAIN PACKAGING LEGISLATION

Australian plain packaging legislation engages a range of human rights considerations, but the disputes have not focused on relevant human rights obligations. The following human rights analysis primarily draws on the frameworks provided by the *International Covenant on Economic, Social and Cultural Rights* ('*ICESCR*'),[48] the *International Covenant on Civil and Political Rights* ('*ICCPR*')[49] and the *Convention on the Rights of the Child* (the '*CRC*')[50] and interpretation of those rights by expert treaty-making bodies. The emphasis of discussion has been on health and, although the right to health is clearly implicated, the discourse has focused on public health considerations.[51] Commercial speech is a form of expression and restrictions on trade marks have been argued to be a restriction on freedom of expression.[52] Moral and material rights of creators of certain tobacco-related trade marks could be protected pursuant to *ICESCR* Article 15(1)(c).[53] Human rights to property not restricted to scientific, literary and artistic productions and rights to development could also be relevant to the disputes. A right to development entitles 'every human person and all peoples to participate in, contribute to, and enjoy economic, social, cultural and political development'.[54] Human rights obligations to property and development are harder to identify as relevant to interpretation

---

under the International Covenant on Economic, Social and Cultural Rights in the Context of Business Activities, UN ESCOR, 61st sess, UN Doc E/C.12/GC/24 (23 June 2017) [19] ('*General Comment 24*').

48 *International Covenant on Economic, Social and Cultural Rights*, opened for signature 16 December 1966, 993 UNTS 3 (entered into force 3 January 1976) ('*ICE SCR*').

49 *International Covenant on Civil and Political Rights*, opened for signature 16 December 1966, 999 UNTS 171 (entered into force 23 March 1976) ('*ICCPR*').

50 *Convention on the Rights of the Child*, opened for signature 20 November 1989, 1577 UNTS 3 (entered into force 2 September 1990) ('*CRC*').

51 See generally Tania Voon, Andrew D Mitchell and Jonathan Liberman (eds), *Public Health and Plain Packaging of Cigarettes: Legal Issues* (Edward Elgar Publishing, 2012).

52 Mariette Brennan, 'Canada's Next Step in Tobacco Control Laws: Is Plain Packaging Legislation a Viable Proposal?' (2013) 51 *Alberta Law Review* 23.

53 *ICESCR* (n 48) art 15(1)(c).

54 *United Nations Declaration on the Right to Development*, GA Res 41/128, UN Doc 41/128 (4 December 1986) art 1.1.

of *TRIPS* obligations in the WTO Disputes as they are less clearly defined in international law.

3.1 Right to Health

Australia has acknowledged the relevance of the human right to the highest attainable standard of health in explanatory material surrounding plain packaging legislation.[55] Compliance with the *FCTC* is an objective of the legislation.[56] The *FCTC* recognises both the human right to health and public health imperatives.[57] There was debate about the extent to which the *FCTC* Guidelines that require states to implement plain packaging constitute binding obligations in international law,[58] yet the requirement of *ICESCR* that states progressively realise the human right to health for individuals is clear.[59] The CESCR's *General Comment 14* interpreting the right to health identifies addressing tobacco marketing and consumption as relevant to the obligation to protect the right to health.[60] Plain packaging legislation engages Australia's obligation to protect the right to health by taking 'all necessary measures to safeguard persons within their jurisdiction from infringements of the right to health by third parties'.[61] The CESCR interprets violations of this obligation to include the failure of states to regulate the activities of corporations that will violate the right to health of others and the failure to protect consumers and workers from activities that are detrimental to health, including marketing and consumption of tobacco.[62] There is well-documented evidence of intentional failure to disclose negative health impacts of tobacco by tobacco companies, which engages additional obligations for states to protect individuals.[63] Australia has

---

[55] Explanatory Statement, Tobacco Plain Packaging: Amendment Regulation 2012 (No 1) (SLI No 29 of 2012) ('Tobacco Plain Packaging Explanatory Statement').

[56] *Tobacco Plain Packaging Act 2011* (Cth) s 3.

[57] *FCTC* (n 18) preamble.

[58] Chang-fa Lo, 'Guidelines and Protocols under the Framework Convention' in Andrew D Mitchell and Tania Voon (eds), *The Global Tobacco Epidemic and the Law* (Edward Elgar Publishing, 2014) 32–45; Jonathan Liberman, 'The Power of the WHO FCTC: Understanding its Legal Status and Weight' in Andrew D Mitchell and Tania Voon (eds), *The Global Tobacco Epidemic and the Law* (Edward Elgar Publishing, 2014) 48–60.

[59] *ICESCR* (n 48) art 12; *General Comment 14* (n 12) [31].

[60] *General Comment 14* (n 12) [51].

[61] Ibid.

[62] Ibid.

[63] Melissa E Crow, 'Smokescreens and State Responsibility: Using Human Rights Strategies to Promote Global Tobacco Control' (2005) 29 *Yale Journal of International Law* 209, 211; Carolyn Dresler and Stephen P Marks, 'The Emerging Human Right to Tobacco Control' (2006) 28(3) *Human Rights Quarterly* 599, 633, 644.

attempted to address this protection obligation through the plain packaging legislation.

A key priority of plain packaging legislation is to reduce the attractiveness and appeal of tobacco products to young people.[64] This also corresponds to Australia's obligations, pursuant to the *CRC*, to protect the rights of children to 'the enjoyment of the highest attainable standard of health'[65] and to ensure that the child has 'access to information and material from a diversity of national and international sources, especially those aimed at the promotion of his or her social, spiritual and moral well-being and physical and mental health'.[66] *General Comment 4* of the COMRC on Adolescent Health and Development interprets this obligation to protect adolescents from information that is harmful to their health and development.[67] States should 'regulate or prohibit information and marketing of … tobacco, particularly when it targets children and adolescents'.[68] This obligation is directly relevant to the restrictions on marketing required by plain packaging legislation. These restrictions are supported by scientific evidence regarding adolescents and plain packaging.[69]

The effectiveness of states' measures to achieve progressive realisation of its human right to health obligations is a relevant consideration to assessing compliance with those obligations. In 2008, the National Health Taskforce Paper identified that declining rates of tobacco consumption in Australia were 'flattening out'.[70] Plain packaging legislation formed part of the policy that responded to concerns of the negative health impacts of continuing tobacco consumption set out in the subsequent report from the National Health Taskforce ('*National Health Taskforce Report*').[71] The key health claims of plain packaging legislation are that it will:

---

64 Tobacco Plain Packaging Bill Explanatory Memorandum (n 29).

65 *CRC* (n 50) art 24.

66 Ibid art 17.

67 Committee on the Rights of the Child, *General Comment No. 4: Adolescent Health and Development in the Context of the Convention on the Rights of the Child*, 33rd sess, UN Doc CRC/GC/2003/4 (1 July 2003) [6], [21–2].

68 Ibid [21].

69 Toebes et al also identify packaging of cigarettes and misleading advertising on cigarettes as important issues for governments to address to protect children's rights: Toebes et al, 'A Missing Voice' (n 14) 4. Sally Dunlop et al, 'Australia's Plain Tobacco Packs: Anticipated and Actual Responses among Adolescents and Young Adults 2010–2013' (2017) 26 *Tobacco Control* 617. See also Richard Edwards et al, 'Impact of Removing Point-of-Sale Tobacco Displays: Data from a New Zealand Youth Survey' (2017) 26 *Tobacco Control* 392.

70 *National Health Taskforce Paper* (n 21) 21.

71 National Preventative Health Taskforce, *Australia: The Healthiest Country by 2020. National Preventative Health Strategy: The Roadmap for Action* (30 June 2009) 19–20, 181–182 https://extranet.who.int/nutrition/gina/sites/default/filesstore/

- reduce the attractiveness and appeal of tobacco products to consumers, particularly young people;
- increase the noticeability and effectiveness of mandated health warnings;
- reduce the ability of the tobacco product and its packaging to mislead consumers about the harms of smoking; and
- through the achievement of these objectives in the long term, as part of a comprehensive suite of tobacco control measures, contribute to efforts to reduce smoking rates.[72]

The substantial scientific basis for these claims was set out in a technical report accompanying the *National Health Taskforce Report*.[73] Additional scientific evidence supported the policy.[74] Competing reports questioned the effectiveness of the proposed measure.[75]

AUS%202009%20National%20Preventative%20Health%20Strategy.pdf ('*National Taskforce Report*').

[72] Tobacco Plain Packaging Bill Explanatory Memorandum (n 29) 1.

[73] See Janne Scheffels, 'A Difference That Makes a Difference: Young Adult Smokers' Accounts of Cigarette Brands and Package Design' (2008) 17(2) *Tobacco Control* 118; M Wakefield et al, 'The Cigarette Pack as Image: New Evidence from Tobacco Industry Documents' (2002) 11(Suppl 1) *Tobacco Control* i73; Becky Freeman, Simon Chapman and Matthew Rimmer, 'The Case for Plain Packaging of Tobacco Products' (2008) 103(4) *Addiction* 580; M A Wakefield, D Germain and S J Durkin, 'How Does Increasingly Plainer Cigarette Packaging Influence Adult Smokers' Perceptions about Brand Image? An Experimental Study' (2008) 17(6) *Tobacco Control* 416; P Beede and R Lawson, 'The Effect of Plain Packages on the Perception of Cigarette Health Warnings' (1992) 106(4) *Public Health* 315; M E Goldberg et al, 'The Effect of Plain Packaging on Response to Health Warnings' (1999) 89(9) *American Journal of Public Health* 1434; E Strahan et al, 'Enhancing the Effectiveness of Tobacco Package Warning Labels: A Social Psychological Perspective' (2002) 11(3) *Tobacco Control* 183; M Wakefield and T Letcher, 'My Pack Is Cuter than Your Pack' (2002) 11(2) *Tobacco Control* 154; Morgan Stanley Research Europe, *Tobacco: Late to the Party* (2007).

[74] Quit Victoria, Cancer Council Victoria, *Plain Packaging of Tobacco Products: A Review of the Evidence* (May 2011) https://www.cancer.org.au/assets/pdf/plain-packaging-of-tobacco-products-a-review-of-the-evidence.

[75] Philip Johnson 'Trademarks Without a Brand: The Proposals on "Plain Packaging" of Tobacco Products' (2012) 34(7) *European Intellectual Property Review* 468–469; British American Tobacco, *British American Tobacco Australia Submission on the Tobacco Plain Packaging Bill 2011* (6 June 2011) http://www.ip-watch.org/weblog/wp-content/uploads/2011/06/BATA-Tobacco-Plain-Packaging-Bill-Submission.pdf; Philip Morris, *Commoditising Tobacco Products through Plain Packaging will Harm Public Health, Violate Treaties, and Does Not Meet the Test of 'Evidence-Based Policy': Submission by Philip Morris Limited on the Tobacco Plain Packaging Bill Exposure Draft* (June 2011) http://webarchive.nla.gov.au/gov/20130329051831/http://www.yourhealth.gov.au/internet/yourhealth/publishing.nsf/Content/Phillip-Morris-Limited~Phillip-Morris-Limited-2.

Following the introduction of plain packaging legislation, early analysis indicated the success of the measure in reducing the appeal of tobacco packaging for adolescents,[76] influencing decisions to cease smoking in adult smokers[77] and causing smokers to conceal their packs.[78] Although the benefits of plain packaging legislation in effecting a decline in smoking are expected to be long term,[79] further evidence establishes the short-term effectiveness of the measures.[80] Multiple tobacco control measures in place in Australia contribute to smoking rates,[81] yet the 2016 Post-Implementation Review concluded that all of the major datasets examined demonstrated sustained drops in national smoking prevalence in Australia.[82] This reduction was expected to have significant long-term impact on public health outcomes and suggested that the legislation was fulfilling its aims.[83] The Post-Implementation Review analysis did not assess whether alternative measures would have been more effective or equally effective.[84] Criticisms of these findings can partly be explained by the fact that tobacco plain packaging is designed to be a long-term measure.[85] At this stage it is difficult to definitively assess the effectiveness of plain packaging legislation in meeting Australia's progressive realisation of the right

---

[76] Victoria White, Tahlia Williams and Melanie Wakefield, 'Has the Introduction of Plain Packaging with Larger Graphic Health Warnings Changed Adolescents' Perceptions of Cigarette Packs and Brands?' (2015) 24(Suppl 2) *Tobacco Control* ii42.

[77] Melanie Wakefield et al, 'Introduction Effects of the Australian Plain Packaging Policy on Adult Smokers: A Cross-Sectional Study' (2013) 3(7) *BMJ Open* e003175.

[78] Meghan Zacher et al, 'Personal Pack Display and Active Smoking at Outdoor Café Strips: Assessing the Impact of Plain Packaging 1 Year Post Implementation' (2015) 24 *Tobacco Control* 94–97.

[79] Tasneem Chipty, *Study of the Impact of the Tobacco Plain Packaging Measure on Smoking Prevalence in Australia* (Australian Government Department of Health, 24 January 2016) http://www.health.gov.au/internet/main/publishing.nsf/content/491CE0444F7B0A76CA257FBE00195BF3/$File/PIR%20of%20Tobacco%20Plain%20Packaging%20-%20with%20Addendum.pdf ('*Post-Implementation Review*').

[80] Ibid app A [6].

[81] *Australia – Certain Measures Concerning Trademarks, Geographical Indications and Other Plain Packaging Requirements Applicable to Tobacco Products and Packaging. Integrated Executive Summary of Australia's Submissions*, WTO Doc WT/DS435/441/458/467 (23 March 2016) [150] ('*Summary of Arguments*').

[82] Davidson and Da Silva contest some of these. Sinclair Davidson and Ashton de Silva, 'Did Recent Tobacco Reforms Change the Cigarette Market?' (2018) 37(1) *Economic Papers: A Journal of Applied Economics and Policy* 55, 69–70 ('Did Recent Tobacco Reforms Change the Cigarette Market?').

[83] *Post-Implementation Review* (n 79) 20.

[84] Ibid.

[85] Davidson and Da Silva, 'Did Recent Tobacco Reforms Change the Cigarette Market?' (n 82).

to health because of this design.[86] If effectiveness is sustained, repeal of the legislation could constitute a retrogression in Australia progressively realising its human right to health obligations unless it is replaced by something equally or more effective.[87]

3.2 Freedom of Expression

The right to freedom of expression includes 'freedom to seek, receive and impart information and ideas of all kinds'.[88] Arguably, the freedom of expression rights of tobacco trade mark owners are restricted by plain packaging legislation as owners cannot use packaging to impart information and ideas about their product.[89] The human right to freedom of expression enshrined in *ICCPR* Article 19, as interpreted by the Human Rights Committee ('HRC') in *General Comment 34*, states that freedom of expression may include commercial advertising.[90] However, the restrictions on the use of trade marks imposed by plain packaging legislation may be permissible restrictions. *ICCPR* Article 19(3) permits restrictions on freedom of expression that are provided in law and necessary for respect of the rights or reputations of others, for the protection of national security, public order, or public health or morals.[91] The HRC confirms[92] that restrictions other than those specified in paragraph 3 are not allowed 'even if such grounds would justify restrictions to other rights protected in the Covenant'.[93] There needs to be a direct relationship between the specified justification and the application of the restriction.[94]

---

[86] Moodie reports ongoing plain packaging effectiveness in international context: see Crawford Moodie et al, 'Plain Tobacco Packaging: Progress, Challenges, Learning and Opportunities' (2022) 31(2) *Tobacco Control* 263; Crawford Moodie et al, 'Plain Packaging: Legislative Differences in Australia, France, the UK, New Zealand and Norway, and Options for Strengthening Regulations' (2019) 28(5) *Tobacco Control* 485.

[87] *General Comment 14* (n 12) [48].

[88] *ICCPR* (n 49) art 19(2).

[89] Tobacco Plain Packaging Explanatory Statement (n 55) 9–13. Brennan considers whether plain packaging legislation would be consistent with the broader freedom of expression protections found in the Canadian Charter: Brennan (n 52) 35–48.

[90] Human Rights Committee, *General Comment No 34: Article 19: Freedoms of Opinion and Expression*, 102nd sess, UN Doc CCPR/C/GC/34 (12 September 2011) ('*General Comment 34*').

[91] *ICCPR* art 19(3).

[92] *General Comment 34* (n 90).

[93] Ibid [22].

[94] Ibid.

The content of Australian plain packaging legislation also suggests that it is necessary for the protection of public health.[95] This is one of the permissible restrictions set out in *ICCPR* Article 19(3). However, a restriction does not meet the test of necessity 'if the protection could be achieved in other ways that do not restrict freedom of expression'.[96] *General Comment 34* does not provide further specific guidance on public health. *General Comment 34* interprets the rights referred to in Article 19(3) to include human rights, so any restriction on freedom of expression posed by plain packaging legislation can be justified as necessary to achieve realisation of the human right to health.[97] The objective of protecting the human right to health has been identified in explanatory materials for plain packaging legislation and its relevance has been explained above.[98] The HRC adopts earlier statements that restrictive measures should not be overbroad and should be consistent with the principle of proportionality, which 'must also take account of the form of expression at issue as well as the means of its dissemination'.[99] Policy documents underlying Australian plain packaging legislation, including the *National Health Taskforce Report* and supporting documentation, set out 'in specific and individualized fashion the precise nature of the threat, and the necessity and proportionality of the specific action taken'.[100] If plain packaging legislation constitutes a restriction on freedom of expression, it can be concluded that the restriction is provided by law and does not appear to be discriminatory to any particular group, so the restriction should not be a basis to modify or restrict the legislation.

3.3 Right to Benefit from Science and Culture

ICESCR Article 15(1)(c) confers limited human rights protection for creators of literary, artistic and scientific productions. Where trade marks constitute literary or artistic productions, Article 15(1)(c) could confer moral and material rights on the authors of those trade marks.[101] Tobacco-related device marks and composite marks can constitute artistic productions, so creators of trade marks could argue that plain packaging legislation impacts on their moral and material rights. However, it is not clear that the rights protected by

---

95 *Tobacco Plain Packaging Act 2011* (Cth) s 3.

96 *General Comment 34* (n 90) [33].

97 Ibid.

98 Tobacco Plain Packaging Explanatory Statement (n 55).

99 *General Comment 34* (n 90) [34].

100 Ibid [35].

101 Cf Peter K Yu, 'The Anatomy of the Human Rights Framework for Intellectual Property' (2016) 69(1) *SMU Law Review* 37, 85–95 ('The Anatomy of the Human Rights Framework for Intellectual Property').

Article 15(1)(c) are directly restricted by plain packaging legislation. There is no pre-existing practice of providing moral rights of attribution to trade mark creators.[102] The human right provided in Article 15(1)(c) does not provide for ongoing remuneration,[103] so it may be assumed that creators of trade marks have already been compensated and their material interest in 15(1)(c) is not impaired. Plain packaging legislation does not appear to be the direct cause of the loss of material or moral rights so, in the present assessment of interrelated rights, it should not be the basis to restrict operation of the legislation to realise the relevant right to health objectives.[104]

3.4 Human Rights to Property and Development

Human rights to property and development have been recognised as relevant to the WTO Disputes.[105] Neither right is enshrined in binding international human rights agreements. Although development concerns are clearly relevant to the object and purpose of *TRIPS*, the status of the human right to development also remains unclear.[106] Importantly, economic development is impacted by

---

[102] See generally *Trade Marks Act 1995* (Cth). See also Genevieve Wilkinson, 'Exploring Moral Interests in the Intellectual Creations Underlying Trade Marks' in Ysolde Gendreau (ed), *Research Handbook on Intellectual Property and Moral Rights* (Edward Elgar Publishing, forthcoming) ('Exploring Moral Interests in the Intellectual Creations Underlying Trade Marks').

[103] Committee on Economic, Social and Cultural Rights, *General Comment No 17: The Right of Everyone to Benefit from the Protection of the Moral and Material Interests Resulting from Any Scientific, Literary or Artistic Production of which He or She is the Author* (article 15, paragraph 1(c), of the Covenant), 35th sess, UN Doc E/C.12/GC/17 (12 January 2006) [16].

[104] Helfer and Austin argue that when we consider potential conflicts between human rights and intellectual property, it is necessary to recognise if the intellectual property legislation that is alleged to be in conflict with the relevant human rights is in fact the reason for the restriction of the rights: Laurence R Helfer and Graeme Austin (eds), *Human Rights and Intellectual Property: Mapping the Global Interface* (Cambridge University Press, 2011) 519–520.

[105] Brigit Toebes, 'Human Rights and Public Health: Towards a Balanced Relationship' (2015) 19(4) *The International Journal of Human Rights* 488, 495 ('Human Rights and Public Health'); Albert Alemanno and Enrico Bonadio, 'Do You Mind My Smoking? Plain Packaging of Cigarettes Under the TRIPS Agreement' (2011) 10 *The John Marshall Review of Intellectual Property Law* 449.

[106] *Marrakesh Agreement Establishing the World Trade Organization*, opened for signature 15 April 1994, 1867 UNTS 3 (entered into force 1 January 1995) annex 1C ('*Agreement on Trade-Related Aspects of Intellectual Property Rights*') preamble ('*TRIPS*'); Uvin questions the status of the right to development: Peter Uvin, 'From the Right to Development to the Rights-Based Approach: How "Human Rights" Entered Development' (2007) 17(4/5) *Development in Practice* 597.

the burden of tobacco-related disease.[107] Health concerns related to tobacco consumption are also problematic for countries that are producers of tobacco.[108] Accordingly, Target 3.a of the United Nations Sustainable Development Goals is to '[s]trengthen the implementation of the World Health Organization Framework Convention on Tobacco Control in all countries, as appropriate'.[109] Consequently, other development considerations undermine arguments that the restrictions imposed by plain packaging legislation impair the economic development of countries who depend on exports of tobacco-related products to Australia for income.[110]

Although property concerns are also clearly relevant to disputes concerning plain packaging legislation,[111] the human right to property has been narrowly interpreted in jurisdictions where protection exists.[112] States are generally given a wide margin of appreciation in European jurisprudence considering whether there has been interference with property rights.[113] Relevant considerations are whether a fair balance has been struck between the interests of the community and those of the applicant, or whether the applicant bears an individual and excessive burden.[114] The right to health concerns, outlined above, suggest that plain packaging legislation supports the interests of the community and this would be important to a human right to property assessment. Even though rights to property and development may be engaged by plain packaging

---

[107] Oscar A Cabrera and Lawrence O Gostin, 'Human Rights and the Framework Convention on Tobacco Control: Mutually Reinforcing Systems' (2011) 7(3) *International Journal of Law in Context* 285, 286.

[108] Oscar A Cabrera and Juan Carballo, 'Tobacco Control in Latin America' in Andrew D Mitchell and Tania Voon (eds), *The Global Tobacco Epidemic and the Law* (Edward Elgar Publishing, 2014) 235, 236.

[109] *Transforming Our World: The 2030 Agenda for Sustainable Development*, GA Res 70/1, UN GAOR, 70th sess, UN Doc A/RES/70/1 (21 October 2015).

[110] Toebes, 'Human Rights and Public Health' (n 105) 495. In the WTO Disputes, Cuba argued that plain packaging measures were detrimental to its economic development because of the importance of its tobacco industries: *Australia – Tobacco Plain Packaging* (n 5) annex B-3, B-62.

[111] *JT International SA v Commonwealth of Australia; British American Tobacco Australasia Limited v The Commonwealth* (n 3).

[112] Marco Ricolfi, 'Trademarks and Human Rights' in Paul Torremans (ed), *Intellectual Property Law and Human Rights* (Kluwer Law International, 2015).

[113] *Anheuser-Busch Inc v Portugal* (European Court of Human Rights, Grand Chamber, Application No 73049/01, 11 January 2007); Laurence R Helfer, 'Regime Shifting: The TRIPS Agreement and New Dynamics of International Intellectual Property Lawmaking' (2004) 29 *The Yale Journal of International Law* 1, 3.

[114] See, for example, the reasoning in *Balan v Moldova* (European Court of Human Rights, Chamber, Application No 19247/03, 29 April 2008).

legislation, the uncertain nature of both rights means that it would be difficult to argue that either right should be considered in the WTO Disputes.[115]

3.5 Monitoring and Accountability

The absence of justiciable rights in Australia for many of the human rights identified in this analysis, impacts the ability of stakeholders to participate and assert their human rights in relation to plain packaging legislation. The *FCTC* was considered by the Joint Senate Committee on Treaties and was subject to National Interest Analysis.[116] However, at the time the agreement was ratified by Australia, the guidelines for Article 11, which form the basis for plain packaging legislation, had not been finalised or formally adopted so they could not be directly scrutinised.[117] The National Interest Analysis did not explicitly consider any human rights. Human rights engaged by Australian plain packaging legislation were eventually considered after the introduction of parliamentary scrutiny processes that require human rights compatibility statements ('HRCS') for new legislative instruments. The HRCS for the *Tobacco Plain Packaging Amendment Regulation 2012* considered plain packaging legislation to be compatible with the human right to health and the human right to freedom of expression.[118] There was no subsequent consideration of this statement by the Joint Committee, indicating that the legislation was considered to raise no further human rights concerns. However, as plain packaging legislation was introduced before parliamentary scrutiny legislation entered into force and only applies to new legislation or amending acts, there is no HRCS for the primary legislation. The subsequent implementation review for plain packaging legislation did not directly address human rights concerns.[119] This is problematic for ongoing monitoring of the human rights implications of the measures. The mandate of Australia's national human rights institution, the Australian Human Rights Commission ('AHRC'), does not include *ICESCR*, so its oversight for economic, social and cultural rights

---

[115] Neither is a clearly defined human right in customary international law or protected by a binding international agreement which lessens the likelihood of their interpretive relevance. See Uvin (n 106); Yu, 'The Anatomy of the Human Rights Framework for Intellectual Property' (n 101) 85–95.

[116] Australian Government Department of Foreign Affairs and Trade, *National Interest Analysis [2004] ATNIA 7* ('*ATNIA*').

[117] *Technical Report 2 – Tobacco Control in Australia* (n 9) 20.

[118] Tobacco Plain Packaging Explanatory Statement (n 55) 10–15.

[119] *Post-Implementation Review* (n 79).

related to plain packaging legislation is limited to overlapping protections in human rights instruments within its mandate, which includes the *CRC*.[120]

Other international bodies can strengthen legislative accountability. The WHO issued a statement to the TRIPS Council Meeting in relation to the WTO Disputes recognising Australia's standardised plain packaging measures as compatible with the provisions of the *FCTC* and the decisions of the COP.[121] In the Uruguayan decision, considered in Section 5, the majority gave weight to an *amicus curiae* brief from the WHO and the *FCTC* Secretariat, as well as the role of the *FCTC* as an agreement giving effect to the right to health.[122]

3.6 Participation, Empowerment and Transparency

Transparency impacts the ability of stakeholders to participate in the process. Analysis of the effectiveness of plain packaging legislation suggests that available data on tobacco consumption is restricted.[123] Data could also improve the effectiveness of accountability measures considered above. The CESCR recognises that the participation of the community at all levels in relation to health-related decisions is an important part of the right to health.[124] Plain packaging legislation engages a number of relevant stakeholders. Diverse stakeholders were consulted in the *Taskforce Report*, in consultation preceding the introduction of plain packaging legislation and for the Post-Implementation Review.[125]

---

120 *Australian Human Rights Commission Act 1986* (Cth) ss 3, 11.

121 World Health Organization, *Statement of The World Health Organization in Relation to the Issue of Standardized Tobacco Product Packaging* (WHO, 2014) http://www.who.int/fctc/mediacentre/news/2014/WHOSTATEMENTWTOTRIPSOCT2014.pdf?ua=1.

122 *Philip Morris Brands Sàrl v Uruguay* (Award, ICSID Arbitral Tribunal, Case No ARB/10/7, 8 July 2016) [304] ('*Arbitral Decision*').

123 Sinclair Davidson and Ashton de Silva, 'The Plain Truth about Plain Packaging: An Econometric Analysis of the Australian 2011 Tobacco Plain Packaging Act' (2014) 21(1) *Agenda: A Journal of Policy Analysis and Reform* 27, 31 ('The Plain Truth about Plain Packaging').

124 *General Comment 14* (n 12) [11].

125 *National Taskforce Report* (n 71) 292–304; Biotext Pty Ltd, *Public Consultation on the Exposure Draft of the Tobacco Plain Packaging Bill 2011: Summary of Submissions* (18 September 2011); Siggins Miller Consultants Pty Ltd, *Consultancy Services to Inform the Development of a Post Implementation Review of the Tobacco Plain Packaging Measure: Stakeholder Consultation Report* (September 2015); *Post-Implementation Review* (n 79) 19–23, app B.

The Australian government is a stakeholder to the extent that it is obliged to protect both public health[126] and the human right to health.[127] Section 3.1 has set out Australia's obligations in relation to the way in which plain packaging legislation respects, protects and fulfils the human right to health for individuals. This protection also has a collective dimension, as a reduced burden on health systems leads to overall benefits, including greater resources available for the realisation of economic, social and cultural rights.[128] Owners of tobacco-related trade marks have been included in the consultations of the National Preventative Health Taskforce[129] and consultations related to plain packaging legislation.[130] To the extent that unjust expropriation laws protect the human right to property in Australia, owners have also been able to assert those rights in *JT International*.[131] However, although the freedom of expression implications identified were considered in the HRCS for plain packaging legislative amendments, no separately justiciable right was available in *JT International* for protection of freedom of expression for this form of commercial advertising.[132] This reflects the problematically limited availability of individually justiciable rights in Australia.[133]

Individuals could participate in legislative development by making submissions to the consultation preceding the introduction of plain packaging legislation.[134] Consultation can be an important mechanism for enhancing the effectiveness of the measure. During a consultation process, smokers or potential smokers may suggest alternative measures or adjustments to proposed measures that they would find a more effective deterrent to tobacco consump-

---

[126] Lawrence O Gostin and Lindsay F Wiley, *Public Health Law: Power, Duty, Restraint* (University of California Press, 3rd ed, 2016) 9.

[127] *ICESCR* (n 48) art 12; *Universal Declaration of Human Rights*, GA Res 217A (III), UN GAOR, 3rd sess, 183rd plen mtg, UN Doc A/810 (10 December 1948) art 25.

[128] Surveys on youth smoking rates were considered but youth do not appear to have been directly consulted: *National Taskforce Report* (n 71) 197, 292–304; Thomas (n 7) 3–5.

[129] Ibid.

[130] Biotext Pty Ltd (n 125).

[131] *JT International SA v Commonwealth of Australia; British American Tobacco Australasia Limited v The Commonwealth* (n 3).

[132] Ibid.

[133] See Gillian Triggs, 'Creating a Human Rights Culture' (2014) 17 *Southern Cross University Law Review* 59.

[134] Department of Health and Ageing, *Consultation Paper: Tobacco Plain Packaging: Proposed Approach to Non-Cigarette Tobacco Products* (30 September 2011) http://webarchive.nla.gov.au/gov/20140215002554/http://www.health.gov.au/internet/yourhealth/publishing.nsf/Content/tpp-noncig-paper.

tion.[135] Some direct consultation of Indigenous groups occurred but there is limited specific evidence that other vulnerable groups who may also disproportionately experience harm from tobacco consumption were consulted.[136]

Children and youth are also affected groups as the measure was directed at adolescent tobacco consumption initiation. Yet youth do not appear to have been directly consulted in the legislative development process.[137] The failure of Australia to transparently conduct a comprehensive human rights assessment of plain packaging legislation during its development may be one of the reasons that the specific human rights of children were not identified. This is important, as children also have special rights to be heard that are relevant to participation and empowerment.[138] Recognising these rights could be significant for effectiveness: the consultation and participation of children can enable unique insights into effective messaging in health promotion.[139] Involvement of children can also empower them to become advocates for measures like tobacco plain packaging and amplify efforts to reduce tobacco consumption and initiation in children.[140]

3.7 International Cooperation and Assistance

General Comment 14 clearly states that the WTO should 'cooperate effectively with States parties, building on their respective expertise, in relation to the implementation of the right to health at the national level, with due respect to their individual mandates'.[141] The CESCR reminds states that they should be mindful of their obligations to realise the right to health in their entry into other agreements.[142] 'Violations of the obligation to respect are those State actions, policies or laws that contravene the standards set out in article 12 of the Covenant and are likely to result in ... preventable mortality.'[143] Examples include 'the failure of the State to take into account its legal obligations regard-

---

[135] Genevieve Wilkinson, 'Using Tobacco Plain Packaging to Protect the Human Rights of Children' (2022) 45(1) *UNSW Law Review* 370, 396 ('Using Tobacco Plain Packaging to Protect the Human Rights of Children').

[136] Indigenous groups were consulted: *National Taskforce Report* (n 71) 292–293.

[137] Some submissions were made on behalf of children: Biotext Pty Ltd (n 125). See also failure to directly consult more recently in Siggins Miller Consultants Pty Ltd (n 125); *Post-Implementation Review* (n 79) 19–23, app B.

[138] *CRC* (n 50) art 12.

[139] Wilkinson 'Using Tobacco Plain Packaging to Protect the Human Rights of Children' (n 135) 395.

[140] Ibid 396–399.

[141] *General Comment 14* (n 12) [64].

[142] Ibid [50].

[143] Ibid.

ing the right to health when entering into bilateral or multilateral agreements with other States, international organizations and other entities, such as multinational corporations'.[144]

The 'essential role of international cooperation', including technical assistance, is emphasised by the CESCR.[145] The Australian government characterised their development of plain packaging legislation as international leadership in tobacco control.[146] Australia's policy of global leadership in developing plain packaging as a health measure could provide valuable technical assistance to other countries seeking to develop and implement analogous legislation.[147] The Australian National Interest Analysis praised the *FCTC* for its potential to promote international acceptance of similar policies and enhance international cooperation.[148] Australia's successful defence of plain packaging legislation in the WTO Disputes may limit the chilling regulatory impact of this litigation on other countries seeking to introduce tobacco plain packaging legislation.

3.8 Balancing of Rights

Tobacco advertising is closely linked to tobacco consumption.[149] States have obligations to address the health impacts of tobacco consumption as part of the human right to health, and the human rights analysis in this chapter demonstrates that this obligation is the most pressing human rights concern engaged by Australian plain packaging legislation. Australian legislative policy regarding tobacco advertising has progressively restricted advertising to attempt to reduce tobacco consumption and its negative health-related impacts.[150] Progressive realisation requires legislation to be effective. Effectiveness is linked to both the appropriateness of the means used by states to realise their

---

[144] Ibid.

[145] *General Comment 14* (n 12) [32].

[146] *ATNIA* (n 116) [6].

[147] Mariette Brennan's analysis of the impact of tobacco consumption in Canada and historical issues with regulating tobacco packaging demonstrates that leadership benefits extend to developed countries: Brennan (n 52).

[148] *ATNIA* (n 116).

[149] David Hammond, '"Plain Packaging" Regulations for Tobacco Products: The Impact of Standardizing the Color and Design of Cigarette Packs' (2010) 52(Suppl 2) *Salud Publica De Mexico* S226; Thomas (n 7) 5, citing Philip Morris Limited, Philip Morris Limited's Submission to the Senate Community Affairs Legislation Committee, Inquiry into *Plain Tobacco Packaging (Removing Branding from Cigarette Packs) Bill 2009*, 30 April 2010; *Summary of Arguments* (n 81) [24]–[35].

[150] See Section 2.1.

obligations[151] and requirements that states move towards full realisation of the right to health 'as expeditiously and effectively as possible'.[152] The effectiveness of plain packaging measures has also been contested by countries challenging the legislation in the WTO.[153] The policy documents underlying plain packaging legislation have established the scientific justification for tobacco plain packaging.[154] Plain packaging was partly designed to ensure that existing health measures, such as graphic health warnings, had increased effectiveness.[155] Although the 2016 Post-Implementation Review presented evidence supporting the effectiveness of the measure, the justification and effectiveness of plain packaging legislation remain contested on several grounds.[156]

Effectiveness also includes consideration of participation and other important rights, including children's human rights. These are ongoing considerations for Australia as it continues to negotiate bilateral and multilateral agreements that can strengthen the rights of intellectual property owners and restrict domestic regulatory autonomy. Although tobacco carve-outs were successfully introduced into the *Comprehensive and Progressive Agreement for Trans-Pacific Partnership*,[157] this would not address emerging public health concerns such as the negative health impacts of e-cigarettes.[158] The chilling regulatory impact of regional and bilateral trade agreements may mean that states do not consider they have the resources needed to respond to legal challenges to associated legislation.[159] Embedding explicit recognition of human rights obligations into bilateral and plurilateral trade agreements could be of significant value when investor–state dispute mechanisms require justification of policies that restrict intellectual property rights. The relevance of human rights to the Philip Morris–Uruguay dispute is considered below.

---

[151] Committee on Economic, Social and Cultural Rights, *General Comment No 3: The Nature of States Parties' Obligations (Art 2, Para 1 of the Covenant)*, UN ESCOR, 5th sess, UN Doc E/1991/23 (14 December 1990) [3] ('*General Comment 3*').

[152] Ibid [9].

[153] *Summary of Arguments* (n 81) [76].

[154] *Technical Report 2 – Tobacco Control in Australia* (n 9) 20.

[155] *Post-Implementation Review* (n 79) 12–15; *Australia – Tobacco Plain Packaging* (n 5) [7.628].

[156] *Summary of Arguments* (n 81) [76]; Davidson and de Silva, 'The Plain Truth about Plain Packaging' (n 123); Davidson and de Silva, 'Did Recent Tobacco Reforms Change the Cigarette Market?' (n 82) 70.

[157] *The Comprehensive and Progressive Agreement for Trans-Pacific Partnership*, signed 8 March 2018, [2018] ATNIF 1 (entered into force on 30 December 2018) art 29.5.

[158] Wilkinson 'Using Tobacco Plain Packaging to Protect the Human Rights of Children' (n 135) 398–399.

[159] Jennifer L Tobin, 'The Social Cost of International Investment Agreements: The Case of Cigarette Packaging' (2018) 32(2) *Ethics and International Affairs* 153, 161–2.

General Comment 14 provides that it is incumbent on capable state parties to the *ICESCR* to assist in providing economic and technical assistance and cooperation to other state parties, in order to assist them to fulfil their core obligations.[160] Relevant obligations to plain packaging legislation include implementation of national health strategies;[161] ensuring child health care;[162] and prevention, treatment and control of diseases.[163] Australia may provide more effective assistance if it uses a human rights framework in the development, implementation and ongoing assessment of plain packaging legislation. This strengthens monitoring of effectiveness: less well-resourced states can then assess whether Australia's approach is appropriate for them to adopt.

4 A HUMAN RIGHTS-BASED ANALYSIS OF *AUSTRALIA – TOBACCO PLAIN PACKAGING*

The WTO Plain Packaging Disputes show that legislative justification is a critical consideration when *TRIPS* Article 20 compliance is disputed in the WTO. Australia's justification focused on public health objectives, including its obligation to implement the *FCTC*. However, this section will explore the way the decisions should provide greater opportunities for use of human rights obligations when justification is considered.

In the WTO Disputes, the complainants asserted that plain packaging constituted multiple breaches of *TRIPS* and, separately, the TBT.[164] Article 20 of *TRIPS* requires that '[t]he use of a trademark in the course of trade shall not be unjustifiably encumbered by special requirements'. Plain packaging legislation only permits use of a trade mark on packaging in a proscribed form, in certain locations on the packaging, in combination with health warnings, graphic photographs and the Quitline mark.[165] The Panel found that plain packaging legislation constitutes special requirements that are an unjustified encumbrance on the use of the relevant trade marks in the course of trade.[166] This section will focus on the Article 20 arguments concerning justifiability of plain packaging measures. These provide scope for interpretation of the term 'unjustifiably' using the *Vienna Convention on the Law of Treaties* ('*VCLT*') interpretative tools. The *VCLT* provides guidelines to the WTO Dispute

---

160 *General Comment 14* (n 12) [45].

161 Ibid [43].

162 Ibid [44].

163 Ibid.

164 See generally *Australia – Tobacco Plain Packaging*.

165 *Tobacco Plain Packaging Act* (Cth) ss 21, 20(3)(a); *Competition and Consumer (Tobacco) Information Standard 2011* (Cth) s 2.2 item 1, pts 3–4, pt 9 divs 3–4.

166 *Australia – Tobacco Plain Packaging* (n 5) [7.2292].

Settlement Body regarding interpretation. The nature of the encumbrance that must be justified is subject to interpretation.[167] *VCLT* Article 31(1) requires interpretation 'in good faith in accordance with the ordinary meaning to be given to the terms of the treaty in their context and in the light of its object and purpose'. The context of a treaty term or provision includes the text, the preamble, annexes and agreements made in connection with conclusion of the treaty.[168] In relation to *TRIPS*, both the Preamble and Articles 7 and 8 are relevant provisions to the object and purpose of the treaty, which will guide interpretation of Article 20.[169] Ruse-Khan argues that it is most important to refer to balancing provisions when the relevant articles contain terms that are not explicit.[170] He identifies a number of 'broad and open legal concepts' within *TRIPS*, including normal exploitation, legitimate interests, (un)reasonableness, necessity and *ordre public*.[171]

4.1 Interpreting the Term 'Unjustifiably' in the WTO Disputes

The Panel approached the interpretative exercise by ascertaining the ordinary meaning of 'unjustifiably' then using other provisions of *TRIPS* to assess justifiability.[172] A broad range of potential meanings for 'unjustifiably' suggests that further interpretative tools provided by the *VCLT* are useful for interpreting its meaning.[173] The Panel determined that the term unjustifiably referenced 'the ability to provide a "justification" or "good reason" for the relevant action or situation that is reasonable in the sense that it provides sufficient support for that action or situation'.[174] The object and purpose of *TRIPS* were also relevant

---

[167] Susy Frankel and Daniel J Gervais, 'Plain Packaging and the Interpretation of the TRIPS Agreement' (2013) 46(5) *Vanderbilt Journal of Transnational Law* 1149, 1172–1174.

[168] *Vienna Convention on the Law of Treaties*, opened for signature 23 May 1969, 1155 UNTS 331 (entered into force 27 January 1980) art 31(2) ('*VCLT*').

[169] Frankel and Gervais (n 167) 1167–1168.

[170] Henning Grosse Ruse-Khan, 'Proportionality and Balancing within the Objectives for Intellectual Property Protection' in Paul L C Torremans (ed), *Intellectual Property and Human Rights* (Kluwer Law International, 2008) 162–3. This is similar to Land's argument that standards provision and textual silence are types of flexibility mechanisms: Molly Land, 'Rebalancing TRIPS' (2011–2012) 33 *Michigan Journal of International Law* 433, 438–442.

[171] Henning Grosse Ruse-Khan (n 170) 162–163.

[172] *Australia – Tobacco Plain Packaging* (n 5) [7.2393]–[7.2431].

[173] Frankel and Gervais have argued that other WTO case law suggests standards ranging from having a rational relationship to the measure to having a substantial or firm evidence base to a near certain correlation: Frankel and Gervais (n 167) 1204–1206.

[174] *Australia – Tobacco Plain Packaging* (n 5) [7.2395].

to understanding what reasons could support justifiability and considered the preamble, Article 7 and Article 8 of *TRIPS*.[175] The preamble notes the importance of protection and enforcement of intellectual property but also recognises public policy objectives underlying domestic systems of intellectual property protection that can be relevant to the object and purpose of the agreement.[176] As part of its analysis, the Panel identified the *Doha Declaration* on Public Health as a subsequent agreement relevant to interpretation of *TRIPS*.[177] The *Doha Declaration* identifies the significance of Articles 7 and 8 to understanding the object and purpose of *TRIPS* and the Panel was guided by this in its assessment that societal interests were relevant to justifiableness.[178] The Panel characterised Article 20 as reflecting an intended balance by drafters of the *TRIPS* Agreement 'between the existence of a legitimate interest of trademark owners in using their trademarks in the marketplace, and the right of WTO Members to adopt measures for the protection of certain societal interests that may adversely affect such use'.[179] In interpreting the justifiability of the encumbrance posed by plain packaging legislation, the content of Articles 7 and 8 influenced the Panel's identification of public health considerations as relevant to societal interests.[180]

The Appellate Body upheld the decision of the Panel that the special requirements that Australia's plain packaging measures placed on the use of a trade mark in the course of trade were not unjustifiable. The weight given by the Panel to the *FCTC* in providing support for Australia's legislative justification was contested by Honduras in the appeal.[181] The Appellate Body found that the Panel recognised Australia's involvement in the *FCTC* as further support for its conclusion that Australia had sufficiently supported its reasons for the introduction of plain packaging.[182] It endorsed the approach taken by the Panel to determining justification but clarified certain points relating to the finding that Australia's measures were justified.

---

[175] Ibid [7.2398]–[7.2402].

[176] *TRIPS* (n 106) preamble.

[177] *Australia – Tobacco Plain Packaging* (n 5) [7.2409]–[7.2410].

[178] Ibid [7.2399]–[7.2402].

[179] Ibid [7.2429].

[180] Ibid [7.2406], [7.2588]. Ruse-Khan notes that the 'unjustifiability' requirement in Article 20 allows the consideration of competing policies and interests, such as public health: Henning Grosse Ruse-Khan (n 170) 344. Frankel recognises 'health' as an open-textured term: Susy Frankel, 'The WTO's Application of 'the Customary Rules of Interpretation of Public International Law' to Intellectual Property' (2006) 46 *Virginia Journal of International Law* 365, 421.

[181] *Appellate Body Reports* (n 8) [6.700].

[182] Ibid [6.707].

The Appellate Body did not adopt the Panel's characterisation of the *Doha Declaration* as a subsequent agreement to *TRIPS*.[183] The Appellate Body determined that this finding was not necessary, as the part of the declaration that the Panel relied on was a reflection of applicable rules of treaty interpretation that each provision should be read in light of the object and purpose of *TRIPS*: 'as expressed, in particular, in its objectives and principles'.[184] Arguably, the Panel goes beyond restating interpretative principles as it confirms that Articles 7 and 8 express the object and purpose of *TRIPS*. The weight given to this in both decisions is important as it recognises that the relevant intention extends beyond the core object and purpose emphasised by Australia: 'to ensure that all WTO Members provide a minimum level of exclusive rights to owners of IP'.[185] The protection and enforcement of intellectual property rights is the primary objective of the *Paris Convention*[186] but the objectives recognised in *TRIPS* reflect the balance negotiated between developed and less-developed countries that is articulated in Articles 7 and 8 of *TRIPS*.[187]

The human rights-focused analysis of plain packaging legislation in this chapter contrasts to the emphasis on public health in the arguments addressing Article 20 in the WTO Disputes. Although the Panel and the Appellate Body recognised the justifiability of the legislation, it did not consider the human rights justifications.[188] This is consistent with the absence of emphasis on human rights by all parties in argument, reflecting the failure of Australia to rely on human rights to support plain packaging legislation.[189] However, the reference to health objectives in plain packaging legislation and the recognition of the role of the legislation in furthering the right to health in explanatory legislative materials indicate that protection of the human right to health is a relevant underlying policy objective of the legislation.[190]

The decisions present opportunities for future recognition of human rights in *TRIPS* disputes. In interpreting the unjustifiableness of the encumbrance posed by plain packaging legislation, the Panel considered the object and

---

183 Article 31(3)(a) provides that a subsequent agreement as something which should be taken into account in interpretation of a treaty term: *VCLT* (n 168).

184 *Appellate Body Reports* (n 8) [6.657].

185 *Australia – Tobacco Plain Packaging* (n 5) [7.2344].

186 Sam Ricketson, *The Paris Convention for the Protection of Industrial Property: A Commentary* (Oxford University Press, 2015) 148–149.

187 Peter K Yu, 'The Objectives and Principles of the TRIPS Agreement' (2009) 46(4) *Houston Law Review* 979, 1000–1008 ('The Objectives and Principles of the TRIPS Agreement').

188 *Australia – Tobacco Plain Packaging* (n 5) [7.2598].

189 Ibid [7.2294]–[7.2392].

190 *Tobacco Plain Packaging Act* 2011 (Cth) s 3; Tobacco Plain Packaging Bill Explanatory Memorandum (n 29) 15.

purpose of *TRIPS* discernible from the preamble, Articles 7 and 8.[191] Taking this approach, it recognised the relevance of societal interests including public health, to assessments of unjustifiableness.[192] This approach to interpretation of societal interests was not disturbed by the Appellate Body.[193]

Article 20 recognises that imposing certain requirements on the use of a trade mark during the course of trade requires justification. This engages human rights concerns when human rights obligations justify regulation of trade mark use. The question of whether human rights obligations can provide sufficient support for the regulation of trade mark use has not been considered by the panel in relation to *TRIPS*.[194] In future disputes, societal interests could be interpreted to directly overlap with the protection of human rights that can be linked to the object and purpose of *TRIPS* such as the right to health.[195] This interpretative approach could be relevant to other 'open textured' terms in *TRIPS*[196] and reduce the impact of fragmentation between different fields of law. Geiger and Desaunnetes-Barbero argue that the decision opens opportunities for use of Articles 7 and 8 as 'transversal interpretation clauses'.[197] This can also impact the interpretation of exceptions to rights: 'understood as horizontal interpretation clauses, Arts 7 and 8 will allow fundamental rights to be taken into account each time a provision of the Agreement opens the possibility of a balancing of interest.'[198]

The balance of rights and obligations referenced in Article 7 of *TRIPS* can be linked to the underlying public policy objectives of the Australian system of intellectual property protection, which include compliance with binding

---

191 *Australia – Tobacco Plain Packaging* (n 5) [7.2398]–[7.2411].

192 Ibid [7.2406], [7.2588].

193 *Appellate Body Reports* (n 8) [6.660].

194 See Christophe Geiger and Luc Desaunettes-Barbero, 'The Revitalisation of the Object and Purpose of the TRIPS Agreement: The Plain Packaging Reports and the Awakening of the TRIPS Flexibility Clauses' in Jonathan Griffiths and Tuomas Mylly (eds), *Global Intellectual Property Protection and New Constitutionalism* (Oxford University Press, 2021) 267, 292–294.

195 Yu also identifies other human rights with links to the object and purpose of TRIPS: Yu, 'The Objectives and Principles of the TRIPS Agreement' (n 187) 1037.

196 Frankel has previously characterised TRIPS provisions where 'the treaty language alone does not determine the scope of the provision' as open textured: Frankel (n 180) 421.

197 Geiger and Desaunettes-Barbero (n 194) 284–286.

198 Ibid 294. See Genevieve Wilkinson, 'Tobacco Plain Packaging, Human Rights and the Object and Purpose of International Trade Mark Protection' in Susy Frankel (ed), *The Object and Purpose of Intellectual Property* (Edward Elgar Publishing, 2019) 182, 212–215.

international obligations.[199] This chapter has identified provisions of the *ICESCR* and the *CRC* that can be interpreted to justify the introduction of plain packaging in Australia. Although there continues to be dispute about the extent of packaging restrictions required by the *FCTC* Guidelines, in the WTO Disputes engaging *TRIPS* Article 20, Australia's *FCTC* obligations were identified by the Panel as relevant to its justification for implementing plain packaging legislation.[200] The objective of protecting health by reducing tobacco consumption is not only relevant to understanding underlying policy objectives and a balance of rights and obligations but is also relevant to social and economic welfare, which is an objective identified in Article 7. Further, in interpreting whether restricting the use of trade marks on tobacco packaging 'unjustifiably' encumbers use of a mark, Australia's obligation to protect the right to health is relevant to a balance of rights and obligations, consistent with the principle articulated in Article 7.

In both decisions, Australia's *FCTC* obligations were considered relevant to their justification for implementation of plain packaging measures.[201] Although it is not a human rights treaty, the *FCTC* preamble does recall the human right to health. The Panel and the Appellate Body were willing to consider that obligations in a non-WTO treaty that functions to protect the human right to health are relevant to assessments that involve a balancing of interests. This indicates future possibilities for protection of human rights in interpretation of trade mark rights and other rights. This presents opportunities for consideration of human rights justifications where consistent interpretation is possible.[202] This is significant for recognition of economic, social and cultural rights within the WTO framework.

4.2 Lessons from the Dispute

Mitchell and Roberts argue that the decision was consistent with the human right to health even though human rights was not the focus of the dispute. They characterise references to public health as a 'clear reflection of the

---

[199] Australian Government Productivity Commission, *Intellectual Property Arrangements*, Inquiry Report No 78 (23 September 2016) 13 http://www.pc.gov.au/inquiries/completed/intellectual-property/report/intellectual-property.pdf ('*Productivity Commission Report*').

[200] *Australia – Tobacco Plain Packaging* (n 5) [7.2595–6], [7.2604].

[201] *Appellate Body Reports* (n 8) [6.707].

[202] Henning Grosse Ruse-Khan, *Protection of Intellectual Property in International Law* (Oxford University Press, 2016) 34.

right to health'.[203] However, as discussed in Chapter 2, the two approaches overlap but differ significantly. It is a core obligation of the right to health for public health systems to be measured against right to health indicators.[204] A systematic human rights assessment of plain packaging legislation would have permitted greater awareness of important human rights issues such as the rights of children. Ensuring the measures were consistent with a rights-based approach could enhance effectiveness and also structure ongoing assessment. The reference to the *FCTC* as evidence of support for Australia's justification also suggests that engagement with human rights principles could have further strengthened the arguments made by Australia that the measures were justified.

The ability to rely on human rights justifications could also be relevant in relation to other *TRIPS* flexibilities.[205] One aspect of the decision that was not appealed by Australia was the finding that the relevant use of a trade mark in the course of trade, protected by *TRIPS* Article 20, was not limited to the point of sale. The relevant meaning of 'in the course of trade' included a broader scope of commercial activities than those associated with the buying and selling of goods for profit, culminating at the point of sale.[206] The relevant use is 'not limited to the use of a trademark for the specific purpose of distinguishing the goods and services of one undertaking from those of other undertakings' and includes 'a wider range of commercial, advertising and promotion activities'.[207] The Panel uses interpretation of Article 17 as relevant guidance for the owner interests that are balanced in an Article 20 assessment,[208] and characterises these as 'the legitimate interest of trademark owners in using their trademarks in the marketplace',[209] which includes interests in extracting economic value from trade marks.[210] These interests align more closely with expanding rights for trade mark owners found in European and American jurisdictions than the more limited protection available in Australia. The following chapter will identify concerns that this expansive approach to protection pose for freedom of expression.

---

[203] Andrew Mitchell and Marcus Roberts, 'Human Rights and Tobacco Plain Packaging in Australia' in Marie Elske Gispen and Brigit Toebes (eds), *Human Rights and Tobacco Control* (Edward Elgar Publishing, 2020) 252, 263.

[204] *General Comment 14* (n 12) [43].

[205] Geiger and Desaunettes-Barbero (n 194) 288–292.

[206] *Australia – Tobacco Plain Packaging* (n 5) [7.2260].

[207] Ibid [7.2285]–[7.2286].

[208] Ibid [7.2425]–[7.2429].

[209] Ibid [7.2429].

[210] Ibid [7.2604].

5 HOW CAN WE BUILD A HUMAN RIGHTS CULTURE?

5.1 Local Conditions

An important limiting feature for protection of human rights in Australian law is the absence of constitutionally enshrined fundamental rights. This is despite Australia's obligations to protect, respect and fulfil human rights enshrined in key international agreements it has ratified, including the *ICESCR*, the *ICCPR* and the *CRC*. The *ICESCR* is largely excluded from the mandate of Australia's national human rights institutions.[211] Australia has also failed to ratify the *Optional Protocol to the International Covenant on Economic, Social and Cultural Rights*,[212] which establishes an individual complaint mechanism. Other mechanisms for monitoring and accountability of these obligations are limited primarily to parliamentary scrutiny of new legislation and amendments, State-focused charters and human rights protection built into ordinary legislation, such as exclusions in discrimination legislation that protect freedom of expression.[213]

Australia is an economically developed country but it is a net importer of intellectual property.[214] Greater benefit may result from less extensive protection for intellectual property for Australia than for a country that is a net exporter of intellectual property.[215] Despite this, Australia has maintained strong intellectual property rights for owners.[216] The introduction of *TRIPS*-plus commitments such as an extended copyright term may reflect a balancing of relative interests in the negotiation of trade agreements, including geo-political interests.[217] Despite this, the monopoly available for well-known trade mark owners in Australia does not include expansive protection against dilution found overseas.[218]

---

211 *Australian Human Rights Commission Act 1986* (Cth) ss 3, 11.

212 *Optional Protocol to the International Covenant on Economic, Social and Cultural Rights*, adopted 10 December 2009, 869 UNTS 34 (entered into force 5 May 2013).

213 See, generally, Triggs (n 133).

214 *Productivity Commission Report* (n 199) 615.

215 Ibid 615–629.

216 For example, it has agreed to a 70 years plus the life of the author copyright term, unlike New Zealand: ibid 128–129.

217 See Australian Government Productivity Commission, *Bilateral and Regional Trade Agreements – Productivity Commission Research Report* (November 2010) https://www.pc.gov.au/inquiries/completed/trade-agreements/report.

218 Advisory Council on Intellectual Property, *Review of Trade Mark Enforcement* (April 2004) 21.

Different local conditions in Uruguay permit a greater understanding of the lessons that tobacco plain packaging provides for development of a human rights culture. Uruguay differs from Australia to the extent that it protects some economic, social and cultural rights in its constitution, including a limited guarantee to provide access to health care as well as autonomy to 'legislate on all questions connected with public health and hygiene, endeavouring to attain the physical, moral, and social improvement of all inhabitants of the country'.[219] It is a state party to all of the international human rights agreements identified by the Office of the High Commissioner for Human Rights,[220] the *FCTC* and the *American Convention on Human Rights*.[221]

5.2 Human Rights Implications for Tobacco Packaging in Different Local Conditions: Uruguay

This section considers the way that Uruguay defended differently formulated tobacco plain packaging in an investment dispute brought by Philip Morris. Arbitration proceedings brought against Uruguay contested two requirements of the Uruguay government: that 80 per cent of tobacco packaging be covered in health warnings and that brands meet single presentation requirements which would not distinguish between sub-brands on packaging.[222] The WTO outcome endorsed Australia's comprehensive and transparent justification for introducing tobacco plain packaging. The approach taken by Uruguay in justifying its packaging requirements in investor–state proceedings was more opaque. Defending tobacco packaging legislation has required significant resource investment. Although concerns were raised about the cost of the Australian disputes about plain packaging, the cost of the Uruguay dispute was of critical importance.[223] Uruguay received philanthropic funding to support its defence and there were fears that it would not have been able to continue its defence without this.[224] This reflects economic differences: although the

---

219 *Constitution of the Oriental Republic of Uruguay*, art 44.

220 'Status of Ratification Interactive Dashboard', *Office of the United Nations High Commissioner for Human Rights* https://indicators.ohchr.org/.

221 See *Sociedad Uruguaya de Tabacología v Estado Poder Ejecutivo*, Juzgados Letrados de Familia [Family Court of Uruguay], IUE 2-54452/2022, 19 October 2022 [tr author].

222 *Arbitral Decision* (n 122) [9]–[11].

223 Cecilia Olivet and Alberto Villareal, 'Who Really Won the Legal Battle between Philip Morris and Uruguay?' *The Guardian* (online, 28 July 2016) https://www.theguardian.com/global-development/2016/jul/28/who-really-won-legal-battle-philip-morris-uruguay-cigarette-adverts.

224 Matthew Rimmer, 'The Chilling Effect: Investor–State Dispute Settlement, Graphic Health Warnings, The Plain Packaging of Tobacco Products, and the Trans-

World Bank categorises it as highly developed, Uruguay is less economically developed than Australia.[225]

5.2.1 Philip Morris–Uruguay Dispute

Philip Morris commenced proceedings under a bilateral investment treaty between Switzerland and Uruguay that protects qualifying foreign investors from the respective parties. The terms of the investment treaty and specific packaging requirements in issue mean that the dispute was quite different from the WTO Plain Packaging Disputes. No objective and principles clauses analogous to *TRIPS* Articles 7 and 8 provided guidance. The treaty provides for 'each other's right not to allow economic activities for reasons of public security and order, public health or morality'.[226] The dispute was commenced in the International Centre for Settlement of Investment Disputes in 2010 by a Swiss company that owned trade mark registrations for tobacco-related brands, Philip Morris Brands Sàrl, and was finally resolved in 2016 in favour of Uruguay.[227]

In the dispute between Uruguay and Philip Morris, two measures were in issue: the requirement for the display of graphic health warnings over 80 per cent of tobacco packaging and the requirement of single presentation of different brand variants on packaging.[228] At the time of the dispute, Uruguay permitted very limited non-plain packaging but removed the ability for tobacco companies to market brand variants.[229] This type of marketing can be used misleadingly to communicate health benefits of certain brands to encourage or increase their consumption.[230] The single presentation requirement for brand families prevented Philip Morris from using more than one brand like Marlboro Gold in addition to Marlboro Red. Uruguay argued that existing consumer associations with these brand variants had been used to mislead consumers that different brands are healthier than others, after the

---

Pacific Partnership' (2017) 7(1) *Victoria University Law and Justice Journal* 76, 79–80.

225 See United Nations Development Programme, *Human Development Report 2021–22: Uncertain Times, Unsettled Lives: Shaping our Future in a Transforming World* (UNDP, 8 September 2022) 272–276 https://hdr.undp.org/content/human-development-report-2021-22.

226 *Agreement Between the Swiss Confederation and the Oriental Republic of Uruguay on the Reciprocal Promotion and Protection of Investments*, 7 October 1988, 1976 UNTS 389 (entered into force 22 April 1991) art 2(1) ('*Swiss–Uruguay Investment Treaty*').

227 *Arbitral Decision* (n 122) [273].

228 Ibid [9].

229 Ibid.

230 Ibid [357]–[367]; FN 482.

use of words such as 'mild' and 'light' on packaging was prohibited.[231] *FCTC* Article 11 required states to implement 'effective measures to ensure that… tobacco product packaging … [does] not promote a tobacco product by any means that are false, misleading, deceptive or likely to create an erroneous impression about its characteristics [or] health effects … [which] … may include terms such as "low tar", "light", "ultra-light", or "mild"'. Marlboro Gold had previously been associated with Marlboro light cigarettes.[232]

The impact of these measures and the way that they were developed by the Uruguay government formed the basis for claims that Uruguay had breached its obligations.[233] The majority judgment by President Piero Bernadini and Arbitrator James Crawford dismissed claims that the measures constituted indirect expropriation because they removed almost all of the value of the brand assets and associated goodwill.[234] Arbitrator Gary Born also dismissed the claim in his dissenting judgment.[235] The majority found that value remained in the assets so the claim failed. It determined further that Uruguay's action could constitute a valid exercise of its police powers to protect public health.[236] Separate allegations that Uruguay breached standards of fair and equitable treatment protected in the bilateral investment treaty resulted in a split decision by the arbitral panel.

Uruguay argued that the single presentation requirement formed part of a comprehensive tobacco control policy.[237] This policy was consistent with recommendations by the WHO and the express obligations on Uruguay as a Member of the *FCTC*. The *FCTC* was supported by scientific evidence.[238] An *amicus curiae* brief from the WHO and the *FCTC* secretariat also supported Uruguay's packaging measures.[239] The majority recognised Uruguay's active participation in the *FCTC* negotiations and development of guidelines that support plain packaging in their determination that fair and equitable treatment standards were not breached.[240] Article 11(a) of the *FCTC* requires states to prevent 'the false implication that a particular tobacco product is less harmful than other products'. Uruguay could rely on evidence underlying the *FCTC*

---

231 Ibid [10].
232 Ibid [113].
233 *Swiss–Uruguay Investment Treaty* art 10.
234 *Arbitral Decision* (n 122) [278]–[279].
235 Ibid [1]–[2] (Born).
236 Ibid [287]–[387].
237 Ibid [107] (Born).
238 Ibid [394].
239 Ibid [391].
240 Ibid [394]–[396].

that supported its legislation because this was appropriate for a Member of the *FCTC* with 'limited technical and economic resources'.[241] For Uruguay:

> adhesion to the FCTC and involvement in the process of scientific and technical cooperation and reporting and of exchange of information represented an important if not indispensable means for acquiring the scientific knowledge and market experience needed for the proper implementation of its obligations under the FCTC and for ensuring the fulfilment of its tobacco control policy.[242]

This meant that Uruguay was not required to support the measure with further evidence. The majority also recognised that Uruguay was entitled to a significant margin of appreciation when making an important public policy decision.[243] This test is commonly used by the European Court of Human Rights to assess claims in which expropriation of property by the state is alleged to be inconsistent with the right to property.[244] Whether or not future arbitration tribunals will adopt a margin of appreciation test in the same way is uncertain. Future tribunals are not bound by precedent.[245] A narrower approach adopted in Born's dissenting opinion could be adopted where states introduce measures that are not consistent with practice in other states.[246]

Uruguay's *FCTC* involvement was particularly important for its defence. However, the dissenting opinion did not find that this support outweighed other considerations. Arbitrator Born found that the development of the single presentation requirement was inconsistent with Uruguay's fair and equitable treatment obligations.[247] Although Uruguay's *FCTC* obligations were relevant to the specific support provided for the use of graphic health warnings in the *FCTC* Guidelines, there was no equivalent support for a single presentation requirement.[248] The measure had not been implemented by any other *FCTC* Member.[249] Born expressed concerns about the effectiveness of the measure. He did not agree that it was appropriate to import the margin of appreciation test used by the majority to assessments of fair and equitable treatment clauses.[250]

---

241 Ibid [393].
242 Ibid [393].
243 Ibid [399], [409].
244 Ibid [85] (Born).
245 See Cynthia Ho, 'A Collision Course Between TRIPS Flexibilities and Investor–State Proceedings' (2016) 6 *UC Irvine Law Review* 395, 452–453.
246 Ibid.
247 *Arbitral Decision* (n 122) [146]–[196] (Born).
248 Ibid [99]–[100] (Born).
249 Ibid [101] (Born).
250 Ibid [87] (Born).

Article 17 of the *CRC* requires states to develop appropriate guidelines for the protection of children from information that is injurious to their wellbeing.[251] Arguably, the single presentation requirement supports Uruguay's obligations to protect Article 17. The measure aimed to prevent tobacco companies from using an advertising approach that could mislead young smokers into believing that certain types of cigarettes have health benefits. If this is the case, detailed reference to human rights justifications in legislative development can overcome arguments of arbitrariness.[252] *Amicus curiae* briefs that support these policies can also be relevant in disputes to establish that human rights considerations justify measures that restrict intellectual property. Justification can also involve mapping how a policy directly meets specific human rights obligations in explanatory material. A rights-based approach supports a more transparent approach to justification of Uruguay's measures based on consultation with key stakeholders. Ensuring the participation of children in health policies impacting them can also be important for effectiveness to ensure that the best interests of the child are met, consistent with the objections focused on in the *CRC*.[253]

Born's judgment also raised concern about Philip Morris's access to a judicial tribunal to contest potentially inconsistent decisions between different decision-makers about the measures and cited human rights obligations underpinning this right.[254] The majority found that the inconsistent decisions between the Supreme Court and a tribunal did not meet the elevated standard required to establish a denial of justice.[255] However, ongoing monitoring and accountability of legal systems should include protection for human rights to a fair trial, supporting a broad rights-based approach for developing policies of this nature within a human rights culture. The majority decision suggests that there may be opportunities for states to use human rights principles to defend measures that are designed to protect human rights. The *FCTC* was characterised by the tribunal as a treaty guaranteeing the human right to health in the determination that the challenged measures were justified by Uruguay's public health objective and the expropriation claim failed.[256]

The weight given by the majority to the *FCTC* provides an example of how local conditions can be relevant to the way that states need to justify policies that restrict the exercise of intellectual property rights. Although effectiveness

---

[251] Wilkinson, 'Using Tobacco Plain Packaging to Protect the Human Rights of Children' (n 135) 380.

[252] Ibid.

[253] Ibid 395–399.

[254] *Arbitral Decision* (n 122) [71]–[71] (Born).

[255] Ibid [499]–[500].

[256] Ibid [304].

is an important consideration in developing policies to protect economic, social and cultural rights, it may not be appropriate to require the same type of evidence to justify measures where precedents exist. States wishing to implement Australian-style plain packaging policies may be able to rely on the *FCTC* or evidence from Australia to support their policies. However, this should not be a substitute for a rights-based approach to implementation of policies that impact intellectual property rights and engage questions of human rights.

5.2.2 Chilling effects and the need for international cooperation and assistance

The Uruguay dispute influenced the chilling impact of the WTO Disputes on other countries considering introducing plain packaging.[257] A number of aspects of the Uruguay arbitration contribute to its chilling effect. The length of the arbitration (over five years) reinforced uncertainty.[258] The ongoing arbitration reinforced threats made by tobacco companies to other states that they would contest tobacco packaging measures.[259] The financial and resource cost of the arbitration deterred other states from introducing legislation that they might have been able to defend only after costly and lengthy arbitration proceedings.[260] Despite Uruguay's overall success, it was only awarded part of its legal fees.[261]

Crosbie has conducted a comprehensive analysis of attempts to prevent tobacco regulation in Uruguay, Australia and New Zealand, and has identified significant evidence of regulatory chill in New Zealand and several other countries, corresponding to activities of tobacco companies in these countries.[262] Crosbie's findings support regulatory chill concerns previously identified by Gruszczynski in New Zealand, Europe and the United Kingdom.[263] New Zealand acknowledged that disputes regarding plain packaging legislation in other countries delayed the introduction and implementation of plain

---

257 Tobin (n 159) 161–162.

258 The request for arbitration was received in February 2010: *Arbitral Decision* (n 122) [15].

259 Lukasz Gruszczynski, 'Australian Plain Packaging Law, International Litigation and Regulatory Chilling Effect' (2014) 5(2) *European Journal of Risk Regulation* 242, 244.

260 Tobin (n 159) 161–162; Eric Crosbie, *Constraining Government Regulatory Authority: Tobacco Industry Trade Threats and Challenges to Cigarette Package Health Warning Labels* (PhD Thesis, University of California, 2016) 284–289 https://escholarship.org/uc/item/7tr077rr#main.

261 *Arbitral Decision* (n 122) [590].

262 Crosbie (n 261) 284–289.

263 Ibid 284–289; Gruszczynski (n 260).

packaging legislation in New Zealand.[264] Tobin provides evidence that the impact of tobacco company campaigns against plain packaging in Australia and Uruguay restricted the implementation of similar policies in Mexico, Guatemala, Honduras and Chile.[265] In arbitration, Uruguay submitted that New Zealand, Costa Rica and Paraguay had been deterred from introducing similar packaging legislation by the threat of litigation.[266] This provides evidence of the strong influence of third-party actors on states, which can restrict the implementation of human rights obligations.

A further chilling aspect was the scrutiny of the processes of the Uruguay government in relation to the implementation of the single presentation requirement. The dissenting judgment found these processes to be inconsistent with standards of fair and equitable treatment as they were arbitrary and disproportionate.[267] Inconsistencies between administrative and judicial decisions about the Uruguay packaging requirements and the failure to provide a judicial means to address these directly were determined to be a further breach of fair and equitable treatment protections.[268] Born's dissenting judgment is important because it recognises some of the justifications for introducing investor–state dispute mechanisms into trade agreements based on concerns about the legal processes of investment states. They also introduce complex human rights considerations. The rule of law considerations raised in relation to inconsistent decisions on packaging requirements are directly relevant to human rights protections for civil rights.[269] In Born's dissenting judgment, the standard applied in assessing whether the measures were arbitrary suggests limited latitude available to states when formulating policies of this nature.[270] The dissenting judgment rejected the use of a 'margin of appreciation' test, which can be found in relation to regional protection for the human right to property in *Article 1, Protocol No 1 of the European Convention of Human Rights*.[271] This margin of appreciation test could address some of the concerns about the democratic impact of foreign investors using investor–state dispute mechanisms to

---

264 Gruszczynski (n 260) 245.

265 Tobin (n 159) 161–162.

266 *Arbitral Decision* (n 122) [367]; William New, 'Australia Accuses Tobacco Industry Of "Regulatory Chill" In WTO Plain Packaging Case' *Intellectual Property Watch* (online, 20 November 2014) http://www.ip-watch.org/2014/11/20/australia-accuses-tobacco-industry-of-regulatory-chill-in-wto-plain-packaging-case/.

267 *Arbitral Decision* (n 122) [146]–[196] (Born).

268 Ibid [81] (Born).

269 Ibid [42] (Born).

270 Ibid (Born).

271 Ibid [85]–[87], [181–191] (Born). Cf *Arbitral Decision* (n 122) [398]–[401], [409].

influence government policy in investment states. The test could also support the integration of human rights laws and investment laws.

5.2.3 Comparison

The findings in the Uruguay dispute and the Plain Packaging Disputes demonstrate that public health is valued as an exception to intellectual property protection. However, both decisions indicate that a public health focus can result in gaps in identifying human rights concerns. Neither decision explicitly considered relevant children's rights, and the lack of transparency in the Uruguayan legislative process was problematic. There was no evidence in either decision that the approaches were measured against human rights benchmarks. Although effectiveness was important, the decisions only demonstrate that the measures met benchmarks related to *TRIPS* and the Uruguayan–Swiss investment agreement.

The *Philip Morris–Uruguay* dispute demonstrates that obligations found in human rights agreements can also be relevant to the determination of investor–state disputes. The finding that the *FCTC* could be used as technical support for Uruguay's agreement aligns with the recognition of the support provided by the *FCTC* for Australia's justification. This may permit the interpretation of international human rights obligations by human rights institutions to underlie the development of some policies. Specific international agreements that support human rights, like the *FCTC*, may be used as justifications in some circumstances without resource-intensive replication of the underlying science. Clear articulation of the relevance of human rights would be valuable to support disputes that require states to demonstrate a supportable justification for restricting intellectual property rights.

Recent WTO dispute decisions, considering the consistency of Turkish measures incentivising local pharmaceutical manufacture by foreign owners with GATT 1994, suggest that transparent consideration of relevant human rights objectives can justify legislative development.[272] The Panel found that Turkey's objective of providing access to medicines was relevant to determining whether the general exception in Article XX(b) of GATT 1994 applied to the breach of national treatment obligations asserted. The objective was supported by a UN Human Rights Council Resolution as well as *TRIPS* Article 8.1 and 31*bis* and the *Doha Declaration*.[273] However, the measure providing reimbursement to Turkish patents only when foreign producers agreed to localise

---

[272] Panel Report, *Turkey – Certain Measures Concerning the Production, Importation and Marketing of Pharmaceutical Products*, WT/DS583/12 (28 April 2022) (affirmed in Turkey – Pharmaceutical Products, WTO Doc WT/DS583/ARB25, (25 July 2022) (Award of the Arbitrators)).

[273] Ibid [7.157]–[7.159].

their pharmaceutical production was not designed to protect human life or health, consistent with the general exception. Documentary evidence did not articulate the objective and the panel did not identify a rational relationship between encouraging domestic production and 'the object of ensuring a continuous supply of safe, effective and affordable pharmaceutical products'.[274] Although the dispute did not adjudicate *TRIPS* compliance claims, it reinforces the value of transparent consideration of human rights concerns where measures impact on the rights of intellectual property owners.

Uruguay subsequently introduced more comprehensive plain packaging requirements in 2018, relying on philanthropic funding to develop evidence to support the introduction of uniform presentation requirements in addition to the single presentation requirement and 80 per cent graphic health warning requirements.[275] More recently, the Uruguayan government identified problems with counterfeit tobacco and issued a decree to amend plain packaging legislation and permit use of trade marks that identify brand by manufacturers inside packaging and on cigarettes.[276] In an administrative appeal, the Uruguayan Tobacco Control Society ('SUT') successfully argued that the decree contravened the *FCTC* and international human rights law, and the Uruguayan Family Court issued an injunction suspending operation of the decree. The government argued that this measure was designed to address the illegal cigarette market in Uruguay. The government asserted that the action was consistent with the requirement for using tracking and tracing in the Protocol for the Elimination of Illicit Trade in Tobacco, which requires affixation of unique identification markings on packaging to enable effective tracking and tracing.[277] The SUT contested this justification and focused its arguments on protection of the human rights of children and adolescents, relying on regional and international human rights instruments, and characterised the decree as retrogressive and inconsistent with *ICESCR* Article 2.1.[278] The Court recognised the relevance of the best interests of the child as a primary consideration when regulating tobacco packaging and found that the health interests of children supported the decree suspension.[279] The decision highlights the clear relevance of human rights concerns to tobacco

---

[274] Ibid [7.210].

[275] Ministerio de Salud Publica, *Decree 806* (29 April 2019) https://medios.presidencia.gub.uy/legal/2019/decretos/04/cm_806.pdf [tr author].

[276] *Sociedad Uruguaya de Tabacología v Estado Poder Ejecutivo*, Juzgados Letrados de Familia [Family Court of Uruguay], IUE 2-54452/2022, 19 October 2022 [tr author].

[277] Ibid.

[278] Ibid.

[279] Ibid.

plain packaging and the problems that plain packaging can pose for states addressing illicit trade in cigarettes. Protocol parties are obliged to implement the tracking and tracing requirements for cigarettes found in the Protocol for the Elimination of Illicit Trade in Tobacco from September 2023.[280]

A rights-based approach can also support effectiveness. Effectiveness of legislative measures is relevant to both the appropriateness of the means used by states to realise their obligations[281] and requirements that states move towards full realisation of the right to health 'as expeditiously and effectively as possible'.[282] It is supported by ongoing monitoring and assessment. This is not a feature of Australian protection for economic, social and cultural rights. Although there was an assessment of plain packaging legislation's effectiveness approximately five years after its introduction, there has not been a similar Post-Implementation Review ten years after introduction. Effectiveness concerns should be monitored. For example, an increase in illicit tobacco use as a consequence of plain packaging legislation would be relevant to the effectiveness of the legislation in realising its right to health objectives.

5.3 Lessons for a Human Rights Culture

The analysis in this chapter suggests that plain packaging measures that restricted intellectual property rights are, on balance, supportive of human rights. The decisions do not demonstrate coexistence between human rights and intellectual property. They may support coexistence between human rights and public health, but this is not the same thing. The absence of extensive, transparent consideration of human rights in either dispute suggests that a human rights culture for trade marks is not yet established. Documentation of human rights assessments during the legislative development process could not be used to support plain packaging measures to benefit the right to health and other rights. Ongoing human rights compatibility is not apparent. The protracted disputes have had a chilling impact on the introduction of plain packaging litigation outside of Australia in Europe, South America and the Asia-Pacific. Although Australia and Uruguay successfully defended their policies in arbitration and Uruguay subsequently introduced more holistic

---

280 Ibid. See WHO Framework Convention on Tobacco Control, *Protocol for the Elimination of Illicit Trade in Tobacco Products* (WHO, 2013) art 8 https://fctc.who.int/protocol/overview; United Nations Treaty Collection, *4. a) Protocol to Eliminate Illicit Trade in Tobacco Products* (4 November 2022) https://treaties.un.org/Pages/ViewDetails.aspx?src=TREATY&mtdsg_no=IX-4-a&chapter=9&clang=_en. Australia is not yet a party to this Protocol.

281 *General Comment 3* (n 151) [3].

282 Ibid [9].

plain packaging following its victory against Philip Morris,[283] the initiation of lengthy investor–state dispute proceedings in Australia and Uruguay increased the palpable risk of disputes occurring in other countries and influenced the introduction of plain packaging legislation in those countries.[284]

How could prescriptive human rights frameworks for intellectual property be useful if Australia or Uruguay had conducted systematic human rights-based assessments of their legislation? Yu's model can be used to consider whether plain packaging legislation restricts the moral and material rights of authors of device marks that are registered in relation to tobacco-related products and constitute artistic productions, in whole or in part. Until there is a practice of recognising creators of trade marks who may be responsible for artistic productions associated with trade marks, it is difficult to understand if the restrictions on intellectual property posed by plain packaging legislation create a conflict with the moral and material rights protected by the CESCR and used in Yu's model. If there was an internal conflict, Yu's mechanisms for resolution, using core minimum protection and progressive realisation standards in this case, are valuable. Progressive realisation of Article 15(1)(c) could support a register for authors of artistic productions underlying some trade marks to be identified and consulted.[285] It is possible they may not wish to assert any moral rights because of the harms associated with tobacco consumption.

Geiger's proposals for recognition of Article 27 are less relevant to plain packaging legislation because of the limited evidence that moral or material interests of creators were impaired. However, English plain packaging legislation was successfully defended against fundamental rights claims brought by Philip Morris and other tobacco companies who alleged that the legislation impaired their right to property.[286] Citing Court of Justice jurisprudence, the Court of Appeal found that the right to property 'can be regulated so far as is necessary in the general interest and to be viewed in relation to its social function'.[287]

In plain packaging disputes in Australia and Uruguay, human rights to benefit from science and culture were less important balances against intellec-

---

[283] 'Uruguay to Require Plain Tobacco Packaging', *Xinhua News Agency* (29 July 2019).

[284] Crosbie (n 261) 286–287.

[285] See Wilkinson, 'Exploring Moral Interests in the Intellectual Creations Underlying Trade Marks' (n 102).

[286] *Philip Morris Brands SARL and Others v Secretary of State for Health* (Court of Justice of the European Union, C-547/14, 4 May 2016).

[287] See Jonathan Griffiths, 'The Tobacco Industry's Challenge to the United Kingdom's Standardised Packaging Legislation – Global Lessons for Tobacco Control Policy' (2017) 17 *Queensland University of Technology Law Review* 66, 78.

tual property rights than health interests. Application of Helfer and Austin's analytical approach to a justification of Australia's plain packaging legislation based on the human rights analysis in this chapter indicates that conducting detailed human rights analysis can justify restrictions on trade marks. However, this does not consider the question of whether intellectual property rights have been modified consistent with Helfer and Austin's thresholds for human rights protection. The protection threshold prescribed by Helfer and Austin for non-interference with civil and political rights is reasonably comprehensive, but the protection guarantee of 'minimum levels of economic and social well-being in areas such as health, food and education' does not seem to engage with different standards of progressive realisation of economic, social and cultural rights between different states.[288]

Retrogression from economic, social and cultural rights is not permitted without careful consideration and excellent justification.[289] This is important. Helfer and Austin are not completely clear about the nature of the minimum standards they advocate protecting. A more recent consideration of standards by Helfer refers to 'the minimum entitlements relating to health, food, education, and so forth that international human right law requires'.[290] Realisation of economic, social and cultural rights needs to be addressed through international cooperation and assistance.[291] The *ICESCR* uses core minimum obligations as a minimum standard but, if these benchmarks are not adopted, minimum entitlements could vary significantly between states. Retrogression is prohibited,[292] so entitlements that are progressively achieved could be considered minimum entitlements in those states. Progressive realisation of economic, social and cultural rights for all states should be an objective of a human rights culture. International assistance and cooperation to assist all states to realise core minimum obligations is a first step. Yet harmonising intellectual property with human rights, particularly economic, social and cultural rights, should support states to protect individuals from harms caused by tobacco consumption as fully as possible. This is also consistent with development objectives recognised as part of the object and purpose of *TRIPS*.

Australia's success in defending disputes may have provided a valuable precedent influencing Uruguay to introduce more holistic plain packaging

---

[288] Helfer and Austin (n 104) 517.

[289] *General Comment 3* (n 151) [9].

[290] Laurence R Helfer, 'Mapping the Interface between Human Rights and Intellectual Property' in Christophe Geiger (ed), *Research Handbook on Human Rights and Intellectual Property* (Edward Elgar Publishing, 2015) 6, 14.

[291] Jonathan Wolff, *The Human Right to Health* (WW Norton & Co, 2012) 11–12.

[292] *General Comment 3* (n 151) [3].

following its victory against Philip Morris.[293] International cooperation and assistance by sharing information about effective approaches can provide valuable support for a human rights culture for trade marks. Integration of human rights principles with intellectual property regulation gives states confidence to assert their human rights objectives. This can be important if domestic trade mark rights continue to expand or registration inconsistencies emerge between jurisdictions, as the next chapter contemplates.

6 CONCLUSION

Disputes about tobacco plain packaging remind us of the incredibly high value that can be attached to certain brands and the trade marks associated with them. Owners of tobacco-related trade marks spent a decade challenging Australian legislation that restricted the use of those trade marks on tobacco packaging in Australian courts, international arbitration and the World Trade Organization. Their failure to overturn the legislation, alongside Uruguay's success against Philip Morris, signals to the global community that intellectual property rights are not an insurmountable barrier to considered, health-based restrictions on the use of trade marks in certain circumstances. These health justifications are relevant to both public health and human rights paradigms, but Australia's human rights obligations could have been more explicitly identified and considered during the development and implementation of plain packaging legislation. The protection of children's human rights in relation to health and health information was underexplored despite Australia's *CRC* obligations.

Applying the analytical framework to Australia's plain packaging legislation also reveals that domestic trade mark legislation can engage important and complex human rights concerns that are not limited to the right to health. A human rights approach requires an integrated analysis of these types of restrictions to safeguard the indivisibility and interdependence of economic, social and cultural rights as well as civil and political rights. Considering these issues for plain packaging legislation ensures that other important human rights such as freedom of expression are not impermissibly restricted. It also engages important human rights considerations such as the ongoing effectiveness of the legislation. The analysis also highlights the more limited protection available for individually justiciable human rights in Australia. This local condition limits the availability of accountability mechanisms if human rights concerns are not addressed through parliamentary scrutiny processes when legislation is initially introduced or subsequently amended. Ongoing monitoring of human rights is more dependent on civil society organisations and the media accessing

293 'Uruguay to Require Plain Tobacco Packaging' (n 284).

transparently available information about the effectiveness of the legislation. Explicit use of human rights indicators and benchmarks to monitor public health measures will also strengthen Australia's ability to ensure that intellectual property protection measures are consistent with binding obligations to implement the right to health in the future.

4 Contrary marks case study: the United States and the European Union

1 INTRODUCTION

The *Paris Convention for the Protection of Industrial Property* ('*Paris Convention*') is the oldest multilateral agreement regarding trade mark registration. It permits states to deny registration to marks that are 'contrary to morality or public order'.[1] Accordingly, the United States Patent and Trademarks Office ('USPTO') has historically rejected applications for scandalous, immoral or disparaging marks.[2] Consequently, it is not surprising that the USPTO rejected musician Simon Tam's application to register his band name, The Slants, as a trade mark, on the basis that the mark is disparaging to Asian people. This is despite the fact that Tam, and other members of his band, are Asian American and that they chose the name in an effort to reclaim a word that had been used to insult them in the past.[3] The USPTO also rejected Erik Brunetti's application to register the clothing brand name FUCT, on the basis that the mark was 'immoral or scandalous'.[4]

Tam and Brunetti appealed. In *Matal v Tam* ('*Tam*'), the United States Supreme Court found that the provision restricting registration of disparaging marks was inconsistent with free speech.[5] In *Iancu v Brunetti* ('*Brunetti*'), the Court reached a similar conclusion, determining that restricting the registration of immoral or scandalous marks was also contrary to free speech protection.[6]

---

1 *Paris Convention for the Protection of Industrial Property*, opened for signature 20 March 1883, 828 UNTS 305 (entered into force 6 July 1884, revised at Stockholm 14 July 1967, amended 28 September 1979) art 6, *quinquies*(B)(III). This chapter uses the term 'contrary marks' to refer to marks prohibited by states consistent with this permission. Diverse terminology is used domestically, including offensive, scandalous, obscene, immoral and contrary to morality or public policy: Lisa P Ramsey, 'A Free Speech Right to Trademark Protection' (2016) 106 *Trade Mark Reporter* 797 ('A Free Speech Right to Trademark Protection').

2 15 USC § 1052(a).

3 *Matal v Tam*, 137 S Ct 1744, 1747 (2017) ('*Tam*').

4 *Iancu v Brunetti*, 139 S Ct 2294, 2297 (2019) ('*Brunetti*').

5 *Tam* (n 3).

6 *Brunetti* (n 4) 22302.

The outcome removed the capacity for the USPTO to bar registration of disparaging, scandalous or offensive marks. The decisions have concerning implications for human rights to freedom of expression, protection from hate speech, non-discrimination and rights to participation in culture.

United States constitutional protection for free speech permits individuals to contest laws that impermissibly restrict expression. Laws that regulate expression based on its content are unconstitutional unless the speech fits into a category where an exception can operate, such as government speech.[7] Some categories provide a comprehensive exemption, such as government speech, but others engage different scrutiny thresholds. For example, the intermediate scrutiny test for commercial speech can permit restrictions narrowly based on substantial government interest.[8] However, restrictions that are based on the viewpoint that is expressed in speech are generally unconstitutional.[9] Although American free speech protection can support human rights protection for the right to freedom of expression, the protection functions differently from international human rights laws. Article 19(3) of the *International Covenant on Civil and Political Rights* ('*ICCPR*') permits freedom of expression restrictions when they are provided in law and necessary:

> (a) for the respect of rights and reputations of others;
> (b) for the protection of national security, or of public order, or of public health or morals.[10]

The Human Rights Committee has applied Article 19(3) to permit restrictions on speech that are viewpoint-based but meet these requirements.[11] In contrast, when American free speech protection was applied in *Tam* and *Brunetti*, the legislative justification for prohibiting the applicants' speech was not determinative. The provisions were unconstitutional because registration refusals restricted expression based on the viewpoint the mark expressed and no excep-

---

7 Lisa P Ramsey, 'Free Speech and International Obligations to Protect Trademark' (2010) 35 *The Yale Journal of International Law* 405, 406–407 ('Free Speech and International Obligations to Protect Trademarks').

8 Central Hudson Gas & Elec Corp v Public Service Commission of New York, 447 US 557, 566 (1980).

9 See Lamb's Chapel v Center Moriches Union Free School District, 508 US 384, 394 (1993).

10 *International Covenant on Civil and Political Rights*, opened for signature 16 December 1966, 999 UNTS 171 (entered into force 23 March 1976) art 19(3) ('*ICCPR*').

11 See, for example, Human Rights Committee, *Views: Communication No 550/1993*, 58th sess, UN Doc CCPR/C/58/D/550/1993 (8 November 1996) ('*Faurisson v France*').

tions operated.[12] The *ICCPR* also requires parties to prohibit 'any advocacy of national, racial or religious hatred that constitutes incitement to discrimination, hostility or violence'.[13] American free speech protection is not equivalently limited as it preserves 'the freedom to express "the thought that we hate"'.[14]

This chapter assesses the human rights implications of protection for contrary marks. The analysis in this chapter suggests that the removal of registration restrictions for contrary marks in the United States has negative implications for human rights protection and is not necessary for protection for freedom of expression. Special protections are given to registered trade mark owners permitting them to limit the freedom of third parties to use signifiers like The Slants. The result of the decisions in *Tam* and *Brunetti* is that marks that could be used to incite hate speech can be protected as registered trade marks, and registration for reclaimed disparaging marks can limit the ability of others to participate in culture where reclamation is part of that culture. Although the Supreme Court rejected the arguments that registered marks were government speech in *Tam* and *Brunetti*, conferral of trade mark privileges means that registration of disparaging marks could be seen as an endorsement of those marks by the state.[15] Concerningly, branded products displaying these marks might be used to incite discrimination, hostility or violence towards the object of that disparagement.[16]

The American approach is not consistent with approaches to registration of contrary marks in other jurisdictions such as Europe, where protections for freedom of expression align with international standards. This disharmony creates a likelihood that a trade mark owner of a contrary mark in one jurisdiction will not be permitted to register that mark in another jurisdiction.[17] The recent decision of the European Court of Justice ('ECJ') in *Constantin* and other European decisions regarding contrary marks demonstrates that it is possible to recognise the human right to freedom of expression in laws regulating registration of contrary marks law, without limiting protection from hate speech. European jurisprudence also indicates that decisions regarding contrary marks may also protect expressive diversity, consistent with rights to

---

12 See *Tam* (n 3); *Brunetti* (n 4) 2302.

13 *ICCPR* (n 10) art 20.

14 *Tam* (n 3) 1770.

15 See Fady J G Aoun, 'Whitewashing Australia's History of Stigmatising Trade Marks and Commercial Imagery' (2019) 42(3) *Melbourne University Law Review* 671, 724–725 ('Whitewashing Australia's History of Stigmatising Trade Marks and Commercial Imagery').

16 Ibid 673.

17 Juliet Dee, 'Sweet Baby Jesus, *the Band Who Must Not be Named*, and Friends U Can't Trust: Disparaging, Immoral and Scandalous Trademarks in the United States and the European Union' (2019) 53 *First Amendment Studies* 91, 111.

participate in culture found in the *International Covenant on Economic, Social and Cultural Rights* ('*ICESCR*').[18]

The second section of this chapter outlines the international legal framework relevant to trade mark registrations for contrary marks. The third section considers the historical approach to registering scandalous, immoral or disparaging marks in the United States and changes that resulted from the *Tam* and *Brunetti* decisions. The fourth section of the chapter conducts a human rights analysis of permitting contrary marks registration in the United States. The fifth section compares this approach with the explicit recognition of human rights in European trade mark registration systems. Finally, it explores the need for change to build a more effective human rights culture for trade marks in relation to contrary marks.

2 INTERNATIONAL LAW

The *Agreement on Trade-Related Aspects of Intellectual Property* ('*TRIPS*') permits but does not require World Trade Organization ('WTO') Members to restrict the registration of certain types of trade marks, consistent with Article 15 of *TRIPS* and the *Paris Convention*.[19] *TRIPS* regulates protection for signs that are capable of distinguishing 'goods or services of one undertaking from those of other undertakings'.[20] *TRIPS* Article 15(1) recognises that states may exclude marks that are not inherently capable of distinguishing relevant goods or permit registration for signs that acquire distinctiveness through use. Members may also deny registration of a trade mark 'on other grounds, provided that they do not derogate from the Paris Convention (1967)'.[21] *TRIPS* binds WTO Members to certain provisions of the *Paris Convention* through incorporation, including the ability to restrict contrary marks that is found in Article 6*quinquies*.[22] This permits but does not require WTO Members to refuse registration of a trade mark or invalidate registration in certain circumstances. Article 6*quinquies* (B) provides that the exception is subject to Article

---

[18] *International Covenant on Economic, Social and Cultural Rights*, opened for signature 16 December 1966, 993 UNTS 3 (entered into force 3 January 1976) art 15 (1) (c) ('*ICESCR*').

[19] See Marrakesh Agreement Establishing the World Trade Organization, opened for signature 15 April 1994, 1867 UNTS 3 (entered into force 1 January 1995) annex 1C Agreement on Trade-Related Aspects of Intellectual Property Rights arts 2.1, 15(2) ('TRIPS').

[20] Ibid art 15.1.

[21] Ibid art 15(2).

[22] Ibid art 2.1

10*bis*, which restricts unfair competition and permits states to prohibit passing off.

Article 6*quinquies* (B)(iii) provides that marks may be 'denied registration or invalidated':

> …when they are contrary to morality or public order and, in particular, of such a nature as to deceive the public. It is understood that a mark may not be considered contrary to public order for the sole reason that it does not conform to a provision of the legislation on marks, except if such provision itself relates to public order.

The original provision was amended to include the words 'in particular, of such a nature as to deceive the public'.[23] Marks that are only objectionable because they are misleading are beyond the scope of this chapter. Even where these grounds for refusal form part of the same provision, as they have in American trade mark law, they are usually considered as separate refusal categories in practice.[24]

State practice in relation to contrary marks shows that the prohibition on the registration of immoral trade marks does not 'specify the theories, nature or principles that form the basis for this concept'.[25] Four categories of marks are often considered to be immoral:

(a) a sexual or vulgar connotation or reference;
(b) an offence to religions or beliefs worthy of respect and veneration;
(c) an offence to the honour of a person or a group of persons; or
(d) a reference to an illegal act or something that causes it or derives from it.[26]

TRIPS limits restrictions on the rights of trade mark owners, but it allows WTO Members to implement such restrictions flexibly. Ramsey argues that *TRIPS* flexibilities enable states to protect freedom of expression in their implementation of the minimum standards for trade marks.[27] The recognition of regulatory autonomy to protect socio-economic welfare and a balance of rights

---

[23] Sam Ricketson, *The Paris Convention for the Protection of Industrial Property: A Commentary* (Oxford University Press, 2015) 545.

[24] Cf Marc J Randazza, 'Freedom of Expression and Morality-Based Impediments to the Enforcement of Intellectual Property Rights' (2015) 16(1) *Nevada Law Journal* 107, 120.

[25] Alysa Arcos Ziemer, Pedro Silveira Tavares and Marc John Randazza, 'Morality and Trademarks: The South American Approach' (2017) 40(2) *Suffolk Transnational Law Review* 221, 226.

[26] Ibid 222.

[27] Ramsey, 'Free Speech and International Obligations to Protect Trademarks' (n 7) 440–443; Ramsey, 'A Free Speech Right to Trademark Protection' (n 1) 821–828.

and obligations in *TRIPS* Articles 7 and 8 can support protection of freedom of expression in domestic implementation of the trade mark provisions found in *TRIPS*.[28] Although these flexibilities provide all states with opportunities to protect freedom of expression and other human rights, the approach to protection in trade mark law can vary significantly.[29]

Granting exclusive rights to use a trade mark restricts the freedom of others to use the underlying signs in commerce: broad trade mark monopolies can also be asserted to limit other expressive uses of the protected signs where the dominant purpose is expression and commercial use is incidental.[30] Intellectual property obligations in plurilateral and bilateral trade agreements do not address freedom of expression. However, some *TRIPS*-plus obligations can directly impact expression, such as requiring protection for owners of well-known marks against dilution by blurring and tarnishment beyond the requirements found in *TRIPS* Article 16(3).[31] Dilution protection expands the monopoly of trade mark rights so that violation can occur even when the use of marks is not confusing.[32] Third parties may face violation actions if their non-confusing reference to another mark in commerce allegedly tarnishes the reputation of the mark or reduces the distinctiveness of the original mark.[33] These rights do not function to reduce consumer search costs or protect the consumer from confusion as to the source of products but can permit trade marks to 'serve as symbolic communication as a basis for publicity and advertising'.[34]

3 DISPARAGING, SCANDALOUS AND IMMORAL MARKS AND UNITED STATES FREE SPEECH PROTECTION

3.1 Registration of Disparaging, Scandalous and Immoral Marks in the United States

The United States acceded to the *Paris Convention* in 1887. Since its inception, the agreement has permitted states to refuse to register the mark on the

[28] Ramsey, 'Free Speech and International Obligations to Protect Trademarks' (n 7) 445–447.
[29] Ramsey, 'A Free Speech Right to Trademark Protection' (n 1) 821–832.
[30] William McGeveran, 'The Trademark Fair Use Reform Act' (2010) *90 Boston University Law Review* 2267, 2308–2309.
[31] Ramsey, 'Free Speech and International Obligations to Protect Trademarks' (n 7) 434.
[32] Ramsey, 'A Free Speech Right to Trademark Protection' (n 1) 838.
[33] 15 USC § 1125(c).
[34] Dee (n 17) 93.

basis that it was immoral or inconsistent with *ordre public*.[35] Historically, 15 U.S. Code § 1052, referred to as section 2 of the *Lanham Act*, implemented Article 6*quinquies* (B)(iii) and required the USPTO to refuse registration of marks on the basis that the trade mark:

> (a) Consists of or comprises immoral, deceptive, or scandalous matter; or matter which may disparage or falsely suggest a connection with persons, living or dead, institutions, beliefs, or national symbols, or bring them into contempt, or disrepute.

Where a mark referenced 'identifiable persons, institutions, beliefs or national symbols', the examiner considered 'whether that meaning may be disparaging to a substantial composite of the referenced group' and if that substantial composite 'would find the proposed mark … to be disparaging in the context of contemporary attitudes'.[36]

Determinations of whether a mark was immoral or scandalous were considered together.[37] The standard applied for rejection of scandalous or offensive marks pursuant to Section 2(a) was that the mark must be 'shocking to the sense of truth, decency, or propriety; … giving offense to the conscience or moral feelings; … [or] calling out [for] condemnation … disgraceful; offensive; disreputable or vulgar'.[38] The threshold was assessed from the standpoint of 'a substantial composite of the general public'.[39]

This chapter considers the implications of trade mark law protection for contrary marks in the United States following the determinations in *Tam* and *Brunetti* that parts of Section 2(a) were inconsistent with free speech protection. The First Amendment of the *Constitution of the United States* provides 'Congress shall make no law … abridging the freedom of speech, or of the press'.[40] A central tenet of free speech protection in the United States is that '[s]peech may not be banned on the ground that it expresses ideas that offend.'[41]

---

[35] In the original agreement, this right was provided in Article 6; it is now found in Article 6*quinquies*. Sam Ricketson, *The Paris Convention for the Protection of Industrial Property: A Commentary* (Oxford University Press, 2015) 537.

[36] *Trademark Manual of Examining Procedure* §1203.03(b)(i) (April 2017) 1200–150.

[37] *Brunetti* (n 4) 2298 (Kagan J).

[38] Ibid.

[39] Ibid.

[40] Constitution of the United States, amend I.

[41] *Tam* (n 3) 1751 (Alito J).

Historically, arguments that the application of these provisions was inconsistent with free speech protections were rejected by American courts.[42]

3.2 *Matal v Tam*

In *Tam*, Simon Tam objected to the refusal by the USPTO to register the sign The Slants for entertainment services. The members of the band, The Slants, were Asian American.[43] The Examiner rejected the application as the mark was inconsistent with the prohibition on disparaging marks.[44] This rejection was confirmed by the Trademark Trial and Appeal Board finding that the mark's reference to people of Asian descent was highly disparaging and a substantial component of the referenced group find the term to be disparaging.[45] Tam argued that the use of the term The Slants by his band was not disparaging but the reclamation of a term that had been used disparagingly in the past.[46] Tam contested the disparagement prohibition underlying the rejection as unconstitutional under the protection for free speech provided in the First Amendment of the *Constitution of the United States*.

It was still possible for Simon Tam to use The Slants without registration so he was not completely restricted from using the sign in commerce.[47] Unfair competition laws can protect unregistered trade marks in the United States and it would be possible to use litigation to protect a mark.[48] In two concurring judgments, the Supreme Court found that although refusal of registration did not prevent Tam from continuing to use the mark, speech was restricted because the refusal prevented the conferral of other significant benefits of registration.[49] The benefits include protection from contestability for lack of distinctiveness after five years; efficient international registration of the mark; and registration for counterfeit detection with United States Customs and Border Patrol.[50]

---

42 Rebecca Tushnet, 'The First Amendment Walks into a Bar: Trademark Registration and Free Speech' (2016) 92(1) *Notre Dame Law Review* 381, 385–387. Ramsey identifies diverse reasons for this: Lisa P Ramsey, 'Free Speech Challenges to Trademark Law after Matal v. Tam' (2018) 56(2) *Houston Law Review* 401, 411–414 ('Free Speech Challenges to Trademark Law after Matal v. Tam').

43 *Tam* (n 3) 1751 (Alito J).

44 Ibid 1754 (Alito J).

45 United States Patent and Trade Mark Office, Trademark Trial and Appeal Board, *In re Simon Shiao Tam* (September 26 2013) 7.

46 *Tam* (n 3) 1754 (Alito J).

47 Ibid 1752.

48 Ramsey, 'A Free Speech Right to Trademark Protection' (n 1) 862.

49 *Tam* (n 3) 1752–1753 (Alito J).

50 *In re Tam,* 808 F 3d 1321, 1328 (Fed Cir, 2015) ('*In re Tam*').

Justice Alito delivered a plurality opinion, joined by Chief Justice Roberts and Justices Thomas and Breyer. Justice Kennedy delivered a separate concurring opinion, joined by Justices Ginsburg, Sotomayor and Kagan. Both opinions rejected the characterisation of trade marks as government speech.[51] Justice Alito did not resolve arguments that registration of a trade mark was a form of commercial speech because he found that the disparagement prohibition would still be subject to a different standard of scrutiny and also could not meet this lower scrutiny threshold.[52] Both opinions found that the disparagement provision restricted free speech because it was based on the viewpoint expressed by the applicant in the relevant speech.[53] For example, the restrictions permit a trade mark expressing a viewpoint that promotes a particular religion such as 'JESUS LOVERS' but would not permit a trade mark that expresses a viewpoint that disparages a religion such as 'JESUS LOVERS SUCK'. Consequently, the USPTO could no longer refuse registration based on the prohibition on disparaging marks as the law was constitutionally invalid. However, the separate decisions 'could not agree on the overall framework for deciding the case'.[54]

3.3 *Iancu v Brunetti*

The Supreme Court's reasoning was then applied to immoral or scandalous marks in *Brunetti*. The Supreme Court considered an appeal against a decision by the USPTO rejecting Erik Brunetti's application to register FUCT for streetwear. The USPTO refused the application as the underlying sign was 'immoral or scandalous'.[55] Brunetti appealed unsuccessfully to the Trademark Appeals Board but was successful in the Federal Circuit Court of Appeals on the basis that the prohibition was inconsistent with free speech protection.[56] The Government appealed to the Supreme Court. Following their decision in *Tam*, the Supreme Court majority determined that the prohibition on registration of immoral marks was viewpoint-based and therefore unconstitutional.[57] There was some division about whether or not the prohibition on scandalous marks could be read down to prohibit 'marks that are offensive [or] shocking to

---

51 *Tam* (n 3) 1758–1760 (Alito J), 1768 (Kennedy J).

52 Ibid 1764–1765 (Alito J).

53 Ibid 1757–1760 (Thomas J, majority opinion), 1763 (Alito J, plurality opinion), 1765–1769 (Kennedy J, concurring).

54 *Brunetti* (n 4) 2298 (Kagan J).

55 Ibid 2297 (Kagan J).

56 Ibid 2298 (Kagan J).

57 Ibid 2299 (Kagan J).

a substantial segment of the public because of their mode of expression'.[58] The majority judgment, delivered by Justice Kagan, joined by Justices Thomas, Ginsburg, Alito, Gorsuch and Kavanaugh, found the statutory language did not permit this. Justice Sotomayor determined that a limited construction of the term scandalous could prohibit 'offensiveness in the mode of expression, apart from any particular message or idea' and Chief Justice Roberts and Justice Breyer agreed.[59]

Brunetti removes the possibility that some marks which were no longer able to be rejected because they were disparaging could nonetheless have been rejected as scandalous or immoral.[60] In oral argument in *Tam* it was suggested that 'at least one particularly egregious racial epithet' could be excluded on the basis not only that it was disparaging but also that it met the standard of scandalous or offensive that was considered in *Brunetti*.[61] Empirical research demonstrates that, during the period following *Tam* when the scandalous or offensive prohibition continued to operate, the provision was used as a basis for rejection for this type of disparaging mark, sometimes with the additional finding that refusal should occur because of 'failure to function'.[62]

4 THE HUMAN RIGHTS IMPLICATIONS OF PERMITTING CONTRARY MARKS REGISTRATION

This section assesses the human rights implications of the removal of the requirement to refuse contrary marks in the American trade mark registration system. The freedom of expression analysis draws on the framework provided by the *ICCPR* and *ICESCR*; guidance on the interpretation of *ICCPR* Article 19(3) in *General Comment 34* and Human Rights Committee ('HRC') determinations of admissible individual complaints; and examples of marks that have been contested under contrary marks legislation in other countries. The HRC individual complaints system does not assess laws in abstract but whether the application of specific laws to individuals impairs their rights, pursuant to the

---

[58] Ibid 2301 (Kagan J).

[59] Ibid 2310 (Sotomayor J), 2303 (Roberts J), 2307–2308 (Breyer J). Breyer J's further criticisms of the categorical approach taken to free speech assessments are discussed below.

[60] Vicki Huang, 'Trademarks, Race and Slur-Appropriation: An Inter-Disciplinary and Empirical Study' [2021] *University of Illinois Law Review* 1605, 1642.

[61] *Brunetti* (n 4) fn 5 of 2312 (Sotomayor J).

[62] Huang (n 60) 1642–1643. Failure to function as a ground for refusal will be discussed further in section 4.10.

ICCPR.[63] This section considers freedom of expression interests for different stakeholders, focusing particularly on the community as a whole, including individuals who may like to make expressive use of the signs underlying registrations such as The Slants and FUCT, and applicants. The following analysis also explores whether other human rights concerns can justify registration of contrary marks as certain freedom of expression restrictions are permissible to protect the rights or reputations of others.[64]

4.1 Right to Freedom of Expression

The *ICCPR* binds the vast majority of WTO Members and provides a common standard for understanding the right to freedom of expression. Article 19 of the *ICCPR* provides:

> 2. Everyone shall have the right to freedom of expression; this right shall include freedom to seek, receive and impart information and ideas of all kinds, regardless of frontiers, either orally, in writing or in print, in the form of art, or through any other media of his choice.
> 3. The exercise of the rights provided for in paragraph 2 of this article carries with it special duties and responsibilities. It may therefore be subject to certain restrictions, but these shall only be such as are provided by law and are necessary:
>   (a) For respect of the rights or reputations of others;
>   (b) For the protection of national security or of public order (ordre public), or of public health or morals.

Protection for the 'freedom to seek, receive and impart information and ideas of all kinds' includes instances where the expression occurs in commercial advertising.[65] Monopolies granted to trade mark owners are, in themselves, restrictions on freedom of expression: competitors would have rights to use the same terms in commercial advertising if they were not restricted by trade mark laws.[66] Any trade mark registration can permit restrictions on freedom

---

[63] *Optional Protocol to the International Covenant on Civil and Political Rights*, opened for signature 16 December 1966, 999 UNTS 302 (entered into force 23 March 1976) art 2.

[64] *ICCPR* (n 10) art 19(3)(a).

[65] Human Rights Committee, *General Comment No 34 on Article 19: Freedoms of Opinion and Expression*, 102nd sess, UN Doc CCPR/C/GC/34 (12 September 2011) [11] ('*General Comment 34*'); Human Rights Committee, *Views: Communication Nos* 359/1989 and 385/1989, 47th sess, UN Docs CCPR/C/47/D/359/1989 and 385/39/Rev 1 (31 March 1993) ('*Ballantyne, Davidson and McIntyre v Canada*').

[66] Genevieve Wilkinson, 'Mitey Marks and Expressive Uses of Culturally Significant Trade Marks in Australia' (2019) 30(1) *Australian Intellectual Property*

of expression. The extent of this restriction on expression depends on the monopoly available to trade mark owners and the way that this monopoly is used. There are some mechanisms built into trade mark registration systems to protect expressive use of registered marks and ensure that trade marks do not pose unnecessary restrictions on all expression. The requirement that signs registered as trade marks are distinctive to the goods and services that they protect establishes a threshold so that the sign 'banana' cannot be registered in relation to fruit: to permit this would limit the ability of competitors to use the normal signifier to describe the product they are selling.[67] The threshold of distinctiveness can vary, depending on whether an applicant has established a reputation in a product.[68] Descriptive uses of marks by non-owners are also permitted.[69] This would permit the use of the phrase The Slants to describe the group and to describe Asian Americans, even though it is a registered trade mark, as long as the sign is used in a non-trade mark manner.[70]

Trade marks are not explicitly set out as permissible restrictions on expression in the *ICCPR* or in interpretation of the right in *General Comment 34* by the HRC but are likely to fit into exceptions for laws which 'are necessary for the respect of the rights or reputations of others'.[71] In interpreting the 'rights of others', *General Comment 34* provides that these include the rights found in the *ICCPR* and 'more generally in international human rights law'.[72] 'Others' is interpreted to include individuals and members of a community, such as 'individual members of a community defined by its religious faith or ethnicity'.[73] Trade mark restrictions may be justified as necessary where they are set out in trade mark law and protection for the rights of owners and consumers is necessary.[74] The HRC has recognised that rights relevant to the interests of the community as a whole can be protected.[75] However, the requirement in Article 19 that a restriction be necessary also requires that relevant laws are consistent

Journal 46, 50 ('Mitey Marks and Expressive Uses of Culturally Significant Trade Marks in Australia').

67 *Lanham Act* 1946, 15 § 1052(e).

68 Ibid § 2(f).

69 Ibid 15 USC § 1115(b)(4).

70 Ibid. Ramsey explains the limitations of the exception: Ramsey, 'A Free Speech Right to Trademark Protection' (n 1) 841–842.

71 *ICCPR* (n 10) art 19(3).

72 *General Comment 34* (n 65) [28].

73 Ibid.

74 Ramsey treats this protection as an assumption: Ramsey, 'Free Speech and International Obligations to Protect Trademarks' (n 7) 451.

75 Human Rights Committee, *Avon Lovell v Australia, Views: Communication No 920/2000*, 80th sess, UN Doc CCPR/C/80/D/920/2000 (24 March 2004) recognised a right to confidentiality.

with principles of proportionality: 'they must be appropriate to achieve their protective function; they must be the least intrusive instrument amongst those which might achieve their protective function; they must be proportionate to the interest protected.'[76] Proportionality is required for both the framing of the laws but also their application by administrative and judicial bodies.[77]

Laws must also relate directly to their specific justification and apply only for the purpose of that justification.[78] Laws restricting expression need to be available to the public and sufficiently precise to enable an individual to regulate their behaviour accordingly.[79] Any restriction of freedom of expression is considered to be 'a serious curtailment of human rights' so must be provided in law rather than form part of customary law.[80] Where laws permit decision-makers to restrict freedom of expression, unfettered discretion should not be conferred on those decision-makers, as '[l]aws must provide sufficient guidance to those charged with their execution to enable them to ascertain what sorts of expression are properly restricted and what sorts are not'.[81]

Criticisms that protections available for contrary marks in different jurisdictions are applied inconsistently should also recognise that considerations of morality are subjective within human rights frameworks.[82] Where there is a restriction on freedom of expression, *ICCPR* Article 19(3) provides a clear mechanism for monitoring that restriction. Detailed, systematic and transparent consideration of expression restrictions and related human rights impacts by decision-makers are particularly important.[83] However, it is difficult to establish clear human rights benchmarks for some justifications, given the subjective nature of the morality standard and the lack of guidance about the extent to which rights of individuals that are not human rights should be protected.

The restrictions that trade mark registration systems impose on the expressive use of certain terms for goods and services for which trade marks are registered are found in law. Mechanisms built into United States trade mark law, including distinctiveness requirements and infringement defences, limit the restrictions trade mark monopolies impose on expression.[84] However,

---

[76] *General Comment 34* (n 65) [34].

[77] Ibid.

[78] Ibid [18], [31].

[79] Ibid [24].

[80] Ibid.

[81] Ibid [25].

[82] Ziemer et al (n 25) 277. See Human Rights Committee, *Views: Communication No 61/1979*, 15th sess, 61/1979, UN Doc CCPR/C/15/D/61/1979 (2 April 1982) ('*Hertzberg v Finland*').

[83] See *Faurisson v France* (n 11).

[84] Ramsey, 'A Free Speech Right to Trademark Protection' (n 1) 838–840.

expanding rights for trade mark owners may mean that a range of expressive uses for non-owners are impaired because they have a commercial use overlapping the expressive use.[85] Ramsey suggests that there should be very narrow monopolies (if any) available for 'trademark rights in certain language and product features that intrinsically communicated a non-source-identifying message before they were adopted or used as marks'.[86] This approach is more consistent with international human rights protection for freedom of expression. It would limit the impact of trade mark protection on expression by third parties and ensure that any restrictions on expression are necessary, direct and proportionate to the objects of consumer protection, and provide an incentive for owners to invest in trade marks as reliable badges of origin.

United States trade mark protection also confers additional, special protections for famous or well-known marks.[87] Owners of famous marks can bring actions against non-owners whose use dilutes the reputation of their mark or tarnishes it, even if there is no risk of consumer confusion.[88] This monopoly expansion is important because one of the primary justifications for permitting trade mark owners to restrict freedom of expression is to ensure that consumers are not confused as to the origin of a product.[89] Legislative defences to dilution and tarnishment can protect certain expressive uses, such as reporting the news, as well as non-commercial uses and parody uses not used as a trade mark to distinguish goods and services.[90] However, the effectiveness of these defences in limiting restrictions on expression depends on non-owners having an understanding of the law and the resources to defend themselves.[91] In practice, the monopoly of a trade mark owner can also be expanded when the registration is used to assert rights that the owner is not in fact entitled to and the threat of litigation chills the use of the mark, even when use could be successfully defended in litigation.[92] Enforcement of a trade mark monopoly

---

85 Ibid 842–842.

86 Ramsey, 'Free Speech Challenges to Trademark Law after Matal v. Tam' (n 42) 402; see also Ramsey, 'A Free Speech Right to Trademark Protection' (n 1) 836.

87 *Lanham Act* 1946, 15 USC § 1125(c).

88 Lisa P Ramsey, 'Non-Traditional Trademarks and Inherently Valuable Expression' in Irene Caboli and Martin Senftleben (eds), *The Protection of Non-Traditional Trademarks: Critical Perspectives* (Oxford University Press, 2018) 337, 354.

89 William M Landes and Richard A Posner, *The Economic Structure of Intellectual Property Law* (Harvard University Press, 2003) 173.

90 *Lanham Act* 1946, 15 USC § 1125(c).

91 Ramsey, 'Free Speech and International Obligations to Protect Trademarks' (n 7) 424.

92 William T Gallagher, 'Trademark and Copyright Enforcement in the Shadow of IP Law' (2011) 28 *Santa Clara Computer & High Technology Law Journal* 453, 487–488.

for any mark can limit expressive use but the scope of the monopoly for famous marks increases the likelihood that limitation on expression can occur. Allowing an owner to restrict the use of that mark on other goods or services because it may dilute the reputation of the mark, even if it is not confusing to consumers, is unlikely to help consumers to distinguish between products and may not be necessary or proportionate to protect goodwill established by traders. Similarly, a law prohibiting tarnishment of marks is unlikely to be necessary to protect consumers, and its necessity to protect the goodwill of traders from tarnishment of their marks should be carefully scrutinised.[93]

4.1.1 Public interests

The Slants example highlights the way that there may be competing groups or individuals with expressive interests in relation to a particular sign that conveys a particular message. Simon Tam and his band members had an interest in using The Slants as both a reliable indicator of origin and a reclaiming of the word. Other groups may have interests in reclaiming the slur in different ways. In the case of The Slants registration, other users of the term that seek to reclaim it might be restricted. Previous reclamation uses of the term include The Slanted Kings of Comedy tour, Slant Magazine and Slant TV.[94] The trade mark registration of the mark in class 41 for entertainment services, in the nature of live performances by a musical band, permits the owners of the mark to restrict use by others. Arguably, these historic reclamation uses overlap with the monopoly conferred by the registration for The Slants.

Individuals or groups of individuals who have had the word 'slants' used against them as a racial slur have interests in its registration as it may restrict their rights to use the mark expressively. They may not wish to reclaim the mark but may wish to use it in another way. The use of a slogan 'Compensate the Slants' on a t-shirt might ultimately be determined by a court to be permissible, but any threat of litigation might effectively chill that expression. Additionally, groups who have had the sign 'the slants' used against them as a racial slur may have interests in the term not being attractive for commercial users because it continues to reinforce stereotypes.[95] There was both support and opposition for the application to register The Slants from individuals in

---

[93] See Michael Handler, 'What Can Harm the Reputation of a Trademark: A Critical Re-Evaluation of Dilution by Tarnishment' (2016) 106 *Trademark Reporter* 639.

[94] April Peavey, 'A Slur or Point of Pride? The Slants' Journey to Litigate their Band Name', *The World* (online, 2 September 2019) https://www.pri.org/stories/2019-09-02/slur-or-point-pride-slants-journey-litigate-their-band-name.

[95] Aoun, 'Whitewashing Australia's History of Stigmatising Trade Marks and Commercial Imagery' (n 15) 679.

the Asian American community, some of whom found the mark offensive.[96] One of the issues that raises concern in trade mark law is the capacity to assign ownership of a mark.[97] The application to register FUCT was assigned to Brunetti by two original applicants.[98] Even where a mark is registered by an individual who intends to use it for reclamation of terminology so that it can no longer be used in a disparaging way, there is always the possibility that that registration ownership can be transferred to a number of different owners through a chain of assignment. Accordingly, the intention of the initial owner may not be the intention of a later owner. Removing the contrary marks prohibition also means that United States law can no longer distinguish between these different types of uses.[99]

Excluding restrictions on speech that are based on viewpoint discrimination is not the same as protecting freedom of expression consistent with international human rights standards. Registration confers special privileges on owners by restricting the expression of non-owners without considering whether that restriction is a necessary, direct and proportionate restriction on non-owners. A mark used for reclamation like The Slants can have a special political purpose: permissible restrictions on political expressions are viewed more strictly than restrictions on commercial expression.[100] Where registration prevents others from using the mark as a symbol of reclamation, human rights to participate in culture protected by *ICESCR* Article 15(1)(a) are also engaged.

4.1.2 Applicants' interests

Analysing the application to register The Slants, Ramsey explains that rather than restricting use of contrary marks, a refusal to register only prevents exercise of the benefits conferred on federal trade mark registration.[101] Protecting access to these benefits is not necessary to permit expressive rights and is problematic 'because of the potential ability of the owner to use that right to suppress expression by others'.[102] United States trade mark laws regulate 'noncommercial expression [including political expression] and commercial

---

[96] En Banc Brief for Appellee, *In re Tam* (n 50).

[97] *Lanham Act* 1946, 15 USC § 1060.

[98] 'Trademark Assignment Abstract of Title: 85310960', *United States Patent and Trademark Office* https://assignments.uspto.gov/assignments/q?db=tm&sno=85310960.

[99] Rochelle Dreyfuss and Susy Frankel, 'Trade Marks and Cultural Identity' in Graeme W Austin et al (eds), *Across Intellectual Property: Essays in Honour of Sam Ricketson* (Cambridge University Press, 2020) 233.

[100] *General Comment 34* (n 65) [34].

[101] Ramsey, 'A Free Speech Right to Trademark Protection' (n 1) 806.

[102] Ibid 834.

expression that is not misleading'.[103] Federal infringement laws protect against use 'in commerce', so even when a third party does not use a mark to identify their goods or services, they may be liable for infringement.[104] Infringement expands beyond likelihood of confusion to circumstances 'where consumers are likely to be confused about affiliation, sponsorship or consent'.[105] Ramsey concludes that the common law speech protection doctrines and exclusions for registration for generic terms or descriptive language are not adequately protected in the United States and that 'protection of trademark rights today is more likely to suppress and chill freedom of expression than the denial of a trademark registration'.[106]

Despite Ramsey's cogent analysis, problems with the inconsistent application of previous restrictions may also raise freedom of expression concerns.[107] Although restrictions on disparaging, scandalous or offensive marks may be permissible on grounds of protection of morals, public order or specific rights such as freedom from discrimination or hate speech or rights to cultural participation, restrictions on expression must be necessary, direct and proportionate.[108] Assessments of necessity require consideration of whether a restriction could be achieved in another way.[109] Relevant to this is assessing how a different mechanism that could protect morality, public order and human rights of others would compare with the Section 2(a) approach.[110] A different exclusion mechanism might be less desirable if it burdened vulnerable groups, such as by allowing them to assert their concerns only if they initiate expensive opposition proceedings. Problematically for assessments of directness and proportionality, the Federal Circuit Court of Appeals recognised the highly inconsistent application of the provision in its decision on Brunetti's application,[111] finding that this 'creates an "uncertainty [that] undermines the likelihood that the [provision] has been carefully tailored"'.[112] Many cases applying Section 2(a) have been decided inconsistently.[113] The disparagement clause was criticised by Justice Alito in *Tam* as a 'happy talk clause' that was not narrowly drawn so that it might only stop discrimination.[114] Importantly, the refusal to register

---

[103] Ibid 836.
[104] Ibid 836–837.
[105] Ibid 837.
[106] Ibid 843.
[107] *General Comment 34* (n 65) [22].
[108] Ibid [33–35].
[109] Ibid [33].
[110] Ibid.
[111] *In re Brunetti*, 877 F 3d 1330, 1353–1354 ('*In re Brunetti*').
[112] Ibid, 1354.
[113] Tushnet (n 42) 414.
[114] Tam (n 3) 1765.

did not constitute an absolute restriction of expression for Tam or Brunetti, as the parties could continue to use the sign in trade. Tushnet identifies inconsistencies in many other trade mark registration assessments.[115]

A human rights-based approach would not necessarily remove all clauses that restrict the registration of contrary marks but would instead ensure there are clear tests for determining whether marks should be refused registration because they are contrary to morality or public order and for explicit protection of freedom of expression. The regulation of contrary marks in the United States following the *Tam* and *Brunetti* decisions engages a number of human rights implications. Although the focus of previous analysis has been on free speech and freedom of expression, other human rights are also relevant to the analysis because the limitation of freedom of expression is permissible if it is found in law and necessary, direct and proportionate to protect the rights of others.

4.2 Right to Protection from Hate Speech

Restrictions on hate speech may be consistent with respect to the human rights of others, such as their right to be free from discrimination.[116] Protection from hate speech is an accepted exception to freedom of expression in international human rights law.[117] Although the HRC recognises that freedom of expression can protect deeply offensive expression, this freedom carries both rights and responsibilities, so there are limits. Deeply offensive expression can be restricted in accordance with both *ICCPR* Article 19(3) exceptions, such as for protection of the rights of others, and the exceptions in *ICCPR* Article 20.[118] *ICCPR* Article 20(2) provides that '[a]ny advocacy of national, racial or religious hatred that constitutes incitement to discrimination, hostility or violence shall be prohibited by law'. This is reinforced by the *International Convention on the Elimination of all forms of Racial Discrimination*, which proscribes racist hate speech.[119]

Restricting contrary mark registrations can also protect public order, which may be particularly relevant to signs containing racial slurs used as hate speech to incite disruption. The refusal to register the sign 'standupifyouhatemanu' in the United Kingdom because of its potential to incite violence provides insight

[115] Tushnet (n 42) 414.

[116] *ICESCR* (n 18) art 19(3).

[117] *General Comment 34* (n 65) [50].

[118] Ibid [11].

[119] *Convention for the Elimination of All Forms of Racial Discrimination*, opened for signature 21 December 1965, 660 UNTS 195 (entered into force 4 January 1969) art 4 ('*CERD*').

into the type of sign that could be a vehicle for hate speech if it was directed at a race or religion rather than the Manchester United football club.[120] The use of the words 'hate' and 'stand up' in the mark was indicative of a 'badge of antagonism': 'such use is liable to increase the incidence of football violence or other offensive behaviour.'[121] Although a registration with the intention of reclamation may be used to prevent use of The Slants in ways that can incite violence such as 'standupifyouhateslants', Dreyfuss and Frankel recognise that the failure of the law to distinguish between users is problematic.[122] The Redskins mark used for decades as an American football team name 'reinforc[ed] hateful stereotypes' about Native Americans,[123] but the decisions in *Tam* and *Brunetti* meant litigation to revoke registration rights for this disparaging mark could not continue.[124] Huang's empirical analysis of registration of racially oriented marks in the United States indicates that new registrations are not limited to those who are likely to have a reclamation purpose or intent to prevent hateful uses.[125] Registrations of Native American signs were primarily 'other-appropriations' by non-Native Americans.[126] There was evidence of more self-appropriation than other-appropriation for most groups,[127] yet even small numbers of other-appropriation could be problematic. False reclamation has been equated with dignity-taking.[128]

A link between refusing contrary marks and preventing hate speech can establish the necessity of restricting regulation of contrary marks. In *Malcolm Ross v Canada*, the HRC found the transfer of a Canadian teacher who had publicly expressed religious opinions to a non-teaching position to be necessary to protect the 'rights or reputations' of people of the Jewish faith as

---

[120] *CDW Graphic Design Ltd v Manchester United Merch Ltd* (Trade Mark Registrar, Application No 2227520, 20 November 2002) [22], [27], [33], [37].

[121] Ibid [39].

[122] Dreyfuss and Frankel (n 99) 233.

[123] Christine Haight Farley, 'Registering Offense: The Prohibition of Slurs as Trademarks' in Irene Caboli and Srividhya Ragavan (eds), *Diversity in Intellectual Property: Identities, Interests, and Intersections* (Cambridge University Press, 2015) 109.

[124] See Fady J G Aoun, 'The Belated Awakening of the Public Sphere to Racist Branding and Racist Stereotypes in Trademarks' (2020) 61(3) *IDEA* 545, 642 ('The Belated Awakening of the Public Sphere to Racist Branding and Racist Stereotypes in Trademarks').

[125] Huang (n 60) 1636.

[126] Ibid 1638.

[127] Ibid 1656–1658.

[128] See Victoria F Phillips, 'Beyond Trademark: The Washington Redskins Case and the Search for Dignity' (2017) 92(3) *Chicago-Kent Law Review* 1061.

the restrictions limited manifestation of beliefs in a particular context.[129] In *Faurisson v France*, the HRC considered restrictions on the expression of an academic who questioned the Nazis' use of gas chambers in World War II and was convicted pursuant to laws prohibiting the denial of crimes against humanity committed by the Nazis.[130] Although the directness and proportionality of the laws was critically analysed because it prohibited 'contestation' of the crimes rather than specifying prohibited acts, the way the laws applied to Professor Faurisson was found to be consistent with Article 19(3) standards.[131] The legislative objectives of preventing racism and anti-Semitism supported the interest of the community as a whole and the detailed examination of the laws by the decision-maker was relevant to its necessity, directness and proportionality.[132]

United States free speech precludes protection against hate speech, although there can be certain overlapping exceptions such as the narrow exception for fighting words used towards specific individuals.[133] Smith argues that the Supreme Court has protected hate speech by defining it as viewpoint in multiple cases, including *Tam*.[134] Minority judgment proposals in *Brunetti*, discussed below, could support future registration prohibitions that provide protection against marks that could be used to incite hate speech.[135] Currently, American law does not offer this protection.

4.3 Right to Non-discrimination and Equal Protection of the Law

Even where hate speech protections are not engaged, freedom from discrimination is expressed as a human right in Article 2 of both the *ICCPR* and the *ICESCR*. The *ICCPR* provides that individuals are entitled to further protection, pursuant to Article 26:

> ...without any discrimination to the equal protection of the law. In this respect, the law shall prohibit any discrimination and guarantee to all persons equal and

---

[129] Human Rights Committee, *Views: Communication No* 736/1997, 70th sess, UN Doc CCPR/C/70/D/736/1997 (18 October 2000) ('*Malcolm Ross v Canada*').

[130] *Faurisson v France* (n 11).

[131] Ibid.

[132] Ibid.

[133] *Brunetti* (n 4) 2311 (Sotomayor J, citing *R A V v City of St Paul*, 505 US 377 (1992); Eric Barendt, *Freedom of Speech* (Oxford University Press, 2nd ed, 2007) 183.

[134] Craig R Smith, 'Circumventing the "True Threat" and "Viewpoint" Protection Tests to Deal with Persistent Campus Hate Speech' (2020) 54(1*) First Amendment Studies* 93, 96–98.

[135] See also Chris Demaske, Free Speech and Hate Speech in the United States: The Limits of Toleration (Routledge, 2020).

> effective protection against discrimination on any ground such as race, colour, sex, language, religion, political or other opinion, national or social origin, property, birth or other status.

The HRC interprets this to mean that 'the law shall guarantee to all persons equal and effective protection against discrimination on any of the enumerated grounds'.[136]

Refusing registration of The Slants or FUCT does not stop Tam, Brunetti or others from using the signifiers. By permitting freedom of expression protection for deeply offensive expression, subject to permissible restrictions, the HRC recognises the value of opportunities to discuss 'the thought we hate'. This is consistent with a marketplace of ideas conducive to societal progress.[137] However, government registration of deeply offensive expression is not essential to a healthy marketplace of ideas. There is an inconsistency within a legal system that prohibits workplace discrimination and requires words not to be used in relation to a person because they are offensive but confers special benefits on trade mark owners that increases the likelihood that they will appear on clothing or other products in the workplace. The latter undermines effective protection of the former. Huang identifies social science research to support the conclusion that 'slurs reinforce discrimination in meaningful and measurable ways'.[138] Aoun identifies that:

> ...exposure to racism leads to social exclusion and shrinks the public sphere for the targeted group. This evidence speaks to a broader argument; specifically, that registered stigmatising trade marks contribute to the inequality faced by marginalised groups in the broader public sphere and provide support for the argument that greater use should be made of the embargo against their registration.[139]

Registration of marks expressing discriminatory viewpoints can entrench patterns of discrimination and can be perceived as government endorsement. The Supreme Court's doctrinal assessment in *Tam* that trade marks did not constitute government speech because the registered rights were the speech of applicants and owners[140] does not mean that registration is not perceived as

---

[136] Human Rights Committee, *General Comment 18: Non-Discrimination*, 37th sess, 1989, UN Doc HRI/GEN/1/Rev.1 at 26 (1994) [12].

[137] The marketplace of ideas in which freedom of expression protects communication supports the pursuit and delivery of truth. See J S Mills, *On Liberty* (1859) and interpretation in *Abrams v United States* 250 US 616, 630 [191] (1919).

[138] Huang (n 60) 1613.

[139] Aoun, 'Whitewashing Australia's History of Stigmatising Trade Marks and Commercial Imagery' (n 15) 726.

[140] *Tam* (n 3) 1757–1760 (Kennedy J). See also *Brunetti* (n 4) 2305 (Breyer J).

endorsement. Registration indicates that certain standards have been met.[141] Aoun argues that 'stigmatising trademarks … reinforce damaging stereotypical representations thereby imposing communicative hurdles in democratic societies'.[142] Concerns that these marks 'shrink the political public sphere for marginalized groups' are also relevant to marks that perpetuate discriminatory gender stereotypes.[143] It may be difficult for other laws that are designed to enhance equality before the law to operate effectively if registration suggests government endorsement.[144] In *Brunetti*, the application to register FUCT was rejected by the board because it was 'highly offensive' and 'vulgar' and had 'decidedly negative sexual connotations'.[145] The Trademark Review Board found that in practice the use of the mark communicated 'misogyny, depravity, violence'.[146] The failure to refuse registration of misogynistic marks can contribute towards a discriminatory culture towards women.

4.4 Rights of Cultural Minorities

Contrary marks also engage questions of the protection of minority rights. *ICCPR* Article 27 provides that:

> In those States in which ethnic, religious or linguistic minorities exist, persons belonging to such minorities shall not be denied the right, in community with the other members of their group, to enjoy their own culture, to profess and practise their own religion, or to use their own language.

Minority rights were relevant to the HRC's assessment of the prohibition of advertising in English that aimed to protect the culture of the francophone minority in Quebec by prohibiting advertising in English.[147] In *Ballantyne, Davidson and McIntyre v Canada*, the majority of the HRC found the prohibition on use of English in advertising to be a restriction that was not necessary to protect the rights of the francophone minority as it would be less restrictive to require advertising in French as well as English.[148] Separate individual

---

[141] Dreyfuss and Frankel (n 99) 231.

[142] Aoun, 'Whitewashing Australia's History of Stigmatising Trade Marks and Commercial Imagery' (n 15) 679.

[143] Aoun, 'The Belated Awakening of the Public Sphere to Racist Branding and Racist Stereotypes in Trademarks' (n 124) 555.

[144] See Aoun, 'Whitewashing Australia's History of Stigmatising Trade Marks and Commercial Imagery' (n 15) 724–725; Tushnet identifies endorsement (n 42) 389–393.

[145] *In re Brunetti* (n 111) 1337.

[146] Ibid.

[147] Ballantyne, Davidson and McIntyre v Canada (n 65).

[148] Ibid [11.2].

opinions criticised the failure of the majority decision to recognise that *ICCPR* Article 27 protection was relevant to assessing Article 19 compliance.[149]

In Europe, human rights protection standards are relevant to assessing whether a mark is contrary to public policy.[150] Minority rights have recently been relevant to contrary marks assessments in Europe. The Norwegian Intellectual Property Office rejected a jewellery company's application in *Tana Gull* because the mark had religious significance and registration could generate moral indignation in those communities contrary to principles of morality.[151] The mark was based on the Sámi sun god Beaivi and had religious significance for the Sámi people. The limited nature of cultural symbols available to the Sámi also meant that it was inconsistent with Norwegian constitutional protections for Indigenous culture and Article 27 of the *ICCPR*, so registration would be inconsistent with public policy.[152]

Registering a mark to reclaim racial slurs like The Slants might not be the best tool to protect minority rights. The exclusive nature of ownership and the expectations that owners demonstrate some control over authorised users could make maintaining protection of such a mark within minority culture an onerous task.[153] A defensive registration could be a better mechanism to protect minorities from commercial use of their culturally significant signs.[154] This could modify requirements of trade mark use to maintain registration: registrants who seek control over use of their culturally significant material by others may not wish to make commercial use of that material in order to avoid removal for non-use.[155] *ICCCPR* Article 27 on protection for minority rights may address all relevant human rights interests, as cultural rights are

---

[149] See ibid (Ndiaye minority).

[150] Constantin Film Produktion GmbH v European Union Intellectual Property Office (Court of Justice of the European Union, C-240/18 P, ECLI:EU:C:2019:553, 2 July 2019) [47] (Opinion of Advocate General Bobek) ('*Bobek Opinion*').

[151] Harriet Jane Deacon, 'Ethics, Intellectual Property and Commercialization of Cultural Heritage' (2020) 64(1) *Правоведение* 93, 103.

[152] Ibid 103–104.

[153] Susy Frankel, 'Trademarks and Traditional Knowledge and Cultural Intellectual Property Rights' in Graeme B Dinwoodie and Marc D Janis (eds), *Trademark Law and Theory: A Handbook of Contemporary Research* (Edward Elgar Publishing, 2008) 433, 445.

[154] See Genevieve Wilkinson, 'Exploring Moral Interests in the Intellectual Creations underlying Trade Marks' in Ysolde Gendreau (ed), *Research Handbook on Intellectual Property and Moral Rights* (Edward Elgar Publishing, forthcoming) ('Exploring Moral Interests in the Intellectual Creations underlying Trade Marks').

[155] Ibid. See Dalindyebo Bafana Shabalala, 'Intellectual Property, Traditional Knowledge, and Traditional Cultural Expressions in Native American Tribal Codes' (2017) 4(5) *Akron Law Review* 1125, 1133–1134.

not restricted to minorities. Separate protection for culture available through *ICESCR* Article 15(1)(a) expands cultural rights protection to all individuals.

4.5 Right to Benefit From Science and Culture

Trade mark owners might assert human rights to protection of contrary marks.[156] However, marks containing words like 'The Slants' or 'FUCT' are well known to the public or parts of the public and unlikely to constitute 'creations of the human mind' and meet the threshold of literary production that is protected in Article 15(1)(c).[157] In some cases, marks could meet threshold protections for artistic productions but copyright can operate to protect relevant moral and material interests.[158] In contrast, word marks with some originality that would be contrary to morals or public order are unlikely to meet the threshold of a literary work required for copyright protection.[159]

Individual rights claimed from Article 15(1)(c) should be balanced against the recognition in Section 15(1)(a) of the right of everyone to take part in cultural life. Granting trade mark rights to marks that reclaim slurs can restrict human rights to participate in culture protected through *ICESCR* Section 15(1)(a). In interpreting this right in *General Comment 21*, the Committee on Economic, Social and Cultural Rights ('CESCR') states that '"Cultural life" is an explicit reference to culture as a living process, historical, dynamic and evolving, with a past, a present and a future'. *General Comment 21* recognises that a broad scope of cultural activities can be included in the right.[160] Culture encompasses 'language, oral and written literature … [and] non-verbal communication through which individuals, groups of individuals and communities express their humanity and the meaning they give to their existence, and

---

156 Anheuser-Busch Inc v Portugal (Merits) (2007) I Eur Court HR 39 ('*Anheuser-Busch Inc*').

157 Committee on Economic, Social and Cultural Rights, *General Comment No 17: The Right of Everyone to Benefit from the Protection of the Moral and Material Interests Resulting from Any Scientific, Literary or Artistic Production of Which He or She Is the Author* (Art 15, Para 1(c) of the Covenant), UN ESCOR, 35th sess, UN Doc E/C.12/GC/17 (12 January 2006) [3] ('*General Comment 17*').

158 Ibid.

159 See Wilkinson, 'Exploring Moral Interests in the Intellectual Creations underlying Trade Marks' (n 154).

160 In the individual complaint regarding Ecuador, AMB, the decision was ultimately about admissibility, but the relevant cultural activity was participation in competitive soccer competitions that led to selection in national teams. Committee on Economic, Social and Cultural Rights, *Views: Communication No 3/2014*, 58th sess, UN Doc E/C.12/58/D/3/2014 (8 August 2016, adopted 24 June 2016) ('*AMB v Ecuador*').

build their world view representing their encounter with the external forces affecting their lives'.[161] Other rights include the right of everyone to contribute to cultural rights, including to 'be involved in creating the … intellectual and emotional expressions of the community'.[162] 'Culture shapes and mirrors the values of well-being and the economic, social and political life of individuals, groups of individuals and communities'.[163] Reclamation symbols fit within this definition: they are mechanisms for expression of meaning and individuals' capacity to encounter external forces affecting their lives.[164] The notion of evolving culture aligns well with reclamation of offensive slurs by minority groups to control the slur's cultural significance. Reclamation can be part of the political life of society, and relevant rights include the right of everyone to participate in that political life and to seek and develop cultural expressions and share them with others.[165] Although reclaiming a racial slur can be a powerful political tool to raise awareness of past and ongoing discrimination and injustice, trade mark registration is not necessary for reclamation.[166] A negative impact of *Tam* suspending the prohibition on registration of disparaging marks was that it undermined the long-running action to revoke the registrations by a famous football team for Redskins that deeply offended Native Americans.[167]

Cultural interests appropriately supported the refusal to register the Tana Gull mark in Norway.[168] Cultural interests were also relevant in *Vigeland.* In *Vigeland*, copyright was about to expire for more than 200 sculptures by Gustave Vigeland, the highly regarded Norwegian artist, depicting the human experience of life and emotion. The owner of the sculptures, the Municipality of Oslo, applied for trade mark registration for a series of marks depicting the sculpture. The application was rejected by the Norwegian Intellectual Property Office as 'non-distinctive, descriptive and functional'.[169] The Norwegian

---

161 Committee on Economic, Social and Cultural Rights, *General Comment No 21: Right of Everyone to Take Part in Cultural Life* (art. 15, para. 1a of the Covenant on Economic, Social and Cultural Rights), 43rd sess, UN Doc E/C.12/GC/21 (21 December 2009) [13] ('*General Comment 21*').

162 Ibid [15].

163 Ibid [13].

164 Aoun, 'The Belated Awakening of the Public Sphere to Racist Branding and Racist Stereotypes in Trademarks' (n 124) 562.

165 See, generally, ibid.

166 Ibid 561.

167 Ibid 644–651.

168 Deacon (n 151) 103.

169 Martin Senftleben, 'Towards a New Copyright/Trademark Interface—Why (and How) Signs with Cultural Significance should be Kept Outside Trademark Law' in Graeme B Dinwoodie and Mark D Janis (eds), *Research Handbook on Trademark Law Reform* (Edward Elgar Publishing, 2021) 100, 132 ('Towards a New Copyright/Trademark Interface').

Board of Appeal endorsed the rejection and identified a further concern that the subjects of the trade mark were works belonging to Norway's cultural heritage so their registration may be contrary to public policy or accepted principles of morality.[170] The Court of Justice of the European Free Trade Association ('EFTA') recognised that there were certain circumstances where the public may find the registration of pieces of art considered to be part of a nation's heritage offensive, which may justify refusal as a community trade mark.[171] Marks may also be contrary to public policy if registration of an artwork 'is regarded as a genuine and serious threat to certain fundamental values or where the need to safeguard the public domain, itself, is considered a fundamental interest of society'.[172]

The marks that were disputed in *Vigeland* could meet the *ICESCR* Article 15(1)(c) threshold for artistic or literary creations but the reasons that they were refused can be characterised as supportive of the right to take part in cultural life protected by *ICESCR* Article 15(I)(a). CESCR guides states to take measures that 'aim at preventing the signs, symbols and expressions of a particular culture from being taken out of context for the sole purpose of marketing'.[173] Article 15(1)(a) can also be restricted by protection of certain contrary marks, such as reclaimed slurs, marks displaying culturally significant material like the Sámi sun symbol and other signs that have entered the public domain after copyright protection expired. Although neither the *Tana Gull* case nor the *Vigeland* case was framed in relation to human rights obligations in article 15(1)(a), the recognition in these cases that the public should have access to language and symbols is relevant to state obligations to promote peoples' right to participate in culture.

4.6 Right to Property

The right to property is not found in either the *ICCPR* or *ICESCR*, although it is recognised in the *Universal Declaration of Human Rights* ('*UDHR*'). Where a right to property is explicitly protected within a human rights framework, it

---

[170] *Municipality of Oslo (Oslo Kommune)* (Decision, Norwegian Board of Appeal for Industrial Property Rights, Case Nos 16/00148, 16/00149, 16/00150, 16/00151, 16/00153 and 16/0015413, 13 November 2017) [14] ('*Vigeland*').

[171] *Municipality of Oslo* (Judgment, EFTA Court, Case No E-5/16, 6 April 2017) [92].

[172] Martin Senftleben, 'Vigeland and the Status of Cultural Concerns in Trade Mark Law—The EFTA Court Develops More Effective Tools for the Preservation of the Public Domain' (2017) 48(6) *IIC International Review of Intellectual Property and Competition Law* 683, 714 ('Vigeland and the Status of Cultural Concerns in Trade Mark Law').

[173] *General Comment 21* (n 161) [43].

is often limited to protection from expropriation of property by the state and the state is given significant discretion in these circumstances.[174] A trade mark owner contesting refusal to register a mark could argue that use as a trade mark without registration creates an entitlement to certain property rights that should be recognised through formal registration.[175] In *Brunetti*, the FUCT mark had been used for 20 years prior to the application for registration.[176] The Slants also had lengthy prior use by Tam and his fellow band members.[177] However, there is a broad margin of discretion in these matters.[178] It is unlikely that refusal of registration of the marks The Slants or FUCT, consistent with *Paris Convention* Article 6*quinquies*, would be arbitrary or unreasonable.[179]

4.7 Monitoring and Accountability

The human rights concerns identified suggest that explicit protection of constitutional free speech applying a viewpoint standard to American trade mark legislation should not be equated to protection for the human right to freedom of expression as found in international human rights law. Free speech jurisprudence does not focus on international human rights obligations, and it is problematic if the application of free speech standards in *Tam* and *Brunetti* suggest that the decision protects human rights when the courts have failed to recognise competing freedom of expression interests and other relevant human rights identified in this chapter. The United States has ratified the *ICCPR* but made a reservation to Article 20, and declared that to the extent of any inconsistency between Article 19(3) and its constitutional protection for free speech, the latter will apply.[180] It has not made any reservation or declaration in relation to Article 27, and stated its understanding that Article 2 prohibitions on discrimination permit distinctions to be made where they are rationally

---

[174] Laurence R Helfer, 'The New Innovation Frontier—Intellectual Property and the European Court of Human Rights' (2008) 49(1) *Harvard International Law Journal* 1, 10–11.

[175] See *Anheuser-Busch Inc* (n 156).

[176] United States Patent and Trademark Office, Trademark Trial and Appeal Board, *In re Brunetti* (Serial No. 85310960, 1 August 2014) 4.

[177] Vicki Huang, 'Comparative Analysis of US and Australian Trade Mark Applications for THE SLANTS' (2018) 40(7) *European Intellectual Property Review* 429, 429.

[178] See *Anheuser-Busch Inc* (n 156).

[179] Cf *Safarov v Azerbaijan* (European Court of Human Rights, Chamber, Fifth Section, Application no. 885/12, 1 September 2022).

[180] Senate Committee on Foreign Relations, *Report on the International Covenant on Civil and Political Rights*, S. Exec. Rep. No. 23, 1 (102nd sess., 1992).

related to a legitimate government objective.[181] The United States has not ratified *ICESCR* but is obliged to avoid acts that would defeat the object and purpose of the agreement, as a signatory.[182] Despite these attempts to avoid binding human rights obligations, the United States is obliged to protect human rights and cooperate to realise them as a member of the United Nations.[183] The declarations made by the United States in relation to *ICCPR* Article 19 make international oversight of constitutional free speech decisions complex.

4.8 Participation and Empowerment and Transparency

A transparent trade mark examination process is particularly important for understanding the relationship between contrary marks registration and human rights. Arguably, the USPTO and its delegates represent the interests of the public in open communication by assessing distinctiveness to ensure that signs are not registered if this would encroach on the language commons by limiting use of ordinary signifiers for goods and services.[184] There are limited in-built mechanisms to protect freedom of expression for stakeholders in trade mark registration systems, but the decision-maker primarily controls these assessments. Accountability for those decisions depends on the willingness of the applicant to invest time and resources in contesting outcomes, or third parties to do so where opposition proceedings or *amicus curiae* interventions are possible.

A contrary marks refusal provision should operate transparently within trade mark registration systems to permit refusal of marks where their registration is inconsistent with morals, public order or the rights or reputations of others. Failure to restrict registration of contrary marks can restrict freedom of non-owners (including reclaimants), entrench discrimination of certain groups and limit participation in culture for some groups. This needs to be carefully balanced against the property rights of owners, consumer interests and any freedom of expression interests for trade mark applicants. A primary concern should be the nature of the restriction imposed by contrary marks and whether it is consistently applied within a framework so that the restriction is necessary, direct and proportionate. Broad monopolies for trade mark owners, particu-

---

[181] Ibid.

[182] Signing obliges states to 'refrain from acts which would defeat the object and purpose of a treaty': *Vienna Convention on the Law of Treaties*, opened for signature 23 May 1969, 1155 UNTS 331 (entered into force 27 January 1980) art 18.

[183] Charter of the United Nations arts 55, 56.

[184] See Patricia Loughlan, 'The Campomar Model of Competing Interests' (2005) 27(8) *European Intellectual Property Review* 289.

larly those of well-known marks, can raise additional freedom of expression concerns that should also be transparently considered

4.9 International Cooperation and Assistance

These decisions raise questions as to what international cooperation to protect human rights is appropriate in relation to trade marks, if freedom of expression and other rights are not adequately protected in other jurisdictions. Principles of international assistance and cooperation predominantly feature in interpretation of the *ICESCR*, and states should ensure relevant international agreements, including *TRIPS*, operate consistently with obligations to protect the right to participate in culture.[185] There is less emphasis on international assistance and cooperation in interpretation of state obligations to protect civil and political rights by the HRC than the obligations identified by CESCR in interpretation of state obligations to protect economic, social and cultural rights. However, read together, *United Nations Charter* Articles 55 and 56 create an obligation for United Nations Members to 'take joint and separate action in co-operation with the Organization' to achieve the promotion of 'universal respect for, and observance of, human rights and fundamental freedoms for all without distinction as to race, sex, language, or religion'. This obligation is important because it applies human rights standards to countries that have not ratified the *ICCPR* and *ICESCR*. Although the United States has signed but not ratified the *ICESCR*, many of the rights it contains are also found in the *UDHR*, which can be understood as an authoritative interpretation of these *United Nations Charter* obligations.[186] Arguably, the United States *ICCPR* declarations described above undermine the purpose of the *ICCPR*.[187]

4.10 Balancing of Rights

This human rights analysis demonstrates that contrary marks registration engages human rights considerations beyond the free speech interests of the applicants protected by the Supreme Court in *Tam* and *Brunetti.* Trade mark

---

[185] *General Comment 21* (n 161) [75].

[186] Khulekani Moyo and Sandra Liebenberg, 'The Privatization of Water Services: The Quest for Enhanced Human Rights Accountability' (2015) 37(3) *Human Rights Quarterly* 707, citing Stephen C McCaffrey, 'A Human Right to Water: Domestic and International Implications' (1992) 5 *Georgetown International Environmental Law Review* 1, 8.

[187] Cf Kristina Ash, 'U.S. Reservations to the International Covenant on Civil and Political Rights: Credibility Maximization and Global Influence' (2005) 3 *Northwestern University Journal of International Human Rights* xxxvi.

registration systems facilitate restrictions on commercial expression of certain information and ideas. The scope of formal and de facto trade mark monopolies may also impact other forms of expression, including political expression. The exclusion of contrary marks within a trade mark registration can be justified on the basis of the rights of others or on the basis of morality or public order where that restriction is necessary, direct and proportionate.[188] The operation and inconsistent application of contrary marks refusal standards in the past is problematic.[189] However, the current failure to provide any equivalent refusal mechanism in the United States trade mark registration system poses serious human rights concerns that existing mechanisms for monitoring and accountability appear inadequate to address. The divergence between United States free speech standards and countries that implement international human rights law standards is highlighted by Justice Alito's statement in *Brunetti* that free speech is 'under attack' in states that limit hate speech, a limitation clearly recognised in human rights law.[190]

Adjustments to United States law could better support a human rights culture. Justice Breyer proposes an alternative approach to assessing free speech protections to determine whether freedom of expression is harmed in a manner 'out of proportion to its justifications' and would test whether 'the regulation at issue wor[ks] harm to First Amendment interests that is disproportionate in light of the relevant regulatory objectives'.[191] This would be more closely aligned with human rights standards but no other judge agreed. However, a proposed narrower prohibition was suggested in Justice Sotomayor's minority judgment.[192] Chief Justice Roberts and Justice Breyer concurred with Justice Sotomayor's finding that it was possible to read down the restriction on scandalous marks so that it was not viewpoint-based and only excluded marks that were obscene, vulgar or profane.[193] This approach would permit marks to be refused where the mode of expression is offensive, rather than through an assessment of the view expressed.[194] Although the majority disagreed with reading down the statute in this way, if the proposed approach was implemented into legislation, the resulting registration decisions may overlap with the operation of contrary marks standards in other countries. It

---

188 *General Comment 34* (n 65) [33]–[35].

189 Barton Beebe and Jeanne C Fromer, 'Immoral or Scandalous Marks: An Empirical Analysis' (2018) 8(2) *NYU Journal of Intellectual Property & Entertainment Law* 169.

190 *Brunetti* (n 4) 2302–2303 (Alito J); Dreyfuss and Frankel (n 99) 231.

191 *Brunetti* (n 4) 2305, 2306 (Breyer J).

192 Ibid 2311 (Sotomayor J).

193 Ibid 2311 (Sotomayor J), 2303 (Roberts J), 2307–2308 (Breyer J).

194 Ibid 2311 (Sotomayor J).

does not permit recognition of the full scope of human rights that may justify restrictions on expression, some of which have been explored in this chapter.

Other changes may address some human rights concerns. Reducing broad trade mark monopolies may limit restrictions on freedom of expression. Ramsey has argued that if the viewpoint-based threshold is applied to dilution and tarnishment protections, those provisions may be found to be viewpoint based and unconstitutional.[195] A similar approach protecting a larger number of vulnerable groups could provide indirect monitoring of some of the human rights concerns identified in this chapter. Some marks that might be considered scandalous or offensive have been rejected because it is determined that there is 'failure to function' as a mark, as the mark does not distinguish goods or services.[196] The failure to function doctrine may also operate to reduce the number of registrations with potentially negative human rights impacts.[197] In *Re Snowflake Enterprises*, the application to register NIGGA for clothing was rejected.[198] Despite the rulings in *Tam* and *Brunetti*, it was determined that the widespread use of the mark by others meant that the mark failed to function because it could not be perceived as a source indicator.[199] In New Zealand, the Māori Trade Mark Advisory Board determines whether certain trade mark applications are offensive to Māori people. A proposal for a Trade Mark Review Board to monitor offensive speech could prevent some negative human rights outcomes. The USPTO could adapt this mechanism for addressing the consequences of *Tam* and *Brunetti.*[200] However, many minorities might be subject to offence in the United States, so determining composition of an analogous board would be difficult and still require clear terms of reference.

These mechanisms can strengthen a human rights culture for trade marks in the United States, although they are unlikely to affect comprehensive monitoring and accountability for all relevant human rights concerns. These protections may also decrease the likelihood that a mark that might be refused protection elsewhere obtains registration in the United States, reducing inconsistencies. Alternatively, there is opportunity for protection of contrary marks

---

[195] Ramsey, 'Free Speech Challenges to Trademark Law after Matal v. Tam' (n 42) 443–445. Cf Jennifer E Rothman, 'Valuing the Freedom of Speech and the Freedom to Compete in Defenses to Trademark and Related Claims in the United States' in Irene Calboli and Jane C Ginsburg (eds), *Handbook on International and Comparative Trademark Law* (Cambridge University Press, 2020) 539.

[196] Huang (n 60) 1643.

[197] See Lisa P Ramsey, 'Using Failure to Function Doctrine to Protect Free Speech and Competition in Trademark Law' (2009) 104 *Iowa Law Review Online* 70.

[198] *In re Snowflake Enterprises, LCC* (Serial No 87496454, 24 June 2021).

[199] Ibid.

[200] Dreyfuss and Frankel (n 99) 237–239.

to occur in a manner consistent with human rights in the existing European framework, which will be explored in the next section.

5 HOW CAN WE BUILD A HUMAN RIGHTS CULTURE?

5.1 Local Conditions

The implementation of human rights standards in the United States means that accountability for human rights concerns engaged by the protection of contrary marks is limited. Constitutional free speech protection relies on a categorisation approach that differs from the systematic assessment of justifications used by the *ICCPR* in assessing permissible restrictions on freedom of expression. Examples of decisions regarding contrary marks registration in Europe and the United Kingdom illustrate that the American approach differs considerably from other jurisdictions.[201]

The United States is a developed country with considerable economic influence. Unlike Australia and Uruguay, it is a net exporter of intellectual property products. It is advantageous for the United States to encourage investment in trade marks to protect these rights. This influences the scope of the monopoly conferred on trade marks. The *Paris Convention* permits states to refuse to register contrary marks but does not require this, so it is possible that other states could agree to adopt American standards if the United States used its geo-political influence and introduced its own contrary marks standards in bilateral and plurilateral trade agreements. However, the following comparison with the European approach demonstrates that net exporters of intellectual property can ensure that their registration systems recognise relevant human rights concerns in relation to contrary marks, if their human rights accountability mechanism effectively realises international human rights standards. This should influence future international discourse regarding contrary marks.

5.2 European Approach to Trade Mark Registration for Contrary Marks

European jurisprudence suggests that states can implement trade mark registration while recognising relevant human rights standards. The European

[201] See also the South American approach in Ziemer et al (n 25); analysis of cases from Australia, the United Kingdom, European Union and United States in Enrico Bonadio, 'Brands, Morality and Public Policy: Some reflections on the Ban on Registration of Controversial Trademarks' (2015) 19(1) *Marquette Intellectual Property Law Review* 39.

Union Intellectual Property Office ('EUIPO') applies an absolute prohibition on registration for 'trade marks which are contrary to public policy or to accepted principles of morality' found in the European Union Trade Mark Directive ('the Directive').[202] The *European Union Charter of Fundamental Rights* ('the *Charter*') binds the EUIPO. *Charter* Article 11(1) protects freedom of expression:

> Everyone has the right to freedom of expression. This right shall include freedom to hold opinions and to receive and impart information and ideas without interference by public authority and regardless of frontiers.

The relevance of freedom of expression has also been noted in the discussion of exceptions in paragraph 21 of the Directive, which provides: '[f]urthermore, this Directive should be applied in a way that ensures full respect for fundamental rights and freedoms, and in particular the freedom of expression.'[203]

The 2020 decision of the European Court of Justice ('ECJ') in *Constantin* recognises the relevance of freedom of expression and other human rights to all aspects of trade mark regulation in Europe, not just infringement proceedings.[204] The European approach suggests that a contrary marks regime can operate to implement *TRIPS* standards and balance competing human rights concerns. In *Constantin*, the EUIPO had refused to register the mark 'Fack Ju Göhte' as an EU trade mark. 'Fack Ju Göhte' was the title of a successful German comedy. The movie title references the famous German author Johann Wolfgang von Goethe. The film used the phrase to encapsulate a joke expressing the occasional frustration of students with their studies.[205] The mark was rejected by the EUIPO on the basis that it was contrary to 'accepted principles of morality'. This decision was unsuccessfully appealed before the EUIPO Appeal Board[206] and then the General Court.[207] It was finally reversed by the ECJ, which had not previously considered the legal test to be applied when assessing whether

---

[202] Directive (EU) 2015/2436 of the European Parliament and of the Council of 16 December 2015 to Approximate the Laws of the Member States Relating to Trade Marks [2015] OJ L 336/1.

[203] See Jens Schovsbo, '"Mark My Words"—Trademarks and Fundamental Rights in the EU' (2018) 8 *UC Irvine Law Review* 555.

[204] *Constantin Film Produktion GmbH v European Union Intellectual Property Office* (Court of Justice of the European Union, C-240/18 P, ECLI:EU:C:2020:118, 27 February 2020) (Judgement of the Court) ('*Constantin*').

[205] *Bobek Opinion* (n 150) [21].

[206] Constantin Film Produktion GmbH, (European Union Intellectual Property Office, Decision of the Fifth Board of Appeal, Case R 2205/2015-5, 1 December 2016).

[207] Constantin Film Produktion v. EUIPO (General Court, T-69/17, 24 January 2018).

to reject an application for a trade mark because it is 'contrary to public policy or to accepted principles of morality'.[208]

The ECJ focused its assessment on the test for marks that are inconsistent with accepted principles of morality. The assessment threshold depends on the viewpoint of the relevant public.[209] The court found that examination of a sign should not be restricted to abstract assessment of a mark or its components but must establish 'that the use of that mark in the concrete and current social context would indeed by perceived by that public as being contrary to the fundamental moral values and standards of society'.[210] This is particularly important where the applicant brings evidence that 'cast[s] doubt on the fact that the mark is perceived by the relevant public as contrary to accepted principles of morality'.[211]

The decision confirms that the approach taken to determining whether or not a mark is contrary to accepted principles of morality includes 'contextual elements capable of shedding light on how the relevant public perceives that mark'.[212] The fact that there was no evidence of negative public response to the film's title that was the subject of the trade mark in their primary markets in Germany and Austria was relevant to the assessment.[213] It was also relevant that the film was successful[214] and that young people accessed the film in German schools.[215] The court found that the legal standard for rejection had not been met in these circumstances, noting the absence of 'concrete evidence ... to explain why the German-speaking public at large will perceive the word sign "Fack Ju Göhte" as going against the fundamental moral values and standards of society when it is used as a trade mark'.[216]

The ECJ recognised that freedom of expression must be taken into account when assessing whether a mark is contrary to accepted morality.[217] It emphasised that the relevant Trade Mark Directive expressly emphasises the need to apply those regulations to ensure 'full respect for fundamental rights and freedoms, and in particular freedom of expression'.[218] This overturned the finding of the General Court that 'there is, in the field of art, culture and literature, a constant concern to preserve freedom of expression which does not exist in

---

208 *Bobek Opinion* (n 150) [4].
209 *Constantin* (n 204) [40].
210 Ibid [43]
211 Ibid.
212 Ibid [51].
213 Ibid [67].
214 Ibid [66].
215 Ibid [67].
216 Ibid [69].
217 Ibid [56].
218 Ibid.

the field of trade marks'.[219] It was determined unnecessary to assess whether freedom of expression concerns were engaged because the ECJ found that the mark was not contrary to accepted principles of morality.[220] The impact of this on freedom of expression for third parties is mitigated by the specific meaning of 'Fack Ju Göhte' derived from the subject matter of the film,[221] compared with known terms such as The Slants or FUCT. Although FCUK was registered in the United Kingdom, it was distinctive as a well-known acronym for French Connection UK.[222]

While the ECJ focused on a morality assessment, the opinion that Attorney-General Bobek provided in relation to *Constantin* explores reasons why a contrary mark might be rejected under European trade mark law where it is contrary to public policy that were not considered in the decision. Public policy assessments depend on views of public regulators and can be determined from laws, policies and official statements of public authorities.[223] The existence of these objective statements are relevant to criteria that are important to a rights-based approach: 'foreseeability, absence of the arbitrary and good administration'.[224] Although the two categories can overlap, an assessment of morality requires 'at least some empirical assessment of what the relevant society (the public in question) considers, at a given point in time, to be acceptable norms of conduct'.[225] Importantly, the public policy exception permits consideration of human rights other than freedom of expression.[226]

Applying American principles, both European tests are viewpoint-based restrictions. However, *Constantin* confirms that these restrictions need to be applied consistently with European protection of freedom of expression. The approach adopted by the ECJ is consistent with the approach that has been taken by the European Court of Human Rights in relation to freedom of expression and trade marks.[227] This depends on the individual circumstances of the case that are balanced against each other, taking into account factors such as the balance between the offensiveness of the mark and the extent to which

---

[219] Ibid.

[220] Ibid [57].

[221] Ibid [54].

[222] *Registered Trade Mark No 2184549 in the name of French Connection Limited* (2006) 70 IPR 438.

[223] *Bobek Opinion* (n 150) [76].

[224] Ibid.

[225] Ibid [80].

[226] Ibid [53], [57].

[227] Christophe Geiger and Elena Izyumenko, 'Shaping Intellectual Property Rights through Human Rights Adjudication: The Example of the European Court of Human Rights' (2019) 46 *Mitchell Hamline Law Review* 527, 585.

a refusal to register would harm the applicant's freedom of expression.[228] *Csibi v Romania* illustrates how this operates for public order: the European Court of Human Rights upheld a refusal to register a mark that could promote separatism, affording broad discretion to Romania.[229] Courts should also consider 'the need to preserve expressive diversity by leaving culturally valuable signs … free for common use'.[230] Consideration of freedom of expression requires a balancing of interests.[231] Arguably, the 'wide margin of discretion which the national authorities enjoy in regulating commercial and advertising speech' is consistent with permitting the rights of others to be balanced by domestic lawmakers against the restriction that trade marks already place on speech.[232]

Although Izyumenko uses the Jewish Monkeys registration in Europe to suggest that an application to register The Slants might be accepted by the EUIPO, this will also depend on context and that assessment is likely to be viewpoint-based.[233] The refusal to register PAKI in the United Kingdom because it was a contrary mark may alternatively guide whether The Slants could be registered. In *PAKI Logistics v OHIM*, the Third Chamber of the ECJ refused an application to register the term PAKI because the term was 'perceived as a racist insult' directed towards the Pakistani community in the United Kingdom.[234] The decision-maker could not rule out that a term could evolve and no longer be regarded as offensive; however, registration could be refused under contrary marks legislation if the evolution is limited and the relevant public continue to regard it as very offensive.[235] Even though there was some evidence of non-racist use, including by Pakistanis, the continuing racist use by others was important.[236] If similar evidence of racist use of The Slants in Europe resulted in rejection of an application to register The Slants, it would be likely to meet the standard required by the HRC. Significant domestic autonomy is permitted in determinations of morality.[237]

---

228 Ibid.

229 *Csibi v Romania* (European Court of Human Rights, Case No 1663212, 4 June 2019).

230 Elena Izyumenko, 'A Freedom of Expression Right to Register ''Immoral'' Trademarks and Trademarks Contrary to Public Order' (2021) 52 *IIC – International Review of Intellectual Property and Competition Law* 893, 903.

231 *Charter of Fundamental Rights of the European Union* [2010] OJ C 83/389 (entered into force 1 December 2009) art 11 ('*ECR*').

232 Gieger and Izyumenko (n 227) 580.

233 See Izyumenko (n 230), 899–900.

234 *PAKI Logistics GmbH v OHIM* (Court of Justice of the European Union, General Court, T-526/09, ECLI:EU:T:2011:5645, October 2011) [37].

235 Ibid [16].

236 Ibid [28].

237 See *Hertzberg v Finland* (n 82).

Even if The Slants did not create offence sufficient for it to be contrary to accepted principles of morality, if registration was inconsistent with public order or the human rights of others, it may not be registered because it is contrary to public policy. This objective standard could permit consideration of the human rights concerns identified in this chapter, such as the impact of government endorsement through registration in perpetuating experiences of discrimination. However, this would rely on the identification of those interests by the relevant stakeholders. Alvaro Fernandez-Mora argues that inconsistencies in the European approach to freedom of expression are influenced by decision-makers' inability to reach consensus on the role that freedom of expression should play in trade mark law generally.[238] There are also discrepancies between the Finnish registration for the Sámi sun symbol by Tana Gull and the Norwegian refusal to register that sign.[239] Although the Norwegian trade mark registration system operates outside of the European Union, it adopts similar principles.[240]

Would a decision to refuse registration for FUCT withstand scrutiny in the HRC? The fact that the refusal does not directly prevent use of the sign in advertising may mean that it is not actually considered a restriction on expression inconsistent with Article 19(2). Restrictions on commercial expression in advertising in *Ballantyne* were far more restrictive as they made the use of English in advertising illegal.[241] A prohibition on material 'celebrating' homosexuality in radio and television broadcasting was not found to be impermissible, despite the chilling impact alleged by journalists whose investigations into social issues impacting homosexuals resulted in charges that were later dropped.[242] A wide discretion was given to Finland to determine questions of morality and whether radio and television were the appropriate forum to discuss the prohibited subject matter.[243]

Even if they found a restriction operated in *Brunetti*, the HRC has balanced restrictions against their impact on the community as whole. In *Faurisson v France*, a restriction on expression denying the findings of crimes against humanity committed in Nazi Germany was permissible because it benefited the community as a whole.[244] Evidence that the term FUCT was sometimes used in misogynistic contexts could similarly demonstrate that refusing regis-

---

238 See Alvaro Fernandez-Mora, 'European Trade Mark Law: The Public Policy and Morality Exclusions' (2020) 4 *Intellectual Property Quarterly* 271.

239 Deacon (n 151) 104.

240 Ibid 98.

241 See Ballantyne, Davidson and McIntyre v Canada (n 65).

242 *Hertzberg v Finland* (n 82) [10.3].

243 Ibid.

244 Faurisson v France (n 11).

tration benefits the interests of the community. The EUIPO's potentially broad power to refuse contrary marks may also mean that in any review of their decisions for *ICCPR* Article 19 consistency, the HRC would consider whether the subsequent decision-makers had carefully determined any refusal, consistent with EUIPO guidelines.[245]

Does the European approach adequately deal with the concerns raised by a human rights analysis of the impact of marks reclaiming slurs on cultural participation? It is possible that this may also be addressed by the prohibition on registration of marks that are contrary to public policy. In *Vigeland*, the EFTA recognised that, in exceptional cases, where a term that is 'offensive' does not meet thresholds of contrary to morality or public order because of the content of that sign, the provision can operate for another purpose to ensure that access to cultural heritage is not impeded.[246] Similar arguments may be made that a reclamation mark registration application presents another exceptional case for protection of expressive cultural diversity, even if the subjective morality standards of offensiveness are not met.

5.3 Lessons for a Human Rights Culture

This chapter illustrates the diversity of human rights concerns that can be associated with contrary marks registration and domestic enforcement and how these are relevant to assessments of restrictions on freedom of expression. The Human Rights Assessment for Trade Marks ('HRATM') framework is valuable for understanding the diversity of rights that are engaged by registration of contrary marks, and for recognising that trade marks engage potentially competing cultural rights protected by *ICESCR* Article 15 and *ICCPR* Article 27. An integrated assessment of civil and political rights and economic, social and cultural rights is important to freedom of expression because permissible exceptions permit justifications to protect the human rights of others. The relationship between intellectual and emotional expressions and the creation of culture[247] means that cultural rights contained in Article 15 can be relevant to restrictions on expression, particularly for contrary marks like The Slants, where commercial expression is likely to intersect with political expression.

Yu's approach to understanding how intellectual property rights can protect human rights can guide analysis of how cultural rights are relevant to contrary mark registrations.[248] The terms FUCT or The Slants are unlikely to qualify as

---

245 Ibid.

246 *Municipality of Oslo* (n 171) [94]–[96].

247 *General Comment 21* (n 161) [15(c)].

248 Peter K Yu, 'The Anatomy of the Human Rights Framework for Intellectual Property' (2016) 69(1) *SMU Law Review* 37.

'literary productions' because they are words or approximations of words that were already well known, and neither Brunetti nor Tam are the authors of these words. In contrast, Vigeland's sculptures are artistic productions and as an author, Vigeland is entitled to protection of moral and material interests in his work. Trade mark protection could protect the moral and material rights associated with a sculpture by Vigeland but Norwegian copyright law has provided protection for material interests for the term of copyright. Norwegian law also permits limited enduring protection of moral rights which would enable the Minister for Culture to bring an action for infringement of derogatory uses of the work after copyright expires.[249]

One justification of copyright protection for material interests is that copyright works eventually enter into the public domain. This creates 'a vibrant public domain of shared cultural heritage, from which all creators are free to draw'.[250] Trade mark protection is likely to restrict use of Vigeland's work within the public domain. Yu notes that protection for the right to own private property in the *UDHR* is not unambiguous.[251] The potential interpretation of the right to own property in association with others could support a 'rich public domain'.[252] Yu concludes that it is ambiguous whether Article 17(1) 'provides the basis for the right to the protection of material interests resulting from intellectual productions in Article 27(2)'.[253] Yu's approach to protection of human rights recognises the role of intellectual property in protecting human rights but does not support expansive protection for private intellectual property rights within a human rights framework for intellectual property.[254]

Where rights to participate in culture are relevant but their protection may overlap with the rights of authors to moral and material interests in their literary or artistic productions, Yu's conflict resolution approach provides useful guidance. This recognises that core minimum protection can be adequate in some circumstances: where the production has already received copyright protection it can be appropriate to privilege *ICESCR* Article 15 protection for the right to participate in culture, particularly in cases attempting to trade mark

---

[249] See *Copyright Act* (Norway) s 5; TerraLex, *Cross-Border Copyright Guide 2018: Norway* (TerraLex, 2018) 3 https://www.rpc.co.uk/-/media/rpc/files/perspectives/ip/norway.pdf.

[250] Farida Shaheed, Report of the Special Rapporteur in the Field of Cultural Rights: Copyright Policy and the Right to Science and Culture, 28th sess, Agenda Item 3, UN Doc A/HRC/28/57 (24 December 2014) 11 [50].

[251] Yu (n 248) 93.

[252] Ibid 94.

[253] Ibid.

[254] Ibid 94–95.

culturally significant works that have already received copyright protection.[255] Yu's framework provides a mechanism to balance between the different parts of Article 15.

The regulation of contrary marks in Europe indicates strengths and weaknesses of a fundamental rights approach to the development of a human rights culture for trade marks. This chapter recognises the strengths of the European human rights protection system for ensuring that assessments regarding registration of potentially contrary marks recognise relevant human rights. However, there are important differences between fundamental rights protection and the rights protected as human rights in international human rights law. The difficulty with these differences is that European laws, including intellectual property law, can confer fundamental rights protection beyond the agreed human rights standards, interfering with human rights balancing mechanisms.[256] Arguably, constitutional protection is not enough as its corrective nature will not be sufficient to address power imbalances between third parties and owners of famous marks.[257] Senftleben identifies the way that trade mark standards have evolved to provide expansive protection for trade marks in Europe. He finds that 'the inherent limits of exclusive trademark rights – use in the course of trade, use as a trademark, use likely to cause confusion and use likely to cause dilution – have become elastic and unreliable safeguards of freedom of use for cultural purposes'.[258] Artistic expression can also be limited by broad trade mark protection. Senftleben argues that commercial use distinctions in determining trade mark law rights can negatively impact cultural innovation as 'sufficient room must be offered not only for art creation but also for art marketing'.[259] Focusing on American and European trade mark law, Ramsey and Schovsbo identify a global expansion of trade mark rights that can harm the public interest and argue that balance needs to be restored to recognise public interests.[260]

---

255 See Senftleben, 'Vigeland and the Status of Cultural Concerns in Trade Mark Law' (n 172).

256 Peggy Ducoulombier, 'Interaction between Human Rights: Are All Human Rights Equal?' in Christophe Geiger (ed), *Research Handbook on Human Rights and Intellectual Property* (Edward Elgar Publishing, 2015) 39, 39–41.

257 See Senftleben, 'Vigeland and the Status of Cultural Concerns in Trade Mark Law' (n 172) 704.

258 Senftleben, 'Towards a New Copyright/Trademark Interface' (n 169) 127.

259 Senftleben, 'Vigeland and the Status of Cultural Concerns in Trade Mark Law' (n 172) 702.

260 Lisa P Ramsey and Jens Schovsbo, 'Mechanisms for Limiting Trade Mark Rights to Further Competition and Free Speech' (2013) 44 *IIC – International Review of Intellectual Property and Competition Law* 671, 697–698.

Geiger's proposals for integrating Article 27/15 protection into the ECR may have some impact on protecting cultural rights. This may strengthen protection within the European Union.[261] The Norwegian Intellectual Property Board recognised that the application to register the Tana Gull mark impacted the right of the Sámi people, but Norway is not part of the European Union and the mark was registered in Finland.[262] However, the *Vigeland* decision by EFTA and Bobek's articulation of European standards support using public policy as a mechanism that permits balancing of relevant human rights as these are standards used to assess compliance with public policy. This has broader significance for international standards as the EUIPO interprets the European provision as equivalent to the *Paris Convention* provision.[263] If the European test for determining whether marks are contrary to public policy embeds human rights standards, this may help establish custom that influences the interpretation of public order set out in the *Paris Convention.* Arguably, in any jurisdiction the registration of a mark could also be considered to be contrary to morality if the public is offended by a failure to protect human rights.[264]

Helfer and Austin argue that it is important to protect human rights considerations while recognising the social benefits of functional intellectual property protection.[265] If trade marks fail to function to preserve human rights ends, this needs to be addressed, but several welfare preservation considerations are relevant to understanding how to do so.[266] Trade mark protection for contrary marks can directly restrict the rights of non-owners to make use of the mark in commerce, and this restriction may overlap with other types of expression, including political and artistic expression. Trade mark protection is positive to the extent that it provides an incentive for owners to invest in maintaining consistent quality to establish goodwill, mechanisms for preventing consumer confusion and means to restrict counterfeit products. However, conferring that protection on contrary marks is negative where it represents government endorsement of marks and facilitates or entrenches discrimination, increasing the potential for marks to be used as hate speech. By potentially limiting

---

[261] Christophe Geiger, 'Implementing Intellectual Property Provisions in Human Rights Instruments: Towards a New Social Contract for the Protection of Intangibles' in Christophe Geiger (ed), *Research Handbook on Human Rights and Intellectual Property* (Edward Elgar Publishing, 2015) 661, 664–665.

[262] Deacon (n 151) 106; the Vigeland decision shows how Norwegian law can be considered when there is an application for a community trade mark, *Vigeland* (n 170).

[263] European Union Intellectual Property Office, *Guidelines for Examination*, (EUIPO, 2023) 544.

[264] See *Bobek Opinion* (n 150) [73].

[265] Laurence R Helfer and Graeme Austin (eds), *Human Rights and Intellectual Property: Mapping the Global Interface* (Cambridge University Press, 2011) 520.

[266] Ibid 519–520.

expressive use that overlaps with commercial use, registration may limit cultural participation, including reclamation activities. Even where the marks are registered to pursue reclamation objectives, they may restrict the activities of others who wish to reclaim the mark. The relative causal contribution of intellectual property to these problems is difficult to assess because trade mark rights can be used by some owners to assert rights that they are not entitled to, and power imbalances between owners and potential expressive users can chill expressive use outside of the legal system, disrupting legislative intent.[267] However, the legitimate exercise of dilution protection by owners of well-known marks is not limited to confusion, and this broader monopoly can also restrict expressive use as the legislative defences fail to protect most commercial uses that may have an overlapping non-commercial expressive purpose.[268]

The human rights concerns identified in this analysis suggest that intellectual property protection should be modified in the United States. Examples explored above of how this could occur do not sufficiently address all the human rights concerns identified in this analysis. A human rights culture could be negatively impacted if the United States attempted to export its approach and required other states to permit registration of contrary marks, as they have negotiated to require other states to protect against dilution and permit registration of marks that are not able to be represented visually.[269] Recognising local conditions is important to an inclusive approach to human rights. It is better to propose partial solutions to the human rights concerns surrounding unlimited protection for contrary marks than simply focus on the broader problems current interpretations of free speech pose for human rights protection. However, United States geo-political influence on trade agreements that include trade mark provisions suggests that addressing present human rights concerns is important, and multilateral dialogue should consider the problems that no restrictions on contrary marks registration can pose for human rights compliance, as well as the impact of broad trade mark monopolies on human rights.

In 2010, Ramsey argued that *TRIPS* flexibilities should enable WTO Members to defend speech-protective trade mark laws in WTO disputes.

---

267 Ramsey, 'Free Speech and International Obligations to Protect Trademarks' (n 7) 424.

268 See Wilkinson, 'Mitey Marks and Expressive Uses of Culturally Significant Trade Marks in Australia' (n 66) 65.

269 Burton Ong, 'The Trademark Law Provisions of Bilateral Free Trade Agreements' in Graeme B Dinwoodie and Marc D Janis (eds), *Trademark Law and Theory: A Handbook of Contemporary Research* (Edward Elgar Publishing, 2008) 229, 242–248.

The protection of public interest in Article 8 requires human rights laws to inform interpretation and application of *TRIPS*.[270] Permitting expressive uses protected by freedom of expression benefits social and economic welfare, consistent with Article 7: dispute settlement bodies should

> "balance" trademark and free speech rights when they interpret the members' trademark obligations in the covered agreements and consider the competing legitimate interests of the markholder and third parties as required by the language in *TRIPS* Article 17.[271]

Where there is flexibility in *TRIPS* provisions, states can argue for treaty interpretation that is consistent with protection for freedom of expression found in international human rights law.[272] Ramsey argued that it would be better to delay explicit recognition of freedom of expression in the *Paris Convention* or *TRIPS* until 'more states recognize that certain trademark laws can harm the free flow of information and ideas'.[273] In 2015, Ramsey recognised problems with insufficient protection for public interest in trade mark laws and advocated for soft laws that would encourage states to amend their national law to permit states to further explore how trade mark law could protect expression.[274]

The impact of broad trade mark monopolies on freedom of expression discussed in this chapter remains very concerning for a human rights culture and may require states to make greater efforts to reach multilateral agreement. The potential human rights impact of very broad protection for owners of well-known marks has been narrowly explored in this chapter in the context of contrary marks, particularly marks with reclamation purposes. However, greater international harmonisation, confirming the importance of permitting states to exclude contrary marks registration, may become increasingly necessary.

6 CONCLUSION

The analysis in this chapter shows that registration of contrary marks raises a range of human rights concerns. Addressing these in a transparent way is not only important for monitoring and accountability but to facilitate international

---

270 Ramsey, 'Free Speech and International Obligations to Protect Trademarks' (n 7) 447.

271 Ibid, 446.

272 Ibid 450–451.

273 Ibid 467.

274 Lisa Ramsey, 'Reconciling Trademark Rights and Free Expression Locally and Globally' in Daniel Gervais (ed), *International Intellectual Property: A Handbook of Contemporary Research* (Edward Elgar Publishing, 2015) 341, 343–345.

cooperation to protect human rights. All analysed examples of trade mark registration involve restrictions on freedom of expression, so the *ICCPR* Article 19(3) mechanism for assessing restrictions is a valuable tool for assessing competing human rights considerations. The inclusion of human rights standards when assessing whether marks are contrary to public policy in Europe provides another mechanism for considering human rights concerns. In some countries, marks that are inconsistent with human rights protection may be considered contrary to morality or, where the relevant concern is hate speech or equality before the law, public order.

There are some limits to European approaches. They appear to be increasingly able to accommodate human rights interests, yet the increasing scope of rights available to European trade mark owners can limit protection for human rights interests, including expression, in other problematic ways.[275] Although the relevant rights engaged by this case study are primarily civil and political rights, economic, social and cultural rights remain relevant, particularly the right to participate in culture. Where there are competing freedom of expression interests, this additional consideration may be relevant to the ultimate balance. In the United States, trade mark registration for contrary marks can be used to restrict human rights ends. Consequently, in countries that have less comprehensive protection for individual human rights and accountability for the exercise of institutional power inconsistent with human rights, including the United States and Australia, a contrary marks exclusion policy is a valuable safeguard for human rights and an important part of human rights culture.

[275] Senftleben, 'Towards a New Copyright/Trademark Interface' (n 169) 127.

5 Anti-counterfeiting legislation case study: Kenya and Australia

1 INTRODUCTION

This chapter explores the human rights implications of counterfeit medical products for Kenya and Sub-Saharan Africa during the Covid-19 pandemic. The pandemic has shown that medical products, including vaccines, treatments, diagnostic testing and personal protective equipment, can be critical tools that enable states to fulfil obligations to treat and control disease, consistent with the human right to health. During the pandemic, global authorities have detected large volumes of imported counterfeit personal protective equipment ('PPE') and counterfeit pharmaceuticals for treatment and management of Covid-19.[1] In 2021 officials seized 20,000 allegedly counterfeit masks from a Kenyan hospital.[2] In South Africa, 2,400 doses of fake Covid-19 vaccine were seized in November 2020.[3] Ineffective counterfeit PPE increases the chance of infection for healthcare workers or others who rely on PPE.[4] Counterfeit pharmaceuticals can be falsified medicines that lack effective ingredients necessary for treatment or contain unspecified ingredients that can gravely endanger lives.[5]

---

1 'Global Operation sees a Rise in Fake Medical Products Related to Covid-19' *Interpol* (19 March 2020) https://www.interpol.int/News-and-Events/News/2020/Global-operation-sees-a-rise-in-fake-medical-products-related-to-COVID-19 ('Global Operation sees a Rise in Fake Medical Products Related to Covid-19').

2 'Counterfeit 3M Co. N95 Face Masks Worth Ksh 21 Million Seized in a Leading Hospital in Nairobi' *Anti-Counterfeit Authority* (6 May 2021) https://www.aca.go.ke/media-center/news-and-events/258-counterfeit-3m-co-n95-face-masks-worth-ksh-21-million-seized-in-a-leading-hospital-in-nairobi.

3 Abdullahi Tunde Aborode et al, 'Fake COVID-19 Vaccinations in Africa' (2022) 98(1159) *Postgraduate Medical Journal* 317.

4 See Mariachiara Ippolito et al, 'Counterfeit Filtering Facepiece Respirators are Posing an Additional Risk to Health Care Workers during COVID-19 Pandemic' (2020) 48(7) *American Journal of Infection Control* 853.

5 Xavier Seuba, *The Global Regime for the Enforcement of Intellectual Property Rights* (Cambridge University Press, 2017) 409.

Counterfeit medical products pose serious health concerns when consumers rely on falsely applied trade marks and use goods that don't meet necessary standards of health and safety. Trade marks are most commonly justified for their contribution to social welfare by reducing search costs for consumers, usually permitting identification of products of known quality standards and incentivising the maintenance of those standards.[6] This quality identification function can be an important mechanism to protect consumers from the potentially negative health impacts of substandard goods manufactured outside known trade channels. This function is weakened by counterfeiting activities in which trade marks are used without the permission of the registered trade mark owner.[7]

The World Trade Organization ('WTO') *Agreement on Trade-Related Aspects of Intellectual Property* ('*TRIPS*')[8] enshrines multilateral standards for enforcement of trade mark rights. *TRIPS* provides the multilateral framework for the detection of imported counterfeit trade marked goods, focusing on liability for the use of trade marks without authorisation, rather than standards of quality or safety. Unsafe and substandard goods engage states' human rights obligations to protect individuals from threats to their health posed by third parties. In a pandemic, substandard medical products also impede state obligations to take measures to control epidemic diseases.[9] However, not all counterfeit goods are substandard and different institutions use different terminology to focus their attention on overlapping problems related to 'substandard' and 'falsified' goods that may or may not also be 'counterfeit' goods that use trade marks without authorisation.[10] A lack of comprehensive data about seized goods makes it difficult to understand the magnitude of the threat that counterfeit goods directly pose to the right to health and the extent to which this can justify directing government resources towards detecting counterfeit goods and enforcing the private rights of individual property owners.

---

6 William M Landes and Richard A Posner, *The Economic Structure of Intellectual Property Law* (Harvard University Press, 2003) 173.

7 Carsten Fink, Keith E Maskus and Yi Qian, 'The Economic Effects of Counterfeiting and Piracy: A Review and Implications for Developing Countries' (Policy Research Working Paper No 7586, World Bank Group, 29 February 2016) 2–3.

8 *Marrakesh Agreement Establishing the World Trade Organization*, opened for signature 15 April 1994, 1867 UNTS 3 (entered into force 1 January 1995) ('*WTO Agreement*') annex 1C ('*Agreement on Trade-Related Aspects of Intellectual Property Rights*') ('*TRIPS*').

9 Committee on Economic, Social and Cultural Rights ('CESCR'), *General Comment No 14: The Right to the Highest Attainable Standard of Health (Article 12 of the Covenant)*, UN ESCOR, 22nd sess, UN Doc E/C.12/2000/4 (11 August 2000) para 43 ('*General Comment 14*').

10 See further discussion in Section 2 of this chapter.

Problematically, widespread counterfeiting can also discourage distribution of intellectual property protected goods and technology transfer to enable their manufacture, which can restrict realisation of the human right to access to applications of scientific progress.[11]

Kenya's response to the widespread domestic prevalence of counterfeit goods focuses on strengthening intellectual property enforcement mechanisms beyond *TRIPS* minimum standards. Legislation adopts and expands some *TRIPS*-plus approaches proposed by developed countries in plurilateral agreements, as well as regional *TRIPS*-plus approaches that have evolved in local regional institutions in East Africa.[12] In 2008, Kenyan anti-counterfeiting legislation empowered the Anti-Counterfeit Agency to enforce the rights of intellectual property owners, regardless of whether those rights were registered in Kenya.[13] *TRIPS* only requires Member States to provide measures for the private owners of intellectual property to enforce the rights conferred on them by that state[14] and focuses additional enforcement obligations on counterfeit trade marks and copyright piracy.[15] The scope of the Kenyan legislation, which also permitted seizure of in-transit goods, was criticised because the legislation could be used to limit access to essential medicines, inconsistent with the human right to health.[16]

In contrast to the prior case studies, Kenya provides constitutional protection for the right to health by recognising individual rights 'to the highest attainable standard of health, which includes the right to health care services, including reproductive health care' and further provides that 'a person shall not be denied emergency medical treatment'.[17] The constitution also protects the right to life and many of the other rights protected by the *International Covenant on Civil and Political Rights* ('*ICCPR*') and the *International Covenant on Economic, Social and Cultural Rights* ('*ICESCR*'). The Kenyan High Court

---

11 See Genevieve Wilkinson and Evana Wright, 'Unblocking the human right to access the benefits of science in the Covid-19 era' in Jens Schovsbo (ed.), *IPR in Times of Crisis: Lessons Learned from the COVID-19 Pandemic* (Edward Elgar Publishing, forthcoming).

12 See Olugbenga A Olatunji, 'How Much is Too Much? Anti-Counterfeit Measures and Access to Medicines in the East African Community' (2021) 43(9) *European Intellectual Property Review* 594, 597.

13 *Anti-Counterfeit Act* No 13 of 2008 (Kenya) s 2.

14 *TRIPS* (n 8) pt III, s 2.

15 Ibid pt III.

16 Johanna Von Braun and Peter Munyi, 'New Enforcement Mechanisms Challenge the Legality of Generics in the Name of Public Health: The Emergence of Anti-Counterfeiting Legislation in East Africa' (2010) 18(2) *African Journal of International and Comparative Law* 238, 248.

17 *Constitution of Kenya* art 43.

recognised the relevance of those rights to the protection and enforcement of intellectual property in 2012 in the case of *Patricia Asero Ochieng* ('*PAO*'). In *PAO*, three individuals who relied on generic medication as treatment for HIV successfully contended that the provisions of Kenya's *Anti-Counterfeit Act* were inconsistent with the rights to health, life and dignity because they could be used to seize generic medicines.[18] They argued that this could force them to rely on branded drugs that would decrease access to essential drugs for HIV treatment.[19] Their case highlighted the risk that an expansive approach to the enforcement of intellectual property rights can limit the availability of essential medicines.[20] Despite the decision, Kenyan anti-counterfeiting legislation still has a very broad scope. In 2018, significant amendments were introduced to improve its effectiveness. However, the amendments entrenched broad enforcement mechanisms and introduced further, resource-intensive requirements for importers.[21] More recently, the *Anti-Counterfeit Act*'s broad scope of protection has been criticised for establishing a system that requires unrealistic resources for Kenyan authorities to effectively police the broad range of counterfeit activities.[22]

The next section of this chapter explores the potential negative impact of counterfeit goods, particularly during the Covid-19 pandemic. The third section explores how Kenyan anti-counterfeiting legislation meets *TRIPS* standards and implements further *TRIPS*-plus protections. The fourth section applies the Human Rights Assessment for Trade Marks framework to the operation of the legislation during the Covid-19 pandemic. The fifth section analyses a country with different local conditions from Kenya – Australia – and explores the serious implications of the enforcement problems identified throughout the chapter for a human rights culture for trade marks.

2 COUNTERFEIT GOODS, SUB-SAHARAN AFRICA AND THE COVID-19 PANDEMIC

Counterfeit goods pose serious health concerns in Kenya and in Sub-Saharan Africa. Long before the Covid-19 pandemic, counterfeit goods threatened health globally. In 2003, a billion fake items were intercepted in Operation

---

[18] *PA Ochieng, M Atieno and J Munjo v Attorney-General* (Petition No. 409 of 2009, Judgment of the Kenyan High Court, 20 April 2012) [15] ('*PAO*').

[19] Ibid.

[20] See Emmanuel K Oke, 'A Triumph for Generic Medicines and the Right to Health in Africa: Patricia Asero Ochieng & Ors. v. Attorney General' (2013) 10(3–4) *Journal of Generic Medicines* 246, 248.

[21] *Statute Law (Miscellaneous Amendments)* No 18 of 2018 (Kenya).

[22] Olatunji (n 12) 606.

Biyela, including 550 million doses of illicit medicine.[23] Imported counterfeit goods in Africa can include clothing and accessories, DVDs, CDs, computer games and software, food products, car parts and pharmaceuticals.[24] These engage a range of concerns for safety and individual health.[25] Counterfeit pharmaceuticals are particularly dangerous to individual health and life: 2,500 deaths have been linked to counterfeit vaccinations in a meningitis epidemic in Niger.[26] There are many reported incidents of falsified medicines severely impacting health in developing and developed countries.[27]

Certain features of counterfeit activities make it difficult for states to effectively detect and deter counterfeiting and protect individuals against the threats to health posed by counterfeiters, who are frequently linked to organised crime.[28] The expanding scope and sophistication of counterfeit activities also poses problems for effective enforcement. Counterfeiters frequently make sales over the internet.[29] Counterfeit medical products can be difficult to monitor, as small quantities ordered online are often sent in surface mail.[30] Limited resources may also restrict the number of imported goods that can be inspected so that counterfeit goods are detected.[31] Even when inspection occurs, counterfeiters have access to sophisticated technology that permit identical packaging to be produced, limiting the effectiveness of visual inspec-

---

[23] Marius Schneider and Vanessa Ferguson, 'Enforcement of Intellectual Property Rights in Africa' (2015) 10(4) *Journal of Intellectual Property Law & Practice* 269, 270–271 ('Enforcement of Intellectual Property Rights in Africa').

[24] Ibid 269–270.

[25] Seuba (n 5) 359.

[26] Klara Dégardin, Yves Roggo and Pierre Margo, 'Understanding and Fighting the Medicine Counterfeit Market' (2014) 87 *Journal of Pharmaceutical and Biomedical Analysis* 167, 169.

[27] Mohammad Sofiqur Rahman et al, 'The Health Consequences of Falsified Medicines – A Study of the Published Literature' (2018) 23 *Tropical Medicine and International Health* 1294, 1295.

[28] 'Global Operation sees a Rise in Fake Medical Products Related to Covid-19' (n 1).

[29] OECD/EUIPO, *Trade in Counterfeit and Pirated Goods: Mapping the Economic Impact* (OECD Publishing, 2016) 19 https://euipo.europa.eu/tunnel-web/secure/webdav/guest/document_library/observatory/documents/ Mapping_the_Economic_Impact_study/Mapping_the_Economic_Impact_en.pdf ('*Trade in Counterfeit and Pirated Goods*'); OECD, *Trade in Fake Medicines at the Time of the Covid-19 Pandemic* (Chair's Note, June 2020) https://www.oecd.org/gov/illicit-trade/oecd-fake-medicines-webinar-june-10-summary-note.pdf.

[30] OECD/EUIPO, *Trade in Counterfeit Pharmaceutical Products* (OECD Publishing, 2020) 44–46 https://www.oecd.org/gov/trade-in-counterfeit-pharmaceutical-products-a7c7e054-en.htm ('*Trade in Counterfeit Pharmaceutical Products*').

[31] See Fink et al (n 7) 31.

tion by customs authorities or consumers for detection of counterfeits.[32] In a pandemic, it may be even harder to detect counterfeit goods, as scarcity may mean that certain recognisable features of counterfeit products, such as lower price, are not present.[33] Increasingly, cross-border cooperation to share intelligence about counterfeit activities is valuable,[34] as the scope of counterfeiting appears to be increasing at a disturbing rate.[35] The serious threats to health that falsified medicines pose are recognised in institutions such as the World Health Organization ('WHO'), the United Nations Office of Drugs and Crime ('UNODC'), Interpol, Afripol[36] and the Council of Europe.[37] But there is no unified inter-agency mechanism for addressing these threats.

The problems with counterfeit goods in Sub-Saharan Africa are not limited to counterfeit medical products, but it is important to recognise that counterfeit pharmaceuticals are particularly prevalent in Africa.[38] Kenya was part of a sample of African countries that Renschler et al. used to estimate that substandard and falsified medications ('SSFM') were responsible for 122,350 deaths in children under five in 2013.[39] SSFM is an umbrella term used by the WHO that can include counterfeit medicines. The term was deliberately adopted instead of the term counterfeit to capture a broader range of medicines

---

32 See Melanie Jose, 'Raising the Bar on Australia's Border Measures: Improvements to the Notice of Objection Scheme Resulting from the IP Laws Amendment (Raising the Bar) Act 2012' (2012) 90 *Intellectual Property Forum* 52, 53; See OECD/EUIPO, *Trade in Counterfeit and Pirated Goods* (n 29) 12.

33 See price inflation of masks in Juliet Linderman and Martha Mendoza, 'Counterfeit Masks Reaching Frontline Health Workers in US' *Associated Press* (online, 13 May 2020) https://apnews.com/850d9e6834fc71967af6d3dda65ad874.

34 *TRIPS* (n 8) art 69.

35 OECD/EUIPO, *Trade in Counterfeit and Pirated Goods* (n 29) 25.

36 'Pharmaceutical Crime: First INTERPOL-AFRIPOL Front-Line Operation sees Arrests and Seizures across Africa' *Interpol* (2 March 2022) https://www.interpol.int/en/News-and-Events/News/2022/Pharmaceutical-crime-first-INTERPOL-AFRIPOL-front-line-operation-sees-arrests-and-seizures-across-Africa ('Pharmaceutical Crime').

37 Stefania Negri, 'The MEDICRIME Convention: Combating Pharmaceutical Crimes through European Criminal Law and Beyond' (2016) 7 *New Journal of European Criminal Law* 350, 366–367.

38 Marius Schneider and Vanessa Ferguson, *Enforcement of Intellectual Property Rights in Africa* (Oxford University Press, 2020) 2 ('Enforcement of Intellectual Property Rights in Africa').

39 See John P Renschler et al, 'Estimated Under-Five Deaths Associated with Poor-Quality Antimalarials in Sub-Saharan Africa' (2015) 92(Sup 6) *The American Journal of Tropical Medicine and Hygiene* 119.

that have negative health implications rather than focus on private intellectual property rights.[40]

Differences in nomenclature highlight fragmentation between the many different international institutions who could regulate goods which use trade marks without authorisation. The WTO characterises these as counterfeit and focuses specifically on goods bearing counterfeit trade marks and copyright piracy, where other organisations have a broader mandate. The WHO focuses on medical products that threaten health, and the World Customs Organization ('WCO') has recently used the term 'dangerous, sub-standard or counterfeit' to focus its activities.[41] There have been criticisms of the contrasting emphasis on intellectual property in the Council of Europe *Medicrime Convention*, which criminalises trade in counterfeit medical products.[42] Afripol, Interpol and UNODC target 'illicit' and 'counterfeit' goods in their activities targeting transnational organised crime.[43] Although these organisations can work together, the different approaches are fragmented. Emphasis on human rights obligations is limited. In this chapter, counterfeit goods references goods bearing false trade marks, consistent with the *TRIPS* standards that Kenya and Australia must implement. Counterfeit goods can be both substandard and falsified, but this is not always the case.

Institutional fragmentation partially explains why enforcement is characterised as the 'weak link' in protecting African consumers.[44] Trade in counterfeit goods between countries is facilitated by free-trade zones within Africa and there are multiple points in the supply chain that provide opportunities for counterfeit goods to enter the market.[45] Yet low numbers of arrests in African states suggest enforcement mechanisms have limited impact.[46]

---

40 World Health Organization ('WHO'), *A Study on the Public Health and Socioeconomic Impact of Substandard and Falsified Medical Products* (WHO, 2017) 1.

41 Ibid. World Customs Organization, *Resolution of the Customs Co-operation Council on the role of Customs in Facilitating the Cross-Border Movement of Situationally Critical Medicines and Vaccines* (December 2020) http://www.wcoomd.org/-/media/wco/public/global/pdf/about-us/legal-instruments/resolutions/resolution-facilitating-cross-border-movement-of-situationally-critical-medicines-and-vaccines.pdf?la=en.

42 *Convention on Counterfeiting of Medical Products and Similar Crimes involving Threats to Public Health (MEDICRIME Convention)*, opened for signature 28 October 2011, CETS No 211 (entered into force 1 January 2016).

43 *Algiers Declaration on the Establishment of the African Mechanism for Police Cooperation – AFRIPOL*. Done at Algiers, 11 February 2014.

44 Marius Schneider and Nora Ho Tu Nam, 'How Pharmaceutical Companies can Prevent Falsified Medicine and Vaccines from Entering African Markets' (2021) 15(6) *Journal of Intellectual Property Law & Practice* 417, 417–418.

45 Ibid.

46 OECD/EUIPO, *Trade in Counterfeit Pharmaceutical Products* (n 30) 34, 39.

Analysis by the WHO of 100 studies from 2007 to 2016, covering more than 48,000 samples, 'assessed 10.5 per cent of drugs in low and middle-income countries to be falsified or substandard' and linked this to thousands of deaths in those countries.[47] Modelling commissioned by the WHO in association with a systematic review of active ingredients in pharmaceuticals for malaria treatment estimated that substandard and falsified anti-malarials contributed an additional 72,000–267,000 deaths annually in Sub-Saharan Africa.[48] Additional modelling estimated that 72,430 annual childhood pneumonia deaths could be attributed to SSFMs if they resulted in reduced antibiotic activity, and 169,271 annual childhood pneumonia deaths could be attributed to SSFMs if they resulted in no antibiotic activity.[49] This is likely to be a significant problem in Kenya, where systematic testing of 53 antibiotic samples in Nairobi found that 37.7 per cent were poor-quality products.[50] All of the poor-quality products were imported.[51] Not all of the pharmaceuticals identified in the review involved counterfeit trade marks: this was not the focus of the study. However, in 2019, the WHO reported the detection in Kenya of a batch of counterfeit Augmentin that did not have any of the expected active ingredients.[52] Counterfeiters have less incentive to build goodwill in their product by maintaining consistent quality.[53] They are unlikely to be accountable for product safety in the way that ordinary visible participants in the supply chain can be subject to regulation and liable if they do not comply with product safety standards.

The OECD recognises that counterfeit and pirated goods '[pose] significant threats to individual and collective health and safety' and illicit trade has accelerated in the Covid-19 pandemic.[54] Covid-19 infection concerns prompted increased use of the Internet and demand for pharmaceuticals and PPE.[55] The

[47] WHO (n 40) 7.

[48] Ibid 13. Graham Kajilwa, 'Poor Quality of Drugs Blamed for Undermining the Fight against Malaria' *The Sunday Standard* (online, 26 April 2018) https://www.standardmedia.co.ke/article/2001278282/poor-quality-of-drugs-blamed-for-undermining-the-fight-against-malaria.

[49] WHO (n 40) 12.

[50] Lilian C Koech et al, 'Quality and Brands of Amoxicillin Formulations in Nairobi, Kenya' (2020) 2020(7091278) *Biomed Research International* 1, 1.

[51] Ibid 5.

[52] 'Medical Product Alert N° 9/2019: Falsified Augmentin' *World Health Organization* (20 August 2019) https://www.who.int/news/item/20-08-2019-medical-product-alert-n-9-2019-(english-version).

[53] See recognition of correlation between consumer safety and some counterfeit good in Seuba (n 5) 359.

[54] OECD/EUIPO, *Global Trade in Fakes: A Worrying Threat* (OECD Publishing, 2021) 3 https://www.oecd.org/publications/global-trade-in-fakes-74c81154-en.htm.

[55] Ibid 61.

treatment and prevention of Covid-19 requires both a 'continuous supply of inexpensive, quality assured medicines' and 'easy-to-use devices for medicine quality screening'.[56] Interpol has reported increases in seizures of counterfeit chloroquine and antivirals that have been used as treatments in the pandemic.[57] Significant quantities of counterfeit medical products were seized by Afripol and Interpol in Africa in Operation Flash-IPPA in late 2021.[58] Interpol has notified law enforcement authorities globally that counterfeit vaccines are likely to be a target for organised crime.[59] PPE, including masks and gowns, also protects medical workers dealing with infected individuals from transmission of Covid-19. During the Covid-19 pandemic there have been reports of seizures of counterfeit PPE that lack important safety features in Kenya, other parts of Sub-Saharan Africa[60] and many other parts of the world.[61] Ineffective masks 'pose an additional risk of contagion to healthcare workers due to the potentially lower protecting capacity'.[62]

3 LAWS PREVENTING COUNTERFEITING IN KENYA

In Kenya, trade mark rights are primarily governed by the *Trade Marks Act 2007* and the *Trade Marks Rules 1956*. These instruments enshrine *TRIPS* minimum standards for trade mark protection. The legislation provides civil and criminal penalties for offences related to forged or falsified registered trade marks.[63] Trade mark enforcement provisions are also regulated by the *Anti-Counterfeit Act 2008* (the '*ACA*') and the *Anti-Counterfeit Regulations 2010* (the '*ACR*').

---

[56] Conor Kavanagh, 'African Countries See Surge in Fake Coronavirus Treatments' *Pharmafile* (14 May 2020) http://www.pharmafile.com/news/548664/african-countries-see-surge-fake-coronavirus-treatments.

[57] 'Global Operation sees a Rise in Fake Medical Products Related to Covid-19' (n 1).

[58] 'Pharmaceutical Crime' (n 36).

[59] 'Interpol Warns of Organized Crime Threat to Covid-19 Vaccines' *Interpol* (2 December 2020) https://www.interpol.int/en/News-and-Events/News/2020/INTERPOL-warns-of-organized-crime-threat-to-COVID-19-vaccines.

[60] 'Africa: Fake Covid-19 Vaccines Seized in SA Just the Start for Africa' *AllAfrica* (online, 17 March 2021) https://allafrica.com/stories/202103170831.html?msclkid=507e8fc6cf3011ecbcab6df469df848a.

[61] Juliet Linderman and Martha Mendoza, 'Counterfeit Masks Reaching Frontline Health Workers in US', *Associated Press* (online, 13 May 2020) https://apnews.com/850d9e6834fc71967af6d3dda65ad874.

[62] Ippolito et al (n 4) 854.

[63] *Trade Marks Act 2007* (Kenya) ss 58C, 58D, 58E.

The legislative objective of the *ACA* is to 'prohibit trade in counterfeit goods, to establish the Anti-Counterfeit Authority, and for connected purposes'.[64] Another objective of the legislation is to protect the public from harms associated with using counterfeit goods.[65] The legislation was introduced to address concerns about the widespread nature of counterfeiting in Kenya.[66] Kenyan manufacturers strongly advocated the need for greater enforcement.[67] Around the same time, the East Africa Community ('EAC') drafted a broad-reaching anti-counterfeiting policy.[68] As a regional economic community, the EAC attempts to harmonise counterfeiting law generally and encourage regional pharmaceutical manufacturing. The EAC 'depends largely on importation to meet its local medical needs, and … the available drug regulatory capacity in the region is weak'.[69] The approach taken to counterfeiting by the EAC has been to strengthen protection of intellectual property rights owners.[70] Originally EAC policy proposed extensive *TRIPS*-plus provisions, including enforcement of all intellectual property rights and seizure of in-transit goods. However, the draft bill intended to implement this has been replaced with a proposed amendment to the *EAC Competition Act*.[71] The harmonised anti-counterfeiting measures now proposed only apply to copyright piracy and counterfeit trade marks and do not apply to goods in transit.[72] Kenya generally applies policies of the EAC on trade and investment[73] but has not indicated that it will narrow the scope of domestic counterfeiting laws following this change of EAC policy.[74]

---

64 *Anti-Counterfeit Act* No 13 of 2008 (Kenya).

65 *PAO* (n 18) [42].

66 Harrington and O'Hare argue that national interest has mobilised state institutions to implement *TRIPS*: John Harrington and Alasdair O'Hare, 'Framing the National Interest: Debating Intellectual Property and Access to Essential Medicines in Kenya,' (2014) 17(1–2) *Journal of World Intellectual Property* 16, 18–19.

67 Nicholas Wadhams, 'Kenya Pressured to Implement Anti-Counterfeit Law despite Access Fears' *IP Watch* (2 July 2009) https://web.archive.org/web/20220120213541/https://www.ip-watch.org/2009/07/02/kenya-pressured-to-implement-anti-counterfeit-law-despite-access-fears/.

68 Olatunji (n 12) 597.

69 Ibid 595.

70 Ibid 598.

71 Ibid 597.

72 Ibid 599–600; EAC Competition (Amendment) Bill 2015.

73 Schneider and Ferguson, Enforcement of Intellectual Property Rights in Africa (n 38) 401.

74 Statute Law (Miscellaneous Amendments) Act 2018 (Kenya).

3.1 The Scope of Protection

The *ACA* and *ACR* provide broad protections for intellectual property owners that extend beyond the enforcement provisions required by *TRIPS*.[75] Inspectors who are appointed under the *ACA* have the power to 'search and enter premises for the purpose of detaining and seizing counterfeit goods and have powers of arrest, without a warrant, any person reasonably suspected of having committed an offence under the Act'.[76] Following seizure, inspectors are required to record an inventory and seal and store the goods before removal to a depot.[77] Aggrieved persons can apply to the court for an order that the goods be returned, or goods are also returned if no charges are laid.[78] This meets the requirements found in Part III of *TRIPS*. However, Kenyan legislation does not always implement *TRIPS* minimum standards. For example, the *ACA* only requires release of seized goods that are suspected to be counterfeit to an importer where proceedings are not implemented within three months.[79] This permits seizure for longer than the 20-day maximum set out in *TRIPS* Article 55.[80]

TRIPS requires states to provide criminal procedures and penalties 'sufficient to provide a deterrent' for 'wilful trademark counterfeiting'.[81] States have discretion to determine the scope of criminal penalties.[82] Breaches of the Kenyan legislation result in severe penalties. Criminal penalties for a first offence under the Act are up to five years, and up to 15 years for subsequent convictions.[83] Fines also increase for subsequent offenders from three times the retail value of seized goods to five times the value for subsequent offences[84] and can be applied with or alternatively to sentences.

The broad definition of counterfeit goods and the scope of available protection for intellectual property rights in the *ACA* and *ACR* has attracted widespread criticism.[85] *TRIPS* standards only require WTO Members to regulate cross-border imports of goods that bear counterfeit trade marks or contain

---

75 Von Braun and Munyi (n 16) 247–248.

76 Schneider and Ferguson, Enforcement of Intellectual Property Rights in Africa (n 23) 276; Anti-Counterfeit Act 2008 (Kenya) ss 22, 23.

77 Anti-Counterfeit Act 2008 (Kenya) ss 44, 25(3).

78 Ibid ss 25(3), 28(1)c.

79 *Anti-Counterfeit Act* No 13 of 2008 (Kenya) s 28.

80 See Seuba (n 5) 300–303.

81 *TRIPS* (n 8) art 61.

82 Panel Report, China — Measures Affecting the Protection and Enforcement of Intellectual Property Rights, WTO Doc WT/DS362/R (26 January 2009).

83 *Anti-Counterfeit Act* No 13 of 2008 (Kenya) ss 44–46.

84 Ibid ss 44–46.

85 See Olatunji (n 12) 601–603; Von Braun and Munyi (n 16) 247–248.

pirated copyright materials for goods that qualify for domestic trade mark and copyright protection.[86] States are required to enforce rights where there is a *prima facie* case of infringement in the country of importation rather than in outside jurisdictions.[87] The *ACA* extends these protections for rights holders both inside and outside Kenya and protects 'intellectual property rights' generally rather than copyright and trade mark protected goods.

The broad scope of goods protected by the *ACA* and the failure of the statute to distinguish between counterfeit goods and generic medicine triggered concerns that authorities would be empowered to seize generic medicines relied on by Kenyans with HIV.[88] In *PAO*, three Kenyans who were reliant on generic HIV anti-viral medications successfully challenged the impact of the legislative definition of counterfeiting on their rights.[89] Article 43 of the Kenya Constitution protects the right to the highest attainable standard of health, providing:

> (1) Every person has the right— (a) to the highest attainable standard of health, which includes the right to health care services, including reproductive health care… (2) A person shall not be denied emergency medical treatment..[90]

The *ACA* originally defined counterfeiting to mean:

> …taking the following actions without the authority of the owner of intellectual property right subsisting in Kenya or elsewhere in respect of protected goods:
>
> (a) the manufacture, production, packaging, repackaging, labelling or making, whether in Kenya or elsewhere, of any goods whereby those protected goods are imitated in such manner and to such a degree that those other goods are identical or substantially similar copies of the protected goods;
>
> (b) the manufacture, production or making, whether in Kenya or elsewhere, the subject matter of that intellectual property, or a colourable imitation thereof so that the other goods are calculated to be confused with or to be taken as being the protected goods of the said owner or any goods manufactured, produced or made under his licence;
>
> (c) the manufacturing, producing or making of copies, in Kenya or elsewhere, in violation of an author's rights or related rights;
>
> (d) in relation to medicine, the deliberate and fraudulent mislabelling of medicine with respect to identity or source, whether or not such products have correct

86 *TRIPS* (n 8) pt III, s 4.

87 Ibid art 52.

88 Seuba (n 5) 365.

89 *PAO* (n 18).

90 The constitution also provides that 'The State shall take legislative, policy and other measures, including the setting of standards, to achieve the progressive realisation of the rights guaranteed under Article 43': *Constitution of Kenya* art 21(2).

> ingredients, wrong ingredients, have sufficient active ingredients or have fake packaging.[91]

The definition is limited by the provision that 'nothing in this paragraph shall derogate from the existing provisions under the Industrial Property Act, [2001 (No. 3 of 2001)]'.[92] The operation of the limitation is unclear.[93] Prior to the introduction of the *ACA*, Kenyans could import generic versions of on-patent drugs, as the Industrial Property Act permitted parallel importation of non-counterfeit goods without permission from the intellectual property owner.[94]

The Court found that the scope of the legislation was inconsistent with constitutional protections for the right to life, human dignity and health. The Court recognised that trade in counterfeit goods needed to be prohibited and that intellectual property owners had rights to benefit from their innovations.[95] However, in prioritising enforcement of intellectual property rights, the legislation had not focused on achieving its stated objective of the protection of individuals from substandard medicine.[96] Although protection of consumers may have been 'a collateral issue in the minds of the drafters', the provisions that attempted to address this were ambiguous and 'those charged with the responsibility of enforcement may not have had a clear understanding of the difference between generic and counterfeit medicines'.[97] The Court agreed with the petitioners' concern that section 2 of the *ACA* was broad enough to include generic medication.[98] This could adversely impact manufacture, sale and distribution of generic medication and impact its availability, posing a genuine threat to the rights to life, dignity and health of the petitioners who relied on this affordably-priced medication to treat HIV and AIDS.[99] The Court declared that the legislation breached the petitioners' right to life, human dignity and health 'in so far as it affects access to affordable and essential drugs and medications particularly generic drugs'.[100]

The decision in *PAO* demonstrates the complex interplay between protecting the public from goods that may negatively impact individual health and safety, and avoiding impeding access to medicines because very broad seizure

---

91 *Anti-Counterfeit Act 2008* (Kenya) s 2.
92 Ibid.
93 Olatunji (n 12) 602.
94 *Industrial Property Act* No 3 of 2001 (Kenya) s 58(2).
95 *PAO* (n 18) [70].
96 Ibid [83].
97 Ibid [83]–[84].
98 Ibid [78].
99 Ibid.
100 Ibid [87].

powers create uncertainty as to the type of goods that can be seized. This is particularly problematic where there are limited resources available to supply medicines to many individuals who require life-prolonging medicine such as HIV retrovirals and rely on generic medicines distributed by not-for-profit organisations.

3.2 Legislative Reform

PAO has been widely recognised as a successful use of constitutional rights to strengthen access to medicine.[101] However, the legislative response to the decision has been problematic. In *PAO*, the Court did not determine that any legislative provision was unconstitutional but found that it was 'incumbent' on the state to review and amend section 2 of the *ACA* to ensure protection of the right to health for individuals, particularly those dependent on generic drugs.[102] Originally the reference to 'or elsewhere' in the definition of anti-counterfeiting was deleted in 2014 amendments.[103] Yet 2018 amendments restored the original scope by introducing the additional words 'or outside Kenya' to the first part of the definition of counterfeiting.[104] This does not address the problem identified in *PAO* and the definition remains too broad.[105] It not only includes patents but products that misrepresent themselves as other products with a reputation, even if a similar trade mark is not used.[106] One of the reasons that these rights are not protected by the enforcement provisions of *TRIPS* is the complexity of assessing breaches of some types of intellectual property, such as patent rights. In contrast, the application of a trade mark by an unauthorised party is more straightforward for customs officials to identify.[107]

Since 2018, the operational approach taken to anti-counterfeiting in Kenya has undergone extensive reform. Reforms undertaken by the Anti-Counterfeit Authority include: developing an inter-agency approach; changing its name

---

[101] See Edward Halle, 'Access to Essential Medicine as Part of the Right to Health in Africa: Access to Essential Medicine under International Human Rights Law, the Case of Kenya and South Africa,' (2018) 11(3) *Asia Pacific Journal of Health Law & Ethics* 105, 128.

[102] *PAO* (n 18) [88].

[103] *Statute Law (Miscellaneous) (Amendment) Act* No 18 of 2014 (Kenya) 283.

[104] Ibid 353.

[105] Wilfrid O Lusi, 'Effective Anti-Counterfeiting Legal System: A Key Enabler for Growth of Kenya's Pharmaceutical Industry' (Doctoral dissertation, Strathmore University, 2020) 52.

[106] See *Republic of Kenya v Anti-Counterfeit Agency and the Department of Public Prosecutions* (Judicial Review Misc No 36 of 2017, Judicial Review Division of the Kenyan High Court, 7 May 2020) ('*Santa King Ice*').

[107] Seuba notes there can be some complexities in this assessment too: (n 5) 297.

from the Anti-Counterfeit Agency to reflect a higher institutional status; expanding border protection and training of judicial staff; conducting a National Baseline Survey about counterfeiting; and introducing a recordal system that requires intellectual property owners to register their products with the Anti-Counterfeit Authority and attach an anti-counterfeit device to all compliant imported products.[108] Recent legislative reforms have also expanded the protection mechanisms available for intellectual property owners who notify the Commissioner of suspected counterfeit imports.[109]

The *Baseline Survey* conducted in 2019 as part of reforms indicates that counterfeit goods are a serious concern, negatively impacting individual health in Kenya.[110] The survey provides insights into consumer attitudes towards counterfeit goods in Kenya. Twenty-four per cent of surveyed respondents said reasons that they would knowingly use counterfeits included 'brand name, low price, easily available, product popularity, origin of product and warranty'.[111] Only 10 per cent of surveyed individuals who had possessed counterfeit products said that they reported the counterfeit products to authorities.[112] For respondents who indicated having not reported to any government agency, the reasons given included their inability to recognise counterfeit products, with the further concerns identified that 'the officials to report to are corrupt; costly and timewasting process; do not know the reporting agencies; do not trust the reporting agencies; fear of reporting; and ignorance'.[113]

There have been significant delays with the implementation of the recordal system for intellectual property rights in addition to intellectual property specific registration systems.[114] In 2019, an *ACA* representative characterised this mechanism as a response to the ongoing growth in fake counterfeits in Kenya, which meant that goods had been less likely to be inspected at the border.[115]

---

[108] See Anti-Counterfeit Agency, *Realigned Strategic Plan 2019–2022* (2019) https://www.aca.go.ke/images/downloads/ACA-Realigned-Strategic-Plan-2019-2022.pdf; *Anti-Counterfeit Act 2008* (Kenya) s 34B.

[109] *Anti-Counterfeit Act 2008* (Kenya) s 34.

[110] Anti-Counterfeit Agency, *The National Baseline Survey on the Extent of Counterfeit and Other Forms of Illicit Trade in Kenya: Executive Brief Summary* (2020) 4 https://www.aca.go.ke/images/2020/National_Baseline_Survey_Counterfeit_and_Illicit_Trade_In_Kenya.pdf ('*National Baseline Survey*').

[111] Ibid 39.

[112] Ibid 40.

[113] Ibid.

[114] Anti-Counterfeit Authority, 'Public Notice No 2/2022 of 24th May 2022 on Commencement of Recordation of Intellectual Property Rights' (Kenyan Anti-Counterfeit Authority, 24 May 2022).

[115] Pauline Mpungu, 'Kenya has a Fake Cosmetics Problem' *Aljazeera* (online, 21 June 2019) https://www.aljazeera.com/features/2019/6/21/kenya-has-a-fake-cosmetics-problem; Pauline Mpungu, 'Fake Cosmetics from China Squeeze Kenyan Producers

However, the legislation has been broadly criticised as unnecessarily onerous for intellectual property owners.[116] It prohibits the import of any unbranded goods into Kenya, unless they are raw materials.[117] This is likely to inflate the cost of previously unbranded goods if it requires changes to labelling, registration of trade mark rights and recordal registration.[118] Engagement between the Anti-Counterfeit Authority and the legal industry indicates that the Anti-Counterfeit Authority currently lacks the resources needed to record all relevant intellectual property rights.[119] Requiring recordal for all imported goods except raw materials extends well beyond the *TRIPS* recordal mechanism. *TRIPS* only requires WTO Members to enable (not require) intellectual property owners to record their copyright and trade mark rights and request suspension of releases of goods that are seized under suspicion that these rights are breached.[120]

4 THE HUMAN RIGHTS IMPLICATIONS OF COUNTERFEIT GOODS IN KENYA DURING THE COVID-19 PANDEMIC

The following analysis uses seizure reports, the legislation and Kenyan anti-counterfeit cases to analyse the human rights implications of anti-counterfeiting legislation that governs imported counterfeit goods in Kenya. The *ACA* estimates that 70 per cent of counterfeit goods detected in Kenya are imported, most frequently from Asia and other countries in Africa.[121] Significant quantities of counterfeit goods are in circulation in Sub-Saharan Africa. In late 2021, a two-month joint operation between Interpol and Afripol in 20 African countries, Flash-IPPA, resulted in seizures of 12 million illicit health products, including significant quantities of counterfeit Covid-19

---

and Officials' *Aljazeera* (online, 22 June 2019) https://www.aljazeera.com/economy/2019/6/22/fake-cosmetics-from-china-squeeze-kenyan-producers-officials.

[116] William Maema, 'Proposed Law on Counterfeits will Hurt Businesses' *Business Daily Africa* (online, 28 May 2018) https://www.businessdailyafrica.com/analysis/ideas/Proposed-law-on-counterfeits-will-hurt-businesses/4259414-4584474-6i1s0t/index.html.

[117] *Anti-Counterfeit Act 2008* (Kenya) ss 32(j), 32(k), 34B.

[118] Maema (n 116).

[119] 'Kenya: 1 January 2023 Deadline Approaching to File Recordals' *Spoor & Fisher* (4 November 2022) https://spoor.com/kenya-1-january-2023-deadline-approaching-to-file-recordals/.

[120] *TRIPS* (n 8) art 51.

[121] Sharon Moambo and Alfred Onyango, 'Kenya Leveraging on Tech to Combat Counterfeits' *The Star* (online, 16 June 2022) https://www.the-star.co.ke/business/kenya/2022-06-16-kenya-leveraging-on-tech-to-combat-counterfeits/.

goods.[122] Seizures included 1,600 rapid Covid-19 tests and more than 208,000 Covid-19 protection masks.[123]

In Kenya, the Anti-Counterfeit Authority has reported seizures of counterfeit face masks, diagnostic tests and sanitisers during the Covid-19 pandemic: if substandard, these products may significantly impair the treatment and control of Covid-19 and place healthcare workers at risk.[124] Compulsory face masks have been an important part of infection control strategy at different times in the pandemic.[125] Primarily the information about these seizures has been communicated in economic terms. For example, the Anti-Counterfeit Authority reported seizing counterfeit Covid-19 consumer goods valued at 13 million KsH in the three months prior to June 2020.[126]

There is a lack of data available to ascertain the true nature of the threat posed by counterfeit goods in Kenya. Media reports indicate there are serious health concerns posed by counterfeit goods. When counterfeit diagnostic tests were seized in March 2020, online reports stated 600 tests had already been sold and may have circulated in the community.[127] 20,000 counterfeit 3M masks were seized in a Nairobi hospital in May 2021 in response to a report of concerns about quality from the hospital to the Anti-Counterfeit Authority, following internal inspection of the Chinese imports.[128] There is no evidence that authorities systematically test seized goods to determine whether they are substandard. Globally, data is incomplete and the reliability of data that is often collected by private actors is treated with caution.[129]

There have been no reported seizures of counterfeit vaccines by the Anti-Counterfeit Authority in Kenya. However, the media reported that Johnson & Johnson vaccines were being administered outside of govern-

122 'Pharmaceutical Crime' (n 36).

123 Ibid.

124 'ACA Destroys Goods Worth 27M KES in Athi River' *Anti-Counterfeit Authority* (30 June 2020) https://www.aca.go.ke/media-center/news-and-events/241-counterfeit-goods-worth-ksh-100-million-destroyed-in-mombasa.

125 Nancy Augutu and Magdalene Saya, 'Kenya Lifts Longstanding Mandatory Wearing of Masks' *The Star* (online, 11 March 2022) https://www.the-star.co.ke/news/2022-03-11-kenya-lifts-longstanding-mandatory-wearing-of-masks/; Hellen Githaiga, 'Kenya Reinstates Mask Mandate Indoors' *The East African* (online, June 20, 2022) https://www.theeastafrican.co.ke/tea/science-health/kenya-reinstates-mask-mandate-indoors-3854140.

126 'ACA Destroys Goods Worth 27M KES in Athi River' (n 124).

127 'Kenya Raids Shop Selling "Fake" Coronavirus Testing Kits' *Aljazeera* (online, 17 March 2020) https://www.aljazeera.com/news/2020/3/17/kenya-raids-shop-selling-fake-coronavirus-testing-kits.

128 'Counterfeit 3M Co. N95 Face Masks Worth Ksh 21 Million Seized in a Leading Hospital in Nairobi' (n 2).

129 See Seuba (n 5) 67–71.

ment channels for a charge, around the time that the government announced increased supply of Johnson & Johnson vaccines.[130] Concerns about counterfeit vaccines prompted a decision in April 2021 to prevent private importation of vaccines in Kenya.[131] Although private providers play an important role in healthcare delivery in Kenya, the import restriction means that private healthcare providers, including philanthropic organisations, are restricted in their ability to increase access to vaccines that can help Kenya control the spread of Covid-19, consistent with its human right to health obligations.[132] The restriction makes it easier for individuals to distinguish between government-issued vaccines, which are issued for free, and counterfeit goods. However, scarcity may still prompt Kenyans to access counterfeit vaccines out of government channels. The concern about state problems with controlling the spread of counterfeit vaccines has broader implications as production capacity for vaccines increases in Kenya and supply of the product increases.[133] In March 2022, Moderna announced an agreement to produce vaccines in Kenya which could expand to include fill/finish and packaging of vaccines.[134] Kenya is also part of the mRNA technology hub established by the WHO to facilitate more equitable distribution of vaccines.[135] A critical part of the effectiveness of this vaccine hub is ensuring secure distribution of the vaccines it aims to produce.[136]

---

[130] Sharon Moambo, 'Don't Pay for Vaccine, Kagwe Says after J&J Fake Jabs Case' *The Star* (online, 9 September 2021) https://www.the-star.co.ke/news/2021-09-09-dont-pay-for-vaccine-kagwe-says-after-jj-fake-jabs-case/.

[131] 'Kenya Blocks Private Covid Vaccine Imports on Fear of Fakes' *New York Times* (online, 3 April 2021) https://www.nytimes.com/2021/04/03/world/kenya-covid-vaccine.html.

[132] See Catherine Kyobutungi, 'The Ins and Outs of Kenya's COVID-19 Vaccine Rollout Plan' *The Conversation* (3 March 2021) https://theconversation.com/the-ins-and-outs-of-kenyas-covid-19-vaccine-rollout-plan-156310.

[133] See Ashley Furlong, 'Moderna to Share Vaccine Tech, Commits to Never Enforce COVID-19 Jab Patents' *Politico* (8 March 2022) https://www.politico.eu/article/moderna-share-vaccine-tech-never-enforce-covid19-patents/.

[134] 'Moderna to Build mRNA Vaccine Manufacturing Facility in Kenya' *Reuters* (online, 8 March 2022) https://www.reuters.com/business/healthcare-pharmaceuticals/moderna-build-mrna-vaccine-manufacturing-facility-kenya-2022-03-07/.

[135] David Walwyn, 'How Drug Companies are Sidestepping the WHO's Technology Transfer Hub in Africa' *The Conversation* (13 March 2022) https://theconversation.com/how-drug-companies-are-sidestepping-the-whos-technology-transfer-hub-in-africa-179029.

[136] See Harsha Chauhan et al, 'Blockchain Enabled Transparent and Anti-Counterfeiting Supply of COVID-19 Vaccine Vials' (2021) 9(1) *Vaccines* 1239.

4.1 Right to Health

In international human rights law, states must address counterfeit activities as part of their obligations to respect, protect and fulfil the human right to health. International human rights law obliges states to protect individuals from the actions of third party counterfeiters who import inferior-quality counterfeit goods that pose potential threats to health and safety.[137] *ICESCR* also obligates states to provide access to quality medication.[138] Obligations of comparable priority to core minimum obligations include '[t]o take measures to prevent, treat and control epidemic and endemic diseases'.[139]

Counterfeiting activities engage the protection requirement of the tripartite obligations to respect, protect and fulfil the human right to health. States must shield individuals from the harmful activities of counterfeiters importing products that are harmful to their health.[140] Counterfeiters do not have the same incentive as trade mark owners to produce quality products and may not comply with health and safety standards.[141] The measures that states are expected to provide to realise the right to health engage a range of actors. Where counterfeit products are involved, protecting the human right to health also engages actors operating outside the sphere of public health, such as customs, counterfeiting and law enforcement agencies. The Anti-Counterfeit Authority has moved to develop an inter-agency approach, but this primarily focuses on other enforcement agencies rather than engagement with public health agencies and does not focus on human rights protection.[142] Public health can and does engage with other actors, but human rights law clearly obliges states to engage with other actors to fulfil their protection obligations pursuant to the human right to health[143] to control and manage the spread of Covid-19. It is a core obligation for the right to health that states ensure that their national public health strategies and plans of action are periodically reviewed using participatory and transparent processes against human rights benchmarks.[144]

---

[137] *General Comment 14* (n 9) [35].

[138] Ibid [12], [17], [43]; *International Covenant on Economic, Social and Cultural Rights*, opened for signature 16 December 1966, 993 UNTS 3 (entered into force 3 January 1976) art 12 ('*ICESCR*').

[139] *General Comment 14* (n 9) [44].

[140] Ibid [35].

[141] The complex nature of this problem is considered in Chapter 6.

[142] 'About Us – Partnerships' *Anti-Counterfeit Authority* (2022) https://www.aca.go.ke/about-us-aca/partners.

[143] Lisa Forman and Gillian MacNaughton, 'Moving Theory into Practice: Human Rights Impact Assessment of Intellectual Property Rights in Trade Agreements' (2015) 7(1) *Journal of Human Rights Practice* 109, 118, 131–132.

[144] *General Comment 14* (n 9) [43](5).

In the Covid-19 pandemic, quality concerns are relevant for diverse medical products that are used to prevent infection, including masks and other personal protective equipment, diagnostic tests and pharmaceuticals for prevention and treatment of the disease. Quality is an essential consideration for realisation of the right to health: 'health facilities, goods and services must also be scientifically and medically appropriate and of good quality.'[145] There have been serious concerns identified about the health risks posed by counterfeit therapeutic goods using trade marks without authorisation.[146] Reported seizures of counterfeit diagnostic test kits, masks and hand sanitiser in Kenya also engage quality concerns. In the Covid-19 pandemic, *ICESCR* obliges states to recognise the critical role of healthcare workers and provide them with 'proper protective clothing and equipment against contagion'.[147]

The discovery of 20,000 counterfeit masks in a Kenyan hospital highlights the need to protect healthcare workers. Ensuring that there is adequate PPE for healthcare workers directly engages states' human rights obligations to 'adopt measures against…occupational health hazards' as part of a 'coherent national policy to minimise the risk of occupational…diseases'.[148] States are also obliged to protect healthcare workers as individuals: the Committee on Economic, Social and Cultural Rights ('CESCR') explicitly identifies failure to protect workers from practices detrimental to health as a violation of the right to health in *General Comment 14*, the body's interpretation of the obligations entailed by the right to health.[149] Where the state does not employ the worker, it is still obliged to take 'all necessary measures to safeguard persons within their jurisdiction from infringements of the right to health by third parties'.[150] Healthcare workers play a critical role in ensuring the state is able to diagnose Covid-19 infection and provide treatment.[151] Increased contagion amongst

---

145 Ibid [12].

146 Kaho Kwok and Lynne S Taylor, 'Analysis of Counterfeit Cialis® Tablets Using Raman Microscopy and Multivariate Curve Resolution' (2012) 66 *Journal of Pharmaceutical and Biomedical Analysis* 126, 126; Dégardin, Roggo and Margot (n 26) 169; World Health Organization and International Medical Products Anti-Counterfeiting Taskforce (IMPACT), *Counterfeit Drugs Kill!* (May 2008) https://www.gphf.org/images/downloads/library/whoimpact2008_counterfeit_drugs_kill.pdf.

147 Committee on Economic, Social and Cultural Rights, *Statement on the Coronavirus Disease (COVID-19) Pandemic and Economic, Social and Cultural Rights*, UN Doc E/C.12/2020/1 (17 April 2020) [13] ('*Statement on the Coronavirus Disease (COVID-19) Pandemic and Economic, Social and Cultural Rights*').

148 *General Comment 14* (n 9) [36].

149 Ibid [51].

150 Ibid.

151 See CESCR, *Statement on the Coronavirus Disease (COVID-19) Pandemic and Economic, Social and Cultural Rights* (n 147) [13].

healthcare workers negatively impacts collective health, as it can increase the likelihood of transmission to other patients in healthcare systems who may be particularly vulnerable to the disease, as well as to healthcare colleagues.[152] Other workers who are integral to the effective functioning of public health responses to the pandemic, including aged care workers, quarantine operational staff and police forces, can be exposed if inadequate PPE enters their supply chains. Concerns about the lack of adequate PPE prompted industrial action by Kenyan healthcare workers during the Covid-19 pandemic.[153]

This analysis highlights the serious threats posed by counterfeit goods in Kenya during the Covid-19 pandemic for the right to health, engaging state obligations to protect individuals from third parties who pose threats to their health, such as counterfeiters.[154] Although it is difficult to determine the direct impact of counterfeit goods on health in the Covid-19 pandemic, the evidence of death from other counterfeit goods used to treat epidemic and endemic diseases in Sub-Saharan Africa indicates that a serious threat exists.[155]

4.2 Right to Life

Problems with the effectiveness of anti-counterfeiting measures in Sub-Saharan Africa pose concerns that existing border control measures that primarily focus on enforcement of private intellectual property rights are inadequate to protect the human right to life enshrined in Article 6 of the *ICCPR*. WHO modelling on deaths from substandard malaria drugs and substandard antibiotics indicates the impact of substandard and falsified medication in Sub-Saharan Africa.[156] Although the right to health is a right subject to progressive realisation, the right to life is a non-derogable right.[157] The right includes a duty on parties to protect life by taking 'appropriate measures to address the general conditions in society that may give rise to direct threats to life' and general conditions may include 'the prevalence of life-threatening disease'.[158] Where necessary, meas-

---

[152] Mariachiara Ippolito et al, 'Medical Masks and Respirators for the Protection of Healthcare Workers from SARS-CoV-2 and Other Viruses' (2020) 26(4) *Pulmonology* 204.

[153] 'Kenya: Pandemic Health Workers Lack Protection' Human Rights Watch (21 October 2021) https://www.hrw.org/news/2021/10/21/kenya-pandemic-health-workers-lack-protection.

[154] *General Comment 14* (n 9) [35].

[155] Dégardin, Roggo and Margot (n 26) 169.

[156] See WHO (n 40).

[157] *International Covenant on Civil and Political Rights*, opened for signature 16 December 1966, 999 UNTS 171 (entered into force 23 March 1976) art 4 ('*ICCPR*').

[158] Human Rights Committee, *General Comment 36, on Article 6 of the International Covenant on Civil and Political Rights, on the Right to Life*, 124th sess, UN Doc CCPR/C/GC/36 (3 September 2019) [26] ('*General Comment 36*').

ures include 'access…to essential goods and services such as…health care…[as well as] bolstering effective emergency health services'.[159] Individuals are entitled 'to be free from acts and omissions that are intended or may be expected to cause their unnatural or premature death'.[160] Where threats are reasonably foreseeable, *ICCPR* Article 6 requires states to exercise 'due diligence to protect the lives of individuals against deprivations caused by persons or entities whose conduct is not attributable to the state' where there are 'reasonably foreseeable threats and life-threatening situations that can result in loss of life'.[161] States should 'establish a legal framework' and 'adopt any appropriate laws or other measures in order to protect life from all reasonably foreseeable threats, including from threats emanating from private persons and entities'.[162] States are obliged to take '[r]easonable positive measures that do not impose disproportionate burdens on them in response to reasonably foreseeable threats to life originating from private persons and entities whose conduct is not attributable to the State'.[163] In the Covid-19 pandemic, substandard counterfeit pharmaceuticals could directly cause death, and substandard counterfeit PPE could indirectly cause death if it fails to protect individuals from infection. However, whether or not investing substantial resources in anti-counterfeiting regimes or other approaches to prevent this is a disproportionate burden on Kenya is difficult to determine in the absence of comprehensive information about the risks posed within the territory and evidence of deaths directly related to counterfeit medical products in the Covid-19 pandemic.

4.3 Rights to a Fair Trial and Procedural Fairness

The inclusion of criminal penalties in the legislation considered in this chapter raises issues regarding the protections provided pursuant to Article 14 of the *ICCPR*.[164] These rights include the human right to a fair trial, including the entitlement to 'a fair and public hearing by a competent, independent and impartial tribunal established by law' in determination of criminal charges.[165] Counterfeit action can engage human rights concerns that effective participation, access to justice and equality of arms in any dispute can be impacted by

---

[159] Ibid [26].
[160] Ibid [3].
[161] Ibid [7].
[162] Ibid [18].
[163] Ibid [21].
[164] Human Rights Committee, *General Comment No 32. Article 14: Right to Equality Before Courts and Tribunals and to Fair Trial*, 90th sess, UN Doc CCPR/C/GC/32 (23 August 2007) [3] ('General Comment 32').
[165] Ibid.

resource disparities between right owners and importers.[166] Various safeguards are enshrined in Kenyan law to protect these rights. The High Court has comprehensively analysed procedural fairness in relation to a seizure pursuant to the *ACA* and found there was no inconsistency, noting that constitutional protection also existed in relation to a fair trial and fair administration.[167] Although case law demonstrates that protection is available for civil and political rights through courts,[168] relevant standards are not always met in practice. The seizure of trade marked goods that were imported before the expungement of a trade mark from the register was in breach of the applicant's constitutional right to fair administrative action.[169] Ongoing monitoring is important. The nature and severity of sentences issued in relation to counterfeit activities[170] should be monitored, in light of the 15-year penalties available for subsequent offenders under the *ACA* regime. The initial five-year penalty is consistent with other jurisdictions such as Australia but it is also considered to be a severe penalty in that jurisdiction.[171]

4.4 Right to Privacy

Investigation and prosecution of counterfeiting activities engages the human right to privacy,[172] which relevantly protects personal information.[173] However, this right can be limited in written law if it is 'reasonable and justifiable in an

---

[166] Ibid [13]. Seuba (n 5) 48.

[167] *Santa King Ice* (n 106) [33].

[168] See *Panyahululu Co. Ltd and Anti-Counterfeit Agency and Another* (Petition No. 59 of 2013, High Court of Kenya at Mombasa, Constitution and Human Rights Division, 11 October 2018).

[169] *Uwin Investments v Registrar of Trade Marks* (Judicial Review Misc. No 60 of 2018, Judicial Review Division of the Kenyan High Court at Mombasa, 10 June 2019) [56].

[170] *General Comment 32* (n 164) [15].

[171] *Ly v The Queen* (2007) 74 IPR 1.

[172] See also *Universal Declaration of Human Rights*, GA Res 217A (III), UN GAOR, UN Doc A/810 (10 December 1948) arts 12, 17 ('*UDHR*').

[173] Jonathan Griffiths, 'Criminal Liability for Intellectual Property Infringement in Europe: The Role of Fundamental Rights' in Christophe Geiger (ed), *Criminal Enforcement of Intellectual Property: A Handbook of Contemporary Research* (Edward Elgar Publishing, 2012) 191, 207–208. See also Human Rights Committee, *CCPR General Comment No 16: Article 17 (Right to Privacy), The Right to Respect of Privacy, Family, Home and Correspondence, and Protection of Honour and Reputation*, 32nd sess (8 April 1988) [10] ('*General Comment 16*'); Alberto J Cerda Silva, 'Enforcing Intellectual Property Rights by Diminishing Privacy: How the Anti-Counterfeiting Trade Agreement Jeopardizes the Right to Privacy' (2011) 26 *American University International Law Review* 601.

open and democratic society based on human dignity, equality and freedom'.[174] Article 31 of the Kenya Constitution protects the right to privacy, including rights for individuals not to have 'persons, home or property searched' and 'possessions seized'. In *Nduba*, the individual complained that the search of their premises and seizure of goods by an *ACA* inspector violated Article 31.[175] The Kenyan High Court rejected the claim, finding the inspector's activities were consistent with the written provisions of the *ACA*. The decision recognised that the legislation had the objective of protecting intellectual property in alignment with the constitutional protection.[176] The inspector's actions were consistent with the emphasis of the Human Rights Committee that restrictions in law not be arbitrary.[177] Proportionate limits on privacy are permitted but this requires 'a sound legal regime integrated by checks and balances'.[178] The provision of an individual, justiciable right to privacy in the Kenya Constitution is an important check and balance on the Kenyan legal regime.

4.5 Right to Property and Right to Benefits from Science and Culture

The Kenya Constitution recognises rights to property, including that '[t]he State shall support, promote and protect the intellectual property rights of the people of Kenya'.[179] This right has been recognised as support for the provisions of the *ACA*.[180] Although there is no human right to property protected in the *ICESCR* and the *ICCPR*, the right of individuals to benefit from their artistic, literary and scientific productions is also protected in *ICESCR* Article 15. The scope of human rights protection for intellectual property in *ICESCR* Article 15(1)(c) has been interpreted quite narrowly by CESCR and limited to individual authors.[181] However, the need for access to applications of benefits of science such as medical products during the Covid-19 pandemic highlights the relevance of Article 15(1)(b). Equitable access to Covid-19

---

[174] *Kenyan Constitution* art 24(1).

[175] *Paul Kihara Nduba T/A Shikanisha Shoes Collection vs The AG and ACA* (Petition No. 17 of 2015, High Court of Kenya at Nakuru, 17 June 2016) (*Nduba*).

[176] *Nduba* 5.

[177] *General Comment 16* (n 173) [4].

[178] Seuba (n 5) 201.

[179] *Kenyan Constitution* art 40(5).

[180] *Nduba*, 5.

[181] Committee on Economic, Social and Cultural Rights, *General Comment No 17: The Right of Everyone to Benefit from the Protection of the Moral and Material Interests Resulting from Any Scientific, Literary or Artistic Production of Which He or She Is the Author (Art 15, Para 1(c) of the Covenant)*, UN ESCOR, 35th sess, UN Doc E/C.12/GC/17 (12 January 2006) [2] ('*General Comment 17*').

vaccines engages questions of how 'balance must be reached between intellectual property and the open access and sharing of scientific knowledge and its applications, especially those linked to the realization of other economic, social and cultural rights, such as the rights to health, education and food'.[182] CESCR has emphasised that states have obligations to cooperate to ensure human rights to access safe vaccines internationally during the pandemic.[183] Preventing vaccine counterfeiting should be recognised as part of this obligation to cooperate: safe vaccines require an assurance of quality that aligns with the obligation to protect individuals from the acts of third party counterfeiters that are harmful to their health.

If there are serious concerns that the legal regime for protection is inadequate to deter counterfeit intellectual property goods, this presents further human rights concerns. Sihanya notes, 'Kenya and other African states have historically suffered challenges in accessing diagnostics, cures, and vaccines, or relevant technologies, and equipment or facilities due to the potentially restrictive nature of IP rights in the pharmaceutical industry.'[184] For intellectual property owners to be willing to both distribute intellectual property-protected products and invest in infrastructure, effective protection is necessary.[185] Effective intellectual property enforcement to detect and deter counterfeit goods incentivises distribution of medical products that are necessary to fulfil the right to health and to access applications of the benefits of science which can support the realisation of related economic, social and cultural rights. Investment in infrastructure is critical to technology transfer for manufacturing certain goods such as mRNA Covid-19 vaccines.[186] The pandemic has benefi-

---

[182] Committee on Economic, Social and Cultural Rights, *General comment No 25 (2020) on Science and Economic, Social and Cultural Rights (Article 15 (1) (b), (2), (3) and (4) of the International Covenant on Economic, Social and Cultural Rights)*, 67th sess, UN Doc E/C.12/GC/25 (30 April 2020) [62] ('General Comment 25').

[183] Committee on Economic, Social and Cultural Rights, *Statement on Universal Affordable Vaccination against Coronavirus Disease (COVID-19), International Cooperation and Intellectual Property*, UN Doc C.12/2021/1 (23 April 2021) [3] ('*Statement on Universal Affordable Vaccination against Coronavirus Disease (COVID-19), International Cooperation and Intellectual Property*').

[184] See Ben Sihanya, 'Intellectual Property, Innovation, and Technology Transfer in Health in Kenya and Africa: Case of COVID-19 and Malaria' in Ben Sihanya, *Intellectual Property and Innovation Law in Kenya and Africa: Cases and Materials* (IPILKA 2) (Sihanya Mentoring & Innovative Lawyering, 2020).

[185] See Keith E Maskus, *Private Rights and Public Problems: The Global Economics of Intellectual Property in the 21st Century* (Peterson Institute for International Economics, 2012) 229–230, 11.

[186] See Siva Thambisetti et al, 'Addressing Vaccine Inequity During the Covid-19 Pandemic: The TRIPS Intellectual Property Waiver Proposal and Beyond' (2022) 81(2) *Cambridge Law Journal* 384.

cially accelerated technology transfer for vaccines but mechanisms to detect, deter and address the circulation of substandard goods remain critical to assure safety and quality. Effective *TRIPS* enforcement mechanisms can aid this where substandard goods are also counterfeit.

4.6 Monitoring and Accountability

Monitoring and accountability is important to ensure that states are meeting their human rights obligations. The consideration of a range of human rights in constitutional challenges surrounding the operation of the *ACA* in relation to civil and political rights evidences monitoring and accountability of human rights. This demonstrates the important role of individual justiciable rights, although their use may depend heavily on availability of resources for individuals who wish to assert those rights. These decisions should not be confined to individual remedies when they identify human rights problems with legislation. Although the High Court identified constitutional issues with the operation of the *ACA* for rights to life, health and dignity in *PAO*, the laws have not been changed to adequately address this, instead entrenching broad protection for intellectual property owners. This indicates problems with accountability for economic, social and cultural rights protection. Failure to implement legislation that is consistent with providing access to essential medication also means that the right to health may not be protected effectively.

4.7 Participation, Empowerment and Transparency

Problems with insufficiently transparent available data associated with counterfeit goods to assess health concerns presents problems for monitoring the human rights impact of counterfeit goods in Kenya. Systematic sample testing of seized goods may provide greater understanding of the scope of the problem and the type of resources required to focus on protection of the right to health as well as protection of property rights.

A human rights framework should also promote stakeholder consultation for decisions that have a significant impact on human rights. The 2019 National Baseline Survey provides information about some of the health impacts of counterfeit goods on individuals in Kenya,[187] and greater understanding of why consumers use counterfeit goods.[188] Reported motivations indicate that knowing use and acceptance of counterfeit goods can be difficult to change

[187] See *National Baseline Survey* (n 110) 40.

[188] Ibid 39.

for complex reasons.[189] Media coverage can be a critical part of stimulating public discourse to focus on change that benefits human rights objectives, by translating complex technical information and jargon about health impacts into plain language that strengthens public awareness and understanding of health impacts associated with regulation of counterfeit goods, particularly when the issue involves complex concepts of access to generic medication.[190] However, concern about recent changes to requirements for recordal suggest limited weight is given to consultation regarding trade mark enforcement.[191]

Consumer education can also influence attitudes to reporting counterfeit goods to authorities, an important part of participation that will better address human rights concerns associated with substandard counterfeit goods. Self-help tools that are already in use in Sub-Saharan Africa, such as using mobile phones to verify the provenance of pharmaceutical products with scratch codes, may be a mechanism to counter some of these issues.[192] Being able to independently verify whether a good is counterfeit could be linked to an app for reporting counterfeit goods to the government that then guides individuals on how to deal with counterfeit products.

4.8 International Cooperation and Assistance

The insufficiency of current Kenyan anti-counterfeiting mechanisms to protect rights to health and life engages the obligations of all states party to *ICESCR* to cooperate to achieve economic, social and cultural human rights.[193] Osei Tutu has argued that the health and safety justification for policing counterfeit goods may not justify the resources committed by states in addressing counterfeiting activities.[194] This is particularly relevant for less developed states

---

189 Ibid.

190 See National Empowerment Network of People Living with HIV/AIDS in Kenya (NEPHAK) et al, 'Joint Press Statement by Health Activists to Engage Government for Review of the Anti- Counterfeit Act' (31 October 2013) http://nephak.or.ke/joint-press-statement-by-health-activists-to-engage-government-for-review-of-the-anti-counterfeit-act/.

191 See Olatunji (n 12) 603–604.

192 Schneider and Ferguson, *Enforcement of Intellectual Property Rights in Africa* (n 38) 24–25.

193 *ICESCR* (n 138) art 2(1). See also *Charter of the United Nations* ss 1(1), 13(1)(b), 55, 56.

194 J Janewa Osei Tutu, 'Corporate "Human Rights" to Intellectual Property Protection?' (2015) 55(1) *Santa Clara Law Review* 1; J Janewa Osei Tutu, 'Private Rights for the Public Good' (2013) 66(4) *SMU Law Review* 767. Maskus recognises health benefits as one of the strongest incentives for poorer countries to invest in expensive machinery to implement effective anti-counterfeiting regimes, but calcu-

with greater resource constraints. CESCR has interpreted the right to health to include a recognition of states' obligations to assist other states in realising the right to health.[195] Part of this requires states to ensure that their engagement in international agreements made subsequent to *ICESCR* is consistent with the right to health.[196] These obligations should influence trade negotiators. If international agreements and organisations enshrine trade incentives that require poorly resourced countries to implement onerous and expensive enforcement machinery, this may divert resources that could be better spent on raising socio-economic standards. Resources are essential to the realisation of the right to health in all countries, and relevant to obligations for international assistance to realise core minimum standards of health in other states.[197] Emphasis on cooperation and intelligence-sharing may be significantly more important and, where countries must choose between competing resource demands, more expeditious and effective.[198]

4.9 Balancing of Rights

Considering the operation of Kenyan anti-counterfeiting legislation in the context of the Covid-19 pandemic engages a range of human rights considerations. Although the clearest impact is on the right to health, a human rights-based approach means that considerations of this right are also integrated with protection of other human rights, as protection of one human right is interdependent with all other human rights.[199] Counterfeit medical products during the pandemic can limit infection control and engage states' obligations to protect third parties from threats to their health resulting from third parties. However, the limited effectiveness of Kenya's anti-counterfeiting regime has also influenced a ban on private importation of Covid-19 vaccines and reduced avenues to access vaccines. This can also limit access to the benefits of applications of science. Although concerns about rights to property, civil rights to a fair trial and privacy have been considered in this analysis, overwhelmingly, human rights concerns relate to the right to health and the right to life and

---

lates the cost to still exceed these health benefits over a 20-year period: Maskus (n 185) 226–228.

195 *General Comment 14* (n 9) [38]–[42].

196 Ibid [39].

197 Ibid [38]–[42].

198 Carlos M Correa, 'Anti-Counterfeiting: A Trojan Horse for Expanding Intellectual Property Protection in Developing Countries?' in Christophe Geiger (ed), *Criminal Enforcement of Intellectual Property: A Handbook of Contemporary Research* (Edward Elgar Publishing, 2012) 59, 74.

199 *Vienna Declaration and Programme of Action: Adopted by the World Conference on Human Rights*, UN GAOR, UN Doc A/CONF.157/23 (25 June 1993) pt 1 para 5.

related concerns about effectiveness, progressive realisation and maximum available resources.

The effectiveness of legislative mechanisms in permitting detection and seizure of counterfeit goods should be consistent with expedient and effective progression towards the right to health and other relevant economic, social and cultural rights.[200] These mechanisms should improve realisation of the right to health for Kenyans by using appropriate means to meet those obligations progressively.[201] This recognises restrictions on maximum available resources, as well as the need to use appropriate means to realise the right to health.[202] Seizures of counterfeit medical products in Kenya and in Sub-Saharan Africa during the pandemic suggest that activities of third-party counterfeiters in Kenya threaten the right to health. Available data in Sub-Saharan Africa frequently suggests a very serious problem, but it is difficult to quantify in the absence of ongoing sampling and testing of relevant products, or even testing of seized products.

If the system is not able to effectively address threats to health and safety, it may not be appropriate to allocate extensive resources to counterfeiting detection which primarily enforces the private rights of intellectual property owners when resources are needed for other, more pressing economic, social and cultural rights concerns.[203] The absence of extensive data and difficulties in detection of counterfeit goods makes it difficult to understand the nature and extent of health threats posed by these goods.[204] The need for these mechanisms to be appropriate and progress towards the realisation of the right to health suggests that careful scrutiny of the prospective and ongoing human rights impacts of anti-counterfeiting legislation is important. The human rights impacts are not limited to the right to health, although the preceding analysis has not identified as extensive problems with other rights in analysis of the *ACA*.

In its response to the pandemic, the CESCR noted states' obligations to devote maximum available resources to the realisation of economic, social and cultural rights, including the highest attainable standard of health.[205] However, where available states resources are not sufficient, the CESCR emphasises that all states are obliged to provide 'international assistance and cooperation,

---

200 Committee on Economic, Social and Cultural Rights, *General Comment No 3: The Nature of States Parties' Obligations (Art 2, Para 1 of the Covenant)*, UN ESCOR, 5th sess, UN Doc E/1991/23 (14 December 1990) [9] ('*General Comment 3*').

201 Ibid [4]–[5].

202 Ibid [3], [10]–[13].

203 Ibid [3], [9].

204 Maskus (n 185) 223–234.

205 CESCR, *Statement on the Coronavirus Disease (COVID-19) Pandemic and Economic, Social and Cultural Rights* (n 147) [14].

especially economic and technical' to enable developing countries to fulfil core obligations and obligations of comparable priority.[206] These include '[t]o take measures to prevent, treat and control epidemic and endemic diseases'.[207]

Kenya's intellectual property legislation enshrines a *TRIPS*-plus approach to enforcement of intellectual property rights but this does not effectively address the human rights implications posed by substandard, counterfeit goods identified in this section. Problematically, for the human right to benefit from science, concerns about enforcement of intellectual property rights can also reduce access to medical products that can be used in the Covid-19 pandemic as rights owners may choose not to permit manufacture or distribution of their products into the region.[208]

5 HOW CAN WE BUILD A HUMAN RIGHTS CULTURE?

5.1 Broader Impact in Sub-Saharan Africa

This analysis has identified serious problems for protection of human rights in Kenya. Some local conditions in Kenya differ within Sub-Saharan Africa. It is a developing country with functioning judicial machinery. Some Sub-Saharan African countries are least developed countries which do not have the resources for administrative bodies like the Anti-Counterfeit Authority or functioning judicial machinery.[209] This contributes to widespread, undetected counterfeiting.[210] There is also evidence of counterfeiting in other developing countries, such as South Africa.[211] South Africa has similarly entrenched human rights protection to Kenya and established administrative and judicial mechanisms but differs from Kenya in the scope of anti-counterfeit activities it addresses, restricting the focus of cross-border activities to trade mark counterfeiting and copyright piracy.[212]

Despite differences in local conditions within Africa, counterfeit Covid-19 treatments and vaccines have been seized throughout Sub-Saharan Africa,

---

206 *General Comment 14* (n 9) [45].

207 Ibid [44].

208 See Maskus (n 185) 229.

209 Schneider and Ferguson, *Enforcement of Intellectual Property Rights in Africa* (n 38) 12–13.

210 Ibid.

211 Schneider and Ferguson, 'Enforcement of Intellectual Property Rights in Africa' (n 23) 270–271.

212 Schneider and Ferguson, *Enforcement of Intellectual Property Rights in Africa* (n 38) 740–742.

along with counterfeit diagnostic tests and PPE.[213] As Africa has the highest global prevalence of falsified medicines, it is at significant risk. There have been seizures of counterfeit medical products used in relation to Covid-19 in Cameroon, Niger, Burkina Faso[214] and Uganda.[215] Fake vaccines have been seized in Uganda and South Africa.[216] The prevalence of counterfeits imported from outside of Sub-Saharan Africa indicates international cooperation to address substandard counterfeit goods is needed.[217]

5.2 Local Conditions

The human rights analysis suggests that the operation of the *ACA* is currently ineffective in permitting Kenya to realise its obligations to protect the right to health. Unlike Australia and the United States, Kenya provides comprehensive protection for international human rights obligations in its constitutional framework that enables judicial adjudication of individual rights. Yet the failure to change the *ACA* to better facilitate access to generic medicines within Kenya following *PAO* suggests that the accountability of the system of constitutional protection for human rights also needs to be closely monitored. An individually justiciable human rights framework is useful for monitoring and accountability of intellectual property rights but remains problematic for a human rights culture for trade marks if findings about compatibility with human rights are not implemented by government.

Socio-economic conditions in Kenya influence its capacity to realise economic, social and cultural rights. They can influence testing rates that permit a greater understanding of the impact of the Covid-19 pandemic on health and data collection about the extent and potential impact of counterfeit goods, beyond concerning modelling regarding counterfeit pharmaceuticals.[218]

---

213 See 'Pharmaceutical Crime' (n 36).

214 'Medical Product Alert N° 4/2020: Falsified Chloroquine (Update)', *World Health Organization* (9 June 2020) https://www.who.int/news/item/09-04-2020-medical-product-alert-n4-2020.

215 Schneider and Nam (n 44) 417.

216 'Medical Product Alert N° 5/2021', *World Health Organization* (31 August 2021) https://www.who.int/news/item/31-08-2021-medical-product-alert-n-5-2021-falsified-covishield-vaccine; 'Fake COVID Vaccine Distribution Network Dismantled after INTERPOL Alert', *Interpol* (3 March 2021) https://www.interpol.int/en/News-and-Events/News/2021/Fake-COVID-vaccine-distribution-network-dismantled-after-INTERPOL-alert.

217 Schneider and Ferguson, 'Enforcement of Intellectual Property Rights in Africa' (n 38) 10.

218 Martin Plaut, 'Why Africa Struggles to Test for Covid-19' *The Economist* (26 May 2020) https://www.economist.com/graphic-detail/2020/05/26/why-africa-struggles-to-test-for-covid-19.

Geo-political conditions can also influence the way that trade mark enforcement is dealt with in trade agreements, resulting in the inclusion of *TRIPS*-plus standards that may also impact the effective protection of human rights in diverse ways, including the requirement of resource-intensive enforcement standards.[219] The current negotiation of a Kenya–US bilateral trade deal is likely to include intellectual property provisions.[220] Kenyan negotiators may give greater weight to favourable trade conditions over human rights-calibrated intellectual property clauses. If new standards require substantial economic investment, this can divert resources away from other social and economic rights concerns.[221] Even if the negotiation does not result in further *TRIPS*-plus obligations, if it entrenches existing *TRIPS*-plus standards, this can reduce flexibility for Kenya to revise current standards.[222]

Although Kenya's local conditions differ significantly from the previous case studies, the evidence of counterfeit products in diverse economies during the Covid-19 pandemic suggests that more extensive change is needed and that the international assistance and cooperation obligations of wealthier states are relevant to achieving that change. The next section identifies potentially negative human rights impacts of counterfeit goods in a developed country and finds that the need for rights-based reforms of the existing approach to protecting individuals from substandard goods is not limited to developing and least developed countries. For example, in 2008, counterfeit heparin was detected in the United States, Europe and other developed nations, illustrating that counterfeit pharmaceuticals pose a global problem.[223] Seizures during the Covid-19 pandemic are not limited to developing and least developed countries. US Customs and Border Protection have seized millions of counterfeit masks during the pandemic, as well as fake respirators, fake treatment

---

[219] See Peter K Yu, 'The Comparative Economics of International Intellectual Property Agreements' in Theodore Eisenberg and Giovanni B Ramello (eds), *Comparative Law and Economics* (Edward Elgar Publishing, 2016) 282, 291.

[220] William Shpiece, 'U.S.–Kenya Strategic Trade and Investment Partnership. A Notice by the Trade Representative, Office of United States' (5 August 2022) 87(15) *Federal Register* 48060, https://www.federalregister.gov/documents/2022/08/05/2022-16798/us-kenya-strategic-trade-and-investment-partnership.

[221] See Yu (n 219) 291–295.

[222] See Kimberlee Weatherall, 'Intellectual Property in the TPP: Not "The New TRIPS"' (2016) 16 *Melbourne Journal of International Law* 257, 280–282.

[223] 'Counterfeit Heparin Blamed for Worldwide Deaths' *Partnership For Safe Medicines* (30 August 2009) https://www.safemedicines.org/2009/08/counterfeit-he.html; 'Information on Heparin' *US Food And Drug Administration* (2 May 2018) https://www.fda.gov/Drugs/DrugSafety/PostmarketDrugSafetyInformationforPatientsandProviders/ucm112597.htm.

tablets and at least 180,000 fake diagnostic tests.[224] Although there have not been comparable seizures in Australia, the following comparison indicates problems with detection of counterfeits and the collection of transparent data about health threats posed by counterfeit goods. This creates uncertainty about the effectiveness of state protection of individuals against the threats posed by counterfeiters to their health, consistent with the human right to health, and suggests the need for reform in countries with well-established judicial machinery with limited evidence of corruption.

5.3 Australian Approach to Anti-counterfeiting

Australia primarily implements its *TRIPS* trade mark enforcement obligations in the *Trade Marks Act 1995* (Cth) and border operations are overseen by Border Force, the Australian government agency empowered to seize counterfeit goods in Australia. The *Therapeutic Goods Act* (Cth) contains additional mechanisms for seizure and regulation of counterfeit therapeutic goods, including goods bearing counterfeit marks, and is overseen by the Therapeutic Goods Administration ('TGA').[225] The TGA explicitly acknowledges the relevance of its provisions to public health but there are no explicit references to human rights in either act. Amending acts can be subject to parliamentary human rights scrutiny but constitutional protection for human rights is extremely narrow in Australia,[226] in contrast to Kenya.

Australia has agreed to some *TRIPS*-plus standards through bilateral and plurilateral trade agreements, such as the requirement of additional criminal enforcement penalties.[227] Intellectual property enforcement legislation focuses on trade marks and copyright infringement.[228] However, therapeutic goods that do not bear a false trade mark can also be subject to the seizure and penalty provisions found in the *Therapeutic Goods Act 1989* (Cth) if they falsely represent key information, including the formulation and strength of the goods, the name of the goods and the manufacturer of the goods.[229]

Effectiveness concerns regarding anti-counterfeiting legislation prompted significant reforms introduced by the *Intellectual Property Laws Amendment (Raising the Bar) Act 2012* (Cth). These reforms strengthened the rights of

---

224 Scottie Andrew, 'Customs Officials have Seized over 20 Million Counterfeit Masks since the Beginning of the Year' *CNN* (online, 8 April 2021) https://edition.cnn.com/2021/04/08/us/millions-counterfeit-masks-seized-trnd.

225 *Therapeutic Goods Act 1989* (Cth).

226 See Chapter 3, section 3.5.

227 Weatherall (n 222) 265, 274–275.

228 *Trade Marks Act* 1995 (Cth) pt 13; *Copyright Act* 1968 pt V div 7.

229 *Therapeutic Goods Act* (Cth) pt 5.2.

trade mark owners by increasing penalties and reforming the notice of objection system that empowers customs officials to seize goods that are suspected to bear counterfeit trade marks or contain pirated copyright material, consistent with *TRIPS*.[230] Following these reforms, seized goods are more likely to be forfeited, reducing the likelihood that trade mark owners would need to initiate court proceedings to assert their rights.[231] The previous system had been criticised for the heavy onus on objectors in the earlier notification system and difficulties regarding making contact with the importer of the relevant goods within the statutory timeframes.[232]

Despite these reforms, there are still ongoing reports of seizures of a range of products that can pose serious concerns for health and safety in Australia, engaging human rights obligations to protect individual rights to health. Data about most seized goods is not systematically reported, so the nature of the threat is very difficult to understand. Border Force sometimes provides media updates regarding seizures. In August 2022, it was reported that Australian Border Force Officers had seized 141,000 counterfeit goods with a value of $63 million.[233] Although publicity can be given in these reports to the type of counterfeit goods that are imported, including mobile phones, watches, power tools and pharmaceuticals, the data about these seizures and any testing of them is not transparent to individuals who may be impacted if these products are substandard.[234] If counterfeit therapeutic goods are detected, the TGA will issue a notification.[235] This was helpful where detections of counterfeit medical products occurred during the Covid-19 pandemic, but there are many other types of counterfeit goods, such as counterfeit mobile phone chargers, that may seriously harm consumers.[236]

---

230 See Jose (n 32).

231 Australian Customs and Border Protection Service, *Annual Report 2013–2014* (Australian Government, 2014) 38 https://www.homeaffairs.gov.au/reports-and-pubs/Annualreports/acbps-annual-report-2013-14.pdf.

232 Explanatory Memorandum, Intellectual Property Laws Amendment (Raising the Bar) Bill 2011 [2012] (Cth) 101–110.

233 Natalie O'Brien, 'Don't Risk Life for Shonky Goods' *Courier Mail* (21 August 2022) 36.

234 Ibid.

235 See, for example, 'Viagra (Sildenafil): Counterfeit 100mg Tablets', *Australian Government Department of Health and Aged Care, Therapeutic Goods Administration* (21 June 2010) https://www.tga.gov.au/alert/viagra-sildenafil-counterfeit-100mg-tablets.

236 Saffron Howden, 'Warning over USB Chargers after Woman Dies from Apparent Electrocution', *Sydney Morning Herald* (online, 27 June 2014) https://www.smh.com.au/national/nsw/warning-over-usb-chargers-after-woman-dies-from-apparent-electrocution-20140626-zsngd.html.

During the Covid-19 pandemic, the TGA has issued notifications regarding imports of counterfeit ivermectin and Covid-19 rapid antigen tests that were not registered in Australia.[237] There have been media reports of border seizures of 800,000 counterfeit or faulty masks in Australia[238] and concerns that substandard masks have entered the hospital system.[239] Seizures in other jurisdictions such as the United States indicate that masks displaying counterfeit trade marks are prevalent globally.[240] The capacity of the Australian system to detect counterfeit masks is not assured. An ongoing post-market review of masks in Australia has identified the presence of imported masks of substandard quality.[241] The review responds to problems identified as a result of the classification of masks as low-risk therapeutic goods, permitting importers to provide assurances that they had evidence that the products being imported met quality standards. This enabled masks to be more rapidly imported at a time of significant demand. Given the periodic high demand for masks during the Covid-19 pandemic, consumers were more likely to purchase them online and outside of ordinary channels. This increased vulnerability to substandard and counterfeit products.

Problems with detection can relate to the sophistication of the imitation packaging and the counterfeit products themselves. The detection of counterfeit Viagra in an Australian hospital in 2010 demonstrates the difficulty of visual inspection by consumers or customs officials as a means of detection.[242]

---

[237] 'TGA Warns about Imports of Ivermectin', *Australian Government Department of Health and Aged Care, Therapeutic Goods Administration* (14 December 2021) https://www.tga.gov.au/news/media-releases/tga-warns-about-imports-ivermectin; 'Ezy Company Pty Ltd Fined $26,640 for Alleged Unlawful Importation of COVID-19 Rapid Antigen Tests and Nicotine Vaping Products', *Australian Government Department of Health and Aged Care, Therapeutic Goods Administration* (14 January 2022) https://www.tga.gov.au/news/media-releases/ezy-company-pty-ltd-fined-26640-alleged-unlawful-importation-covid-19-rapid-antigen-tests-and-nicotine-vaping-products.

[238] Andrew Greene, 'Australia Seizes Faulty Coronavirus Protective Equipment Imported from China', *ABC News* (online, 1 April 2020) https://www.abc.net.au/news/2020-04-01/coronavirus-chinese-ppe-border-force-intercepted/12085908.

[239] Liam Mannix and Kate Abusson, 'Counterfeit Face Masks Sold to Australian Hospitals', Sydney Morning Herald (6 May 2020).

[240] See, for example, '108,000 Counterfeit 3M Surgical Masks Stopped by Cincinnati CBP', *US Customs and Border Protection* (18 February 2021) https://www.cbp.gov/newsroom/local-media-release/108000-counterfeit-3m-surgical-masks-stopped-cincinnati-cbp#:~:text=CINCINNATI%E2%80%93%2DLast%20Thursday%2C%20U.S.,fill%20an%20entire%20sea%20container.

[241] 'Post-Market Review of Face Masks: Overview', *Australian Government Department of Health and Aged Care, Therapeutic Goods Administration* (17 December 2021) https://www.tga.gov.au/post-market-review-face-masks-overview.

[242] See *Health Care Complaints Commission v Attia* [2016] NSWCATOD 167.

Although it is most famous for the treatment of erectile dysfunction, the active ingredient in Viagra is also used for the treatment of paediatric hypertension. The counterfeit products were identified by a pharmacist crushing the tablets who noted a different consistency when the tablets were crushed. In disciplinary proceedings for the supplier of the product it was accepted that a pharmacist could not have detected the difference between the counterfeit and genuine product by 'checking the normal parameters'.[243] This sophistication of reproduction impacts on the effectiveness of Border Force in identifying counterfeit products.

The TGA issued a notification regarding the entry of counterfeit Viagra into the wholesale pharmacy supply chain.[244] The active ingredient, sildenafil, was present in an incorrect dose. In subsequent litigation, a medical expert identified a health risk associated with incorrect dosages.[245] Where sildenafil is used in the treatment of hypertension in infants and children, incorrect dosages could place patients at significant risk.[246] The counterfeit product was estimated to be in circulation for 12 weeks before detection.[247]

Resources remain a significant issue for the effectiveness of the Australian anti-counterfeiting detection system. The cost of surveillance and the potential delays that surveillance poses for the importation of goods[248] mean that inspection of goods is a selective exercise,[249] complicated by new approaches of sending counterfeit goods in small quantities.[250] Border Force increasingly uses intelligence to identify imports bearing counterfeit trade marks.[251] However, there is acknowledgement that it is difficult to detect counterfeit goods effectively.[252] There is no publicised systematic process for testing seized goods for health and safety dangers, although this testing does occur in

---

[243] *Health Care Complaints Commission v Attia* [2016] NSWCATOD 167, [69].

[244] 'Viagra (Sildenafil): Counterfeit 100mg Tablets' (n 235).

[245] *Attia v Health Care Complaints Commission* [2017] NSWSC 1066, [111].

[246] Ibid.

[247] *Health Care Complaints Commission v Attia* [2016] NSWCATOD 167, [69].

[248] See Andrew Hosking, 'Australian Customs Service: Working to Improve Facilitation of International Trade and Security of the Supply Chain within the APEC Region' (2007) 1(2) *World Customs Journal* 67.

[249] The Australian Border Force emphasises that this is risk-based and intelligence led: Australian Government Department of Immigration and Border Protection, Submission No 52 to the Productivity Commission, *Inquiry into Intellectual Property Arrangements*, 30 November 2015.

[250] See Jose (n 32) 53.

[251] See ibid.

[252] The New South Wales Fair Trading Commissioner acknowledged 'the task of protecting the public from cheap, imported, unapproved products remains a challenge for regulators': 'Fair Trading Raids Net Thousands of Unapproved USB Phone Chargers', *New South Wales Department of Finance, Services and Innovation* (14 April

certain circumstances.[253] Problematically, testing can involve damage to the relevant goods if their seizure is disputed.[254] Without that systematic testing, it is difficult to determine the extent to which these goods pose a threat to health and safety. As the nature of the threat is unclear, it is difficult to determine what resources should be devoted to testing. This complicates assessment of the cost-effectiveness of the system. An initial approach is to comprehensively analyse a dataset of imports, testing a sample of those that are identified as potentially counterfeit.[255]

The undetected Viagra example in this section illustrates the potentially negative human rights impacts related to substandard and falsified medical products in a developed country in the Covid-19 pandemic. Although widespread distribution of substandard pharmaceuticals in Australia is not evident, the risks posed by individual cases such as the counterfeit Viagra, which had been circulating for 12 weeks when detected, engage concerns about effective protection for individuals from third parties posing threats to their right to health. It is not clear that the seizures of counterfeit products reported by the TGA in the Covid-19 pandemic involved the use of counterfeit trade marks, given the differing use made of the term counterfeit in the *Therapeutic Goods Act*.[256] However, these seizures indicate human rights concerns that need to be addressed, as part of Australia's obligations to protect the right to health.

The Australian comparison suggests global problems with the detection of counterfeits and transparency about the health impacts, which creates uncertainty about the effectiveness of state protection of individuals against the threats posed by counterfeiters to their health. These impacts suggest that the need for rights-based reform of existing international approaches to protecting individuals from substandard counterfeit goods is not limited to developing and least developed countries.

2016) https://www.doesitcomply.com.au/article/compliance-news/fair-trading-raids-net-thousands-of-unappro-ved-usb-phone-chargers.

[253] See Connor Duffy and Nikki Tugwell, 'Global Crime Gangs Behind Surge in Counterfeiting, Customs Says: Fake Pharmaceuticals Laced with Rat Poison', *ABC News* (online, 8 October) http://www.abc.net.au/news/2014-10-08/global-crime-gangs-behind-counterfeiting-surge-customs-says/5799660.

[254] This can engage liability of the objector if infringement is not proved: *Trade Marks Act 1995* (Cth) s 137.

[255] See Fink et al (n 7) 34–35.

[256] *Therapeutic Goods Act 1989* (Cth) s 42E.

5.4 Lessons for a Human Rights Culture

In Kenya, attempted implementation of high intellectual property enforcement standards has not produced a regime that effectively protects the right to health. This chapter identifies reports of extensive seizures of counterfeit PPE in the pandemic. Given the estimated prevalence of counterfeit goods in Kenya following the National Baseline Survey,[257] it is likely that many counterfeit goods have not been seized. The threats that substandard goods like masks may have on infection control is very difficult to estimate but are likely to restrict Kenya's ability to control Covid-19 during the pandemic.

The human rights analysis in this chapter suggests that existing intellectual property-based mechanisms in Kenya to address problems caused by counterfeit goods using intellectual property means do not achieve human rights ends.[258] The *Baseline Survey* suggests that multiple structural factors prevent effective counterfeiting control. Additional structural problems impede the effectiveness of trade mark enforcement. Jarrells argues that even where trafficking in counterfeit medicines is criminalised in Sub-Saharan African countries 'political instability, weak governance, and weak law enforcement mechanisms make it difficult to enforce these laws'.[259] However, the preceding comparison suggests that problems with detection and deterrence of counterfeit goods is not limited to states with these characteristics. Reform of these intellectual property means should not be limited to Kenya, nor to Sub-Saharan Africa, where there are similar concerns about widespread counterfeit products.[260] The following chapter considers a rights-based, technological approach for global reform of anti-counterfeiting measures and explains the way that this type of reform aligns with existing frameworks for human rights.

The *ACA* implements both *TRIPS* minimum standards and *TRIPS*-plus standards. The East African Community supports a *TRIPS*-plus approach, and other bilateral and regional trade agreements could further entrench this in the future. But many states that promote *TRIPS*-plus mechanisms, such as the United States, have reported detection of counterfeit and substandard medical products during the Covid-19 pandemic, impacting control of the disease and posing threats to individual health that engage obligations to protect the

---

[257] *National Baseline Survey* (n 110) 14.

[258] See Laurence R Helfer and Graeme Austin (eds), *Human Rights and Intellectual Property: Mapping the Global Interface* (Cambridge University Press, 2011) 517.

[259] Hannah Elizabeth Jarrells, 'History, TRIPS, and Common Sense: Curbing the Counterfeit Drug Market in Sub-Saharan Africa' (2014) 43 *Georgia Journal of International and Comparative Law* 557, 563.

[260] Schneider and Ferguson, Enforcement of Intellectual Property Rights in Africa (n 38) 1–2.

human right to health. Simultaneously, states that limit adoption of *TRIPS*-plus standards, such as South Africa, have reported seizures of counterfeit medical products during the pandemic.[261] Worldwide, problems with enforcement of intellectual property rights have been identified repeatedly but an acceptable global solution remains undetermined.

In the Covid-19 pandemic, the anti-counterfeiting system raises a number of human rights concerns. Vaccine availability has been limited and the option of private imports was rejected by the government, which cited concerns that this would encourage trade in counterfeits, suggesting that the current system is ineffective.[262] The WHO initiative to increase mRNA manufacturing capacity in Kenya and other parts of Africa will require effective controls to ensure that counterfeit goods do not proliferate.[263] Schneider and Ferguson find that the problems with the effectiveness of anti-counterfeiting legislation are not limited to Kenya but widespread in Sub-Saharan Africa.[264] Attempts to strengthen enforcement mechanisms continue to be a feature of regional and bilateral trade agreements, but the presence of *TRIPS*-plus features in the Kenyan *ACA* have not resulted in effective mechanisms to prevent trade in counterfeit goods. The widespread proliferation of substandard and false pharmaceuticals in Kenya suggests that the intellectual property means do not seem to be effective to achieve even the minimum standard of human rights ends that Helfer and Austin seek to protect.[265] However, expanding the scope of counterfeiting protection is counterproductive if it fails to recognise resource constraints surrounding implementation.[266] Determining the extent to which intellectual property protection causes the human rights concerns is extremely difficult to assess without data, but modelling demonstrates that the social welfare benefits of trade marks as a badge of origin and quality are being undermined by counterfeit goods in Sub-Saharan Africa.

An important part of a human rights culture is an integrated assessment of competing human rights that recognises both the limited human rights protection available for intellectual property rights and the important instrumental

---

[261] 'Fake COVID Vaccine Distribution Network Dismantled after INTERPOL Alert (n 216).

[262] 'Kenya Blocks Private Covid Vaccine Imports on Fear of Fakes' (n 131).

[263] 'WHO Announces First Technology Recipients of mRNA Vaccine Hub with Strong Support from African and European partners', *World Health Organization* (18 February 2022) https://www.who.int/news/item/18-02-2022-who-announces-first-technology-recipients-of-mrna-vaccine-hub-with-strong-support-from-african-and-european-partners.

[264] Schneider and Ferguson, *Enforcement of Intellectual Property Rights in Africa* (n 38) 1–2.

[265] Helfer and Austin (n 258) 517.

[266] Olatunji (n 12) 606.

role of intellectual property for realisation of human rights. The recognition of intellectual property rights within the Kenya Constitution should not mean that they are treated as rights of equal status to those that are found in international human rights agreements. Failing to address the concerns identified in *PAO* suggests that the Kenyan government could be elevating intellectual property protection over rights to health, life and dignity. Geiger proposes reformulation of the protection for intellectual property in the European fundamental rights model to recognise its social function.[267] Reformulation would recognise that *UDHR* Article 27 (and its counterpart in *ICESCR* Article 15) is an integrated right and includes access to the benefits of scientific progress and their applications, as well as providing some rights to intellectual property owners. Analysis of economic, social and cultural rights within an integrated human rights analytical framework is also important because the way that specific rights engaged are balanced against each other can result in competition for maximum available resources. Progressive realisation of the right to access the benefits of science may not justify the same allocation of resources as the right to health. However, the Covid-19 pandemic highlights the tension in this balance. Incentivising innovation is critical to scientific progress to address the pandemic and enforcement of intellectual property rights used as incentives can influence willingness of intellectual property owners to locally produce or import intellectual property-protected products and provide local access to applications of the benefits of scientific progress.

Recognition that intellectual property rights should be balanced against human rights concerns aligns with Yu's interpretation of the weight that should be given to the right to property. Yu's model provides only limited human rights protection for products that can be protected by intellectual property.[268] This aligns with the characterisation of intellectual property as a social product by the CESCR in its interpretative comments regarding Article 15 and its statements about the pandemic.[269]

This social function of intellectual property is important. To be valuable in a human rights framework, intellectual property should provide sufficient incentive to stimulate scientific innovation that promotes human flourishing. The CESCR recognises that intellectual property can restrict access to benefits and applications of scientific progress to the detriment of human rights and

---

[267] See Christophe Geiger, 'Building an Ethical Framework for Intellectual Property in the EU: Time to Revise the Charter of Fundamental Rights' in Gustavo Ghidini (ed), *Reforming Intellectual Property* (Edward Elgar Publishing, 2022) 80.

[268] See Peter K Yu, The Anatomy of the Human Rights Framework for Intellectual Property' (2016) 69(1) *SMU Law Review* 37.

[269] CESCR, *Statement on Universal Affordable Vaccination against Coronavirus Disease (COVID-19), International Cooperation and Intellectual Property* (n 183) [7].

that intellectual property needs to be viewed in terms of its social function. This relates to the CESCR's interpretation of the obligation for international cooperation associated with Article 15(b):

> the benefits and applications resulting from scientific progress should be shared, with due incentives and regulations, with the international community, particularly with developing countries, communities living in poverty and groups with special needs and vulnerabilities, especially when the benefits are closely related to the enjoyment of economic, social and cultural rights.[270]

Yu recognises that the existing system has supported the rapid development of tools to address Covid-19, including vaccines.[271] Previous work on finding treatments and vaccines for SARS and other respiratory diseases, developed within an intellectual property-focused incentive regime, was important in expeditiously developing treatments and vaccines for Covid-19.[272] However, the limitations of the existing system have been apparent in the pandemic, including failure to support development in developing and least developed countries through technology transfer.[273] Technology transfer is recognised in Article 7 as a *TRIPS* objective, but there is also a specific obligation for WTO Members to transfer technology to least developed countries in *TRIPS* Article 66.2. Although mechanisms have developed within the *TRIPS* regime to encourage this to occur, including a reporting regime to encourage accountability for WTO Members,[274] the Covid-19 pandemic has highlighted serious inadequacies of technology transfer globally.[275] Even though Moderna announced that it would not enforce its patent applications in Africa, it did not agree to participate in the mRNA vaccine hub initiated by the WHO to develop capacity to produce mRNA vaccines.[276] This impeded production because

---

270 *General Comment 25* (n 182) [80].

271 Peter K Yu, 'Intellectual Property Paradoxes in Pandemic Times' (Research Paper No 22-04, Texas A&M University School of Law Legal Studies, 5 January 2022).

272 Ibid.

273 Thambisetti et al (n 186) 385–388.

274 David M Fox, 'Technology Transfer and the TRIPS Agreement: Are Developed Countries Meeting their End of the Bargain?' (2019) 10 *Hastings Science & Technology Law Journal* 1, 19–20.

275 See Thambisetti et al (n 186) 385–388.

276 Kerry Cullinan, 'Moderna Waives Its Covid Patent Permanently but Won't Share Tech With mRNA Hub', *Health Policy Watch* (9 March 2022) https://healthpolicy-watch.news/moderna-waives-its-covid-patent-permanently-but-wont-share-tech-with-mrna-hub/#:~:text=Moderna%20CEO%20Stephane%20Bancel%20said%20that%20it%20was,and%20middle-income%20countries%20identified%20for%20support%20by%20COVAX.

of the critical role of know-how in technology transfer for vaccines and treatment.[277] In addition to these concerns, problems with technology transfer extend beyond sharing core technologies and include associated infrastructure technology that supports distribution of these applications of scientific progress. Not only do many developing and least-developed countries lack the manufacturing capacities to produce the vaccines and treatments that have emerged in response to Covid-19, but they lack the infrastructure necessary to transport, store and distribute these medical products.[278] They often also lack the means to ensure the provenance of these goods, prompting policies such as Kenya's decision not to permit private imports of vaccines.

Effective solutions to this provenance problem can be an important part of rights-based reform of the intellectual property enforcement system. Kenya's new requirement to attach an anti-counterfeit security device to all imported products may require unrealistic government resources and burden importers if Kenya is the only country to implement the requirement, but there is increasing recognition of the importance of tracing the provenance of goods. The next chapter will explore how tamper-evident technology has potential for reforming protection and enforcement of intellectual property for a range of goods within a broader rights-based mechanism. Yu recognises that 'the more the intellectual property system has been shaped to provide fair protection to both the developed and developing worlds, the more interests and incentives both sides will have in fostering a more robust and effective intellectual property enforcement regime'.[279]

In considering how to address the human rights concerns identified in this chapter, it is critical to note that not all substandard goods are counterfeit. It is also important that the effectiveness of intellectual property machinery is only one structural factor contributing to widespread counterfeiting in Africa.[280] Schneider and Ferguson identify multiple contributing factors, including porous borders, corruption and bribery, limited resources available or enforcement agencies, limited cooperation between authorities domestically and between African states, perceptions of counterfeiting as a victimless

---

277 Thambisetti et al (n 186) 398–399.

278 See Susy Frankel, 'COVID-19, Vaccines and International Knowledge Governance on Trial' (2022) 12(4) *Queen Mary Journal of Intellectual Property* 441.

279 Peter K Yu, 'Enforcement: A Neglected Child in the Intellectual Property Family' in Susy Frankel and Daniel Gervais (eds), *The Internet and the Emerging Importance of New Forms of Intellectual Property* (Kluwer Law International, 2016) 279, 300.

280 See Helfer and Austin (n 258) 519–520.

crime, and a lack of specialised courts for intellectual property infringements.[281] Schneider and Ferguson argue that the WCO has an important role to play to support anti-counterfeiting measures and the enforcement of intellectual property rights in Africa.[282] They also emphasise the importance of rights holders working with public institutions to effect enforcement measures.[283] Given the number of human rights issues identified as relevant to anti-counterfeiting legislation in this chapter, reform also needs to embed a rights-based approach. Chapter 6 explores the way that technology could underpin an expanded and innovative approach to detection of counterfeits that permits individuals to work with authorised trade mark users to confirm authenticity using technology. This should not be limited to countries with funds to invest in research and development nor should it be limited to medical products. Kenyans are exposed to health risks from counterfeits from a broad range of products.[284]

6 CONCLUSION

Human rights analysis in this chapter indicates that Kenyan anti-counterfeiting legislation is not operating effectively to protect individual rights in the Covid-19 pandemic and raises questions about how trade mark enforcement standards can be compatible with a global human rights culture for trade marks. Trade marks can support state obligations to protect the right to health by providing a means for consumers to efficiently identify goods of an acceptable quality and provide an incentive for producers of applications of the benefits of scientific progress to distribute intellectual property protected goods in states with systems that effectively protect intellectual property rights. Evidence of substandard goods linked to widespread counterfeiting in Sub-Saharan Africa indicates that developing and least developed states are not able to meet their human right to health obligations to protect individuals from third party threats to their health.

Counterfeit pharmaceuticals were prevalent in Sub-Saharan Africa long before the Covid-19 pandemic.[285] Counterfeits can impact effective control of other prevalent infectious diseases, including HIV, malaria and tuberculosis.[286]

---

[281] Schneider and Ferguson, *Enforcement of Intellectual Property Rights in Africa* (n 38) 9–19.

[282] Ibid 29–30.

[283] Ibid 29.

[284] 'Commemoration of the World Anti-Counterfeit Day', *Anti-Counterfeit Authority* (23 June 2021) https://www.aca.go.ke/media-center/news-and-events/264-commemoration-of-the-world-anti-counterfeit-day-wacd-2021.

[285] World Health Organization (n 40).

[286] Ibid 7.

This threatens individual and population health. International and regional institutions have recognised threats posed by counterfeit medical products in divergent ways but do not focus on the way that counterfeit medical products engage states' individual and collective obligations to protect individual rights to health[287] and to cooperate to address and solve international health problems.[288] Counterfeiting in the Covid-19 pandemic expands beyond pharmaceuticals, indicating the importance of addressing the provenance of a broad range of goods so that threats to individual health can be addressed.

Resources play a critical role in the ability of states to progressively realise economic, social and cultural rights. Yet the way that they should be used to address counterfeits is particularly complex because many counterfeit goods are undetected and insufficient data is available to understand the extent of their threat to individual health and safety. The resources required to effectively enforce anti-counterfeiting measures so that they adequately protect human rights obligations are critical considerations for developing and least developed countries that comprise Sub-Saharan Africa.[289] As net importers of intellectual property, these countries receive limited direct economic benefit from expending resources on administrative and judicial machinery to enforce private intellectual property rights.[290]

It is difficult to assess the scope of the problem and determine its extent because of problems with detection and collection of transparent data about the extent to which these products harm health. This is also a problem in developed countries like Australia, but modelling based on sampling in Sub-Saharan Africa suggests that the human rights threat is significantly more serious. In Kenya, attempts to implement *TRIPS*-plus reforms to deter counterfeits have not effectively reduced widespread counterfeiting. Proposals to resolve this embed additional *TRIPS*-plus approaches that may further deter producers of applications of science to distribute intellectual property protected goods in Kenya. Resources need to be redirected towards reform of the anti-counterfeiting system and embed mechanisms that collect data about health threats and enable secure tracing of provenance. These changes will facilitate more effective detection of counterfeit goods and enable states to more effectively allocate resources to address the risks that counterfeit goods pose for human rights.

---

287 *ICESCR* (n 138) art 12; *Charter of the United Nations*; *UDHR* (n 172) art 27.

288 *Charter of the United Nations* preamble, arts 55, 56.

289 Yu (n 219) 291–294.

290 Ibid.

PART III

BUILDING A HUMAN RIGHTS CULTURE FOR TRADE MARKS

6 Innovating trade mark enforcement approaches in a human rights culture

1 INTRODUCTION

In the international legal order, legal standards prohibiting counterfeiting rely heavily on intellectual property enforcement provisions found in the World Trade Organization ('WTO') *Agreement on Trade-Related Aspects of Intellectual Property* ('*TRIPS*').[1] The extent to which states should be obliged to meet further resource-intensive standards for protection of intellectual property rights is a controversial and unresolved issue.[2] However, the existing intellectual property regime has proven ineffective in deterring trade in counterfeit medical products that pose serious threats to health, engaging human rights obligations of great significance in the Covid-19 pandemic.[3] Institutional innovation is needed.

This chapter considers how these issues can be addressed within a human rights culture for trade marks, drawing on the Human Rights Assessment for Trade Marks ('HRATM') framework developed in Part I of this book. Part II has used the HRATM framework to analyse the human rights implications of examples involving registration, exercise and enforcement of trade mark rights. The case studies of tobacco plain packaging, contrary marks and anti-counterfeiting demonstrate that there are important and often under-explored human rights concerns associated with international trade mark standards and their domestic implementation. Human rights benchmarks

---

1 *Marrakesh Agreement Establishing the World Trade Organization*, opened for signature 15 April 1994, 1867 UNTS 3 (entered into force 1 January 1995) ('*WTO Agreement*') annex 1C ('*Agreement on Trade-Related Aspects of Intellectual Property Rights*') ('*TRIPS*').

2 See Peter K Yu, 'Intellectual Property, Global Inequality and Subnational Policy Variations' in Daniel Benoliel et al (eds), *Intellectual Property, Innovation and Global Inequality* (Cambridge University Press, 2023, forthcoming).

3 See United Nations Office on Drugs and Crime ('UNODC'), *Covid-19-Related Trafficking of Medical Products as a Threat to Public Health* (Research Brief, 8 July 2020) https://www.unodc.org/documents/data-and-analysis/covid/COVID-19_research_brief_trafficking_medical_products.pdf.

should be used to guide countries to develop corrective mechanisms where they are needed to limit trade mark protection, but they are also important to structure changes that may expand trade mark rights or make them more effective. This chapter draws together key findings from the case studies and explores how the rights-based approach underpinning the HRATM framework can be used transformatively to address human rights concerns about substandard goods. Data is critical to this project. Although not all counterfeit goods are substandard, there is evidence that many counterfeit goods are substandard.[4] The Framework Convention on Goods Provenance ('FCGP') proposed in this chapter establishes reporting mechanisms so that states can better understand the prevalence of both counterfeit goods and substandard goods.

Many counterfeit goods are imported. Traditionally, detection of imported counterfeit goods involved physical inspection by customs and border officials who used trade mark registrations to justify seizure of suspected counterfeit goods. Counterfeiters increasingly use technology to undermine this approach, aided by increasing online trade in goods. Counterfeit goods can harm the human rights to health and life, if they are substandard or unsafe, and widespread counterfeiting can deter foreign intellectual property owners from importing or investing in domestic production, reducing access to applications of the benefits of scientific progress.[5] This chapter explores how provenance-tracing mechanisms could be effectively used in a rights-based multilateral framework to protect individuals from substandard goods that may harm their health, using blockchain technology to securely provide information about provenance and intellectual property rights. This approach supports the functional role played by trade marks as a badge of origin, which assures consumers that products have been manufactured consistent with quality standards,[6] by using technology to assure provenance.

Building on the case study findings that domestic implementation of the current international system for trade mark enforcement presents serious concerns for human rights, this chapter proposes a new international agreement to facilitate the widespread adoption of technological mechanisms to track and trace goods. Although this chapter recognises that health concerns

---

4 Keith E Maskus, *Private Rights and Public Problems: The Global Economics of Intellectual Property in the 21st Century* (Peterson Institute for International Economics, 2012) 227. See discussion of differences in terminology and institutional approaches for addressing counterfeit, substandard and falsified goods in Chapter 5.

5 See ibid 229. Maskus argues 'greater transparency and certainty in trademarks can offer incentives for product development and commercialization. Finally weak enforcement can be a powerful barrier to legitimate trade'.

6 William M Landes and Richard A Posner, *The Economic Structure of Intellectual Property Law* (Harvard University Press, 2003) 173.

posed by counterfeit medical products require urgent attention, the approach is intended to expand to facilitate detection of other counterfeit products that can be harmful to health.[7] Where the products that they purchase are ordinarily part of an international system for tracking and tracing, consumers will know that quality is not assured for goods that do not demonstrate secure provenance that is consistent with the system. A tamper-evident documented supply chain can permit self-verification using widespread mobile phone technology and encourage better reporting about counterfeit goods and product safety concerns. Blockchain and other technology-based innovations can further improve supply chain security to better deter counterfeiting.

Actors in the supply chain, including consumers, can use mobile phone technology to confirm the source of the product. Reporting can link to this system so that substandard goods detected within the tracing system can be reported and goods that are not traceable can also be reported. This new multilateral approach can facilitate understanding of the relationship between counterfeiting and substandard goods that pose threats to individual health, embedding rights-based principles and human rights standards into the governance framework. Secure tracking and tracing technology will empower individuals to protect their own rights to health and life and could encourage market investment so rights of access to applications of the benefits of science are progressively realised.[8]

The second section of this chapter identifies key findings from the case studies that help us to understand the relationship between human rights and trade marks in domestic law. The seriousness and uncertain nature of the human rights problems identified in the assessment of trade mark enforcement laws in the anti-counterfeiting chapter indicate that reform is needed. The third section considers previous approaches to reform and the human rights implications of reform. The fourth section proposes a novel rights-based approach to reforming anti-counterfeiting regimes, integrating innovative technology into a rights-based approach that will better address the serious threats to health posed by counterfeit products that are substandard. The section then proposes the FCGP, which translates the rights-based principles underlying the HRATM framework into an institutional mechanism that strengthens human rights and deters trade mark infringement.

---

[7] See types of goods in Xavier Seuba, *The Global Regime for the Enforcement of Intellectual Property Rights* (Cambridge University Press, 2017) 372–373.

[8] See Maskus (n 4) 11.

2 UNDERSTANDING THE RELATIONSHIP BETWEEN TRADE MARKS AND HUMAN RIGHTS IN DOMESTIC LAW

2.1 Foundations for Understanding the Relationship

This book proposes a human rights culture for trade marks, using a variety of approaches so that trade mark protection can be consistent with the realisation of human rights. Chapter 1 identified fragmentation between the fields of intellectual property and human rights law. This fragmentation has concerning implications for human rights protection because institutional enforcement mechanisms for protection for intellectual property are more likely to compel states to comply with intellectual property obligations than human rights obligations.[9] Chapter 2 analysed conceptual models of the relationship between human rights and intellectual property that engage with this fragmentation. Models which harmonise the relationship prescribe useful approaches to understanding how intellectual property rights may need to change to respect, protect and fulfil human rights but paid limited attention to trade marks.[10] These mechanisms only give limited attention to rights-based approaches which ensure that human rights protection is consistent with economic, social and cultural rights.

Consequently, Chapter 2 developed an analytical framework drawing on the assessment mechanisms used to embed a human rights culture into public health so states could more comprehensively recognise human rights implications for trade marks. This HRATM framework is important to establishing an environment where trade mark laws can aid realisation of human rights, particularly economic, social and cultural rights.[11] Certain rights-based principles that have been identified as important in the process of developing a human rights culture for health are useful to guide effective protection of human rights for trade marks and recognise the transformative potential of economic, social and cultural rights for 'promoting human welfare objectives'.[12] These include transparency, participation and empowerment, monitoring and accountability, effective progressive realisation of economic, social and cultural rights con-

---

[9] See Samuel Murumba, 'Foxes and Hedgehogs at the Intersection of Human Rights and Intellectual Property' (2012) 38(1) *Monash University Law Review* 119, 124–125.

[10] See Chapter 2, section 3.3.

[11] Compare Ruth Okediji, 'Does Intellectual Property Need Human Rights?' (2018) 50(1) *New York University Journal of International Law and Politics* (JILP) 1.

[12] Ibid 4.

sistent with maximum available resources, and international cooperation and assistance to realise human rights.[13]

2.2 Using Case Studies to Understand the Relationship

Part II of this book identifies fragmentation between human rights protection and trade mark protection in domestic case studies of trade mark protection. It applies the HRATM framework in three cases studies considering the registration, exercise and enforcement of trade mark rights. Local conditions can significantly influence the human rights impact of domestic trade mark law so each case study uses comparative examples to explore additional human rights concerns in states where different legal, economic and geo-political conditions can operate. The HRATM framework guides assessment of human rights implications and relevant rights-based principles in each case study. The examples highlight circumstances where broad protection for trade marks can have concerning human rights implications. Simultaneously, third parties distribute products bearing counterfeit trade marks internationally, making enforcement of any rights difficult and posing human rights concerns when the counterfeit goods are substandard because they are manufactured by third parties with reduced incentives to maintain quality standards consistent with ordinary trade channels.

2.2.1 Plain packaging case study

Rights-based analysis of Australia's tobacco plain packaging legislation in the plain packaging case study determined that tobacco companies exercising trade mark rights to advertise brands on packaging can seriously harm the human right to health. Restrictions on trade mark rights to restrict advertising also engage specific children's human rights as well as rights to freedom of expression, property, benefit from science and culture and development. The human rights implications are not confined to Australia: the case study also explored disputes about tobacco plain packaging in Uruguay. The plain packaging case study concludes that restricting the scope of trade mark rights to permit states to prescribe specific requirements for use of marks or limit use completely for non-word marks is consistent with human rights protection. Yet human rights obligations were not explored in Australia's successful defence

---

13 See Paul Hunt, 'Interpreting the International Right to Health in a Human Rights-Based Approach to Health' (2016) 18(2) *Health and Human Rights* 109.

of its packaging legislation in WTO disputes brought by Honduras, Indonesia, Cuba and the Dominican Republic.[14]

Policy justification is also important when defending policies that limit trade mark rights in international trade and investment mechanisms. Both Australia's justification of its plain packaging legislation in the WTO disputes and Uruguay's defence of its tobacco packaging legislation in an investor–state dispute with Philip Morris relied on their obligations to implement the *Framework Convention on Tobacco Control (FCTC)*, a non-WTO agreement.[15] Decision-makers recognised this support as relevant to both defences and upheld the domestic regulatory autonomy of Australia and Uruguay to implement these policies. Considering and articulating the positive impact of these measures for realisation of human rights could have benefited the domestic defences of the legislation. A well-articulated human rights basis for limitation of trade mark rights could also address the chilling impact of the disputes in other countries and support adjustments to domestic intellectual property protection to protect rights to health and life. Early adopters like Australia and Uruguay can assist implementation of these types of policies in other countries.

The examples analysed indicate that human rights obligations could be used to justify limitations of trade mark rights, if *TRIPS* disputes result.[16] The WTO plain packaging decisions suggest opportunities for relying on human rights obligations as a justification for limitation of intellectual property rights in the future. Rights-based principles should encourage ongoing monitoring of human rights concerns such as the effectiveness of the legislation in achieving human rights objectives. However, *Australia – Tobacco Plain Packaging* also confirms that *TRIPS* can protect broad trade mark owner rights.[17] States need to balance these broad powers so that they can realise human rights obligations

---

14 See generally Panel Report, *Australia – Certain Measures Concerning Trademarks, Geographical Indications and Other Plain Packaging Requirements Applicable to Tobacco Products and Packaging*, WTO Doc WT/DS435/R, WT/DS441/R, WT/DS458/R, WT/DS467/R (28 June 2018) ('*Australia – Tobacco Plain Packaging*').

15 Appellate Body Reports, *Australia — Certain Measures Concerning Trademarks, Geographical Indications and Other Plain Packaging Requirements Applicable to Tobacco Products and* Packaging, WTO Docs WT/DS435/AB/R and WT/DS441/AB/R (9 June 2020) ('*Appellate Body Reports*') [6.707]; *Philip Morris Brands Sàrl v Uruguay* (Award, ICSID Arbitral Tribunal, Case No ARB/10/7, 8 July 2016) [105], [304] ('*Arbitral Decision*').

16 Christophe Geiger and Luc Desaunettes-Barbero, 'The Revitalisation of the Object and Purpose of the TRIPS Agreement: The Plain Packaging Reports and the Awakening of the TRIPS Flexibility Clauses' in Jonathan Griffiths and Tuomas Mylly (eds), *Global Intellectual Property Protection and New Constitutionalism* (Oxford University Press, 2021) 267, 292–294.

17 See *Australia – Tobacco Plain Packaging* (n 14) [7.2285].

even where well-resourced trade mark owners systematically oppose restrictions of their trade mark rights.

2.2.2 Contrary marks case study

The contrary marks case study analysed the removal of legislative power for the United States Patent and Trade Mark Office to refuse to register scandalous, immoral and disparaging marks following the United States Supreme Court's decision in *Tam* and *Brunetti.*[18] Removing the prohibition has concerning human rights implications for rights to freedom of expression and to participate in culture, as well as effective protection from hate speech and discrimination. The *Paris Convention* expressly permits members to refuse registration of marks that are contrary to public order and principles of morality, and this permission extends to WTO Members.[19] Accordingly, fragmentation has resulted between the United States and other jurisdictions, including the European Union.[20] Prohibitions on registrations for trade marks that are contrary to morality or public policy should limit registration in a manner consistent with international standards of freedom of expression. This permits consideration and balancing of a complex range of human rights in addition to freedom of expression interests.

The contrary marks case study also highlights the impact of broad trade mark monopolies on expression. This concern exists in a range of jurisdictions and is exacerbated by a practice of well-resourced trade mark owners asserting ever broader monopolies in letters of demand eliciting compliance from less well-resourced individuals.[21] Trade mark protection already restricts expression but assertions of broad monopolies may further chill artistic or political expression. The practice of asserting rights that may be unjustified can extend the scope of expression that trade mark monopolies can restrict, particularly if there is a commercial dimension to political or artistic expres-

---

[18] *Matal v Tam*, 137 S Ct 1744, 1747 (2017); *Iancu v Brunetti,* 139 S Ct 2294, 2297 (2019).

[19] *Paris Convention for the Protection of Industrial Property*, opened for signature 20 March 1883, 828 UNTS 305 (entered into force 6 July 1884, revised at Stockholm 14 July 1967, amended 28 September 1979) art 6, *quinquies*(B)(III).

[20] See *Constantin Film Produktion GmbH v European Union Intellectual Property Office* (Court of Justice of the European Union, C-240/18 P, ECLI:EU:C:2020:118, 27 February 2020) (Judgement of the Court) ('*Constantin*').

[21] William T Gallagher, 'Trademark and Copyright Enforcement in the Shadow of IP Law' (2011) 28 *Santa Clara Computer & High Technology Law Journal* 453, 487–488. See also William McGeveran, 'Rethinking Trademark Fair Use' (2008) 94 *Iowa Law Review* 49.

sion.[22] The European comparison demonstrates that the constitutional human rights accountability framework can be an important corrective mechanism. However, the human rights impact of broad trade mark monopolies available in Europe remains concerning[23] and should be scrutinised, particularly in any proposals to expand the rights of trade mark owners in bilateral or plurilateral agreements. The utilitarian, social planning and natural law justifications for trade marks do not clearly support broad protections, so considerations of justice underpin this caution.[24] Similarly, additional protections for trade marks that use publicly funded mechanisms to protect the private property rights of trade mark owners should be monitored closely, and human rights frameworks should guide whether this protection is justified.[25]

2.2.3 Anti-counterfeiting case study

The anti-counterfeiting case study identifies further concerns for human rights protection. The chapter focuses on threats posed by trade in counterfeit pharmaceuticals, diagnostic devices and personal protective equipment during the Covid-19 pandemic in Kenya. States are obliged to protect the human right to health with measures that protect individuals from harms to their health posed by third parties, including counterfeiters.[26] Many counterfeit goods are manufactured outside traditional quality assurance chains so they are more likely to pose harms to human health.[27] The case study determined that there is a serious problem with the enforcement of trade mark rights that can facilitate distribution of substandard goods that negatively impact human rights to life and health. Technological developments mean that counterfeiting is more difficult to detect and expertly reproduced trade marks can become false assurers of quality for poorly manufactured counterfeit goods. However, trade mark enforcement rights can also impact on civil rights to a fair trial and to privacy. Requiring states to develop administrative and judicial infrastructure to detect

---

22 Martin Senftleben, 'Vigeland and the Status of Cultural Concerns in Trade Mark Law—The EFTA Court Develops More Effective Tools for the Preservation of the Public Domain' (2017) 48(6) *IIC International Review of Intellectual Property and Competition Law* 683, 695, 702.

23 See ibid.

24 See Chapter 1, section 3.2.

25 See J Janewa Osei Tutu, 'Private Rights for the Public Good?' (2013) 66(4) *SMU Law Review* 767, 787–788.

26 Committee on Economic, Social and Cultural Rights, *General Comment No 14: The Right to the Highest Attainable Standard of Health (Article 12 of the Covenant)*, UN ESCOR, 22nd sess, UN Doc E/C.12/2000/4 (11 August 2000) [39], [51] ('*General Comment 14*').

27 OECD/EUIPO, *Global Trade in Fakes: A Worrying Threat* (OECD Publishing, 2021) 3 https://www.oecd.org/publications/global-trade-in-fakes-74c81154-en.htm.

and prosecute counterfeits can negatively impact economic, social and cultural rights.

Multilateral attempts to address the problem have proposed mechanisms that extend beyond the minimum standards in *TRIPS*, strengthening penalties and expanding the scope of intellectual property protected.[28] Although *TRIPS*-plus mechanisms have been implemented in Kenya since the *Anti-Counterfeit Act 2008* (Kenya) was introduced, widespread prevalence of counterfeit goods persists.[29] Recent Kenyan law requires mandatory intellectual property rights recordation for all imported goods and that an anti-counterfeit security device can be attached to compliant goods.[30] Implementing this *TRIPS*-plus measure without widespread international cooperation will be very difficult. These new requirements are likely to make the import of goods into Kenya difficult[31] and raise questions about the utility of individual *TRIPS*-plus approaches in the context of a problem that is international in nature.[32] Even where widespread *TRIPS*-plus mechanisms do not operate in other parts of Sub-Saharan Africa, there are still significant problems with counterfeit goods.[33] Widespread counterfeiting restricts effective control of epidemic diseases and engages an obligation for other states to cooperate and assist less well-resourced states to address this core obligation.[34] The comparative study of undetected counterfeits in Australia, global seizure statistics and estimates of worldwide trade in counterfeit goods considered in Chapter 5 further indicates that effective detection of counterfeit goods and resulting health threats are an international problem. A multilateral response is also supported by obligations of international assistance and cooperation for all parties to ICESCR.[35]

---

28 Peter K Yu, 'TRIPS and its Achilles Heel' (2011) 18(2) *Journal of Intellectual Property Law* 479, 504–521 ('TRIPS and its Achilles Heel').

29 See Anti-Counterfeit Agency, *The National Baseline Survey on the Extent of Counterfeit and Other Forms of Illicit Trade in Kenya: Executive Brief Summary* (2020) 4 https://www.aca.go.ke/images/2020/National_Baseline_Survey_Counterfeit_and_Illicit_Trade_In_Kenya.pdf ('*National Baseline Survey*').

30 *Anti-Counterfeit Act 2008* (Kenya) 34B; Olugbenga A Olatunji, 'How Much is Too Much? Anti-Counterfeit Measures and Access to Medicines in the East African Community' (2021) 43(9) *European Intellectual Property Review* 594, 603.

31 See Olatunji (n 30) 603.

32 OECD/EUIPO (n 27) 64.

33 See Marius Schneider and Vanessa Ferguson, *Enforcement of Intellectual Property Rights in Africa* (Oxford University Press, 2020) 2.

34 *General Comment 14* (n 26) [44]-[45].

35 Ibid [38]–[39].

2.3 The Need for Transformative Change

The plain packaging and contrary marks case studies identified legislative and policy approaches that can address the human rights concerns identified with trade mark registration and the exercise of trade mark rights. The problems with trade mark enforcement identified in the anti-counterfeiting case study are significantly more difficult to address, in part because of the incomplete information available about the nature and prevalence of counterfeit goods. Although modelling estimates that substandard medications can result in tens or hundreds of thousands of deaths,[36] there is limited data to understand the extent to which these substandard medications bear counterfeit marks and engage state trade mark enforcement obligations. Greater attention should be given by states to preventing circulation of substandard goods. Yet, without more information about whether these goods are also counterfeit, it is difficult to understand if states should direct resources to strengthening trade mark enforcement which also protects private trade mark rights and benefits states that are net exporters of intellectual property-protected goods.

The plain packaging and contrary marks case studies identify ways that expanded rights can harm intellectual property. In contrast, the anti-counterfeiting case study has identified human rights problems that could justify allocating further state resources to protection of trade mark rights against counterfeiting. The FCGP proposal addresses the problem of insufficient data and will permit states to understand how extensive the human rights threat posed by counterfeit goods is globally.[37] Assessment is complex. Not all counterfeit medication is of substandard quality, but there have been serious concerns identified about the health risks posed by counterfeit therapeutic goods using trade marks without authorisation.[38] Risks include the negative

---

[36] World Health Organization ('WHO'), *A Study on the Public Health and Socioeconomic Impact of Substandard and Falsified Medical Products* (WHO, 2017) 12–13 https://apps.who.int/iris/handle/10665/331690.

[37] Seuba (n 7) 70–73; Fink, Maskus and Qian 'observe that capturing the impacts of global infringement of IPR is a complex and uncertain problem that could use far more analytical and data attention': Carsten Fink, Keith E Maskus and Yi Qian, 'The Economic Effects of Counterfeiting and Piracy: A Review and Implications for Developing Countries' (Policy Research Working Paper No 7586, World Bank Group, 29 February 2016) 23.

[38] Kaho Kwok and Lynne S Taylor, 'Analysis of Counterfeit Cialis® Tablets Using Raman Microscopy and Multivariate Curve Resolution' (2012) 66 *Journal of Pharmaceutical and Biomedical Analysis* 126, 126; Klara Dégardin, Yves Roggo and Pierre Margo, 'Understanding and Fighting the Medicine Counterfeit Market' (2014) 87 *Journal of Pharmaceutical and Biomedical Analysis* 167, 169; World Health Organization and International Medical Products Anti-Counterfeiting Taskforce

health impacts of harmful substances found in the goods and the consequences of not receiving expected therapeutic benefits.[39] The types of counterfeit goods seized during the Covid-19 pandemic also show that the problem is not limited to pharmaceuticals and greater attention should be given to a range of goods that may be counterfeit.[40] The potential human rights consequences of the distribution of substandard, counterfeit goods are sufficiently serious to engage states' human rights obligations to act. However, the Kenyan case study explored in Chapter 5 indicates that stronger trade mark enforcement mechanisms are unlikely to be appropriate to do this in many countries where resources are limited.[41] Helfer and Austin emphasise the beneficial function of intellectual property to support creativity and innovation and argue that other structural influences on human rights outcomes need to be recognised when changes to intellectual property protection are considered.[42] The following sections engage with this concern and explore an approach that deters trade mark infringement in a rights-based framework by strengthening accurate provenance identification which can communicate intellectual property rights associated with goods. The proposed FCGP translates the questions underpinning the HRATM framework into a guide for developing a mechanism that can be part of a human rights culture for trade marks.

The case studies suggest that counterfeit goods have diverse impacts on the human rights implications of trade mark protection. The volume of counterfeit goods seized in the Covid-19 pandemic considered in Chapter 5 indicates the existing approach for detecting and preventing counterfeit goods is ineffective.[43] The counterfeit Viagra detected in an Australian hospital was such a sophisticated reproduction that it was estimated to have circulated undetected

---

(IMPACT), *Counterfeit Drugs Kill!* (May 2008) https://www.gphf.org/images/downloads/library/whoimpact2008_counterfeit_drugs_kill.pdf.

[39] See Erwin A Blackstone, Joseph P Fuhr and Steve Pociask, 'The Health and Economic Effects of Counterfeit Drugs' (2014) 7(4) *American Health & Drug Benefits* 216, 217; Tim K Mackey et al, 'After Counterfeit Avastin – What Have We Learned and What Can Be Done?' (2015) 12(5) *Nature Reviews Clinical Oncology* 302; William L Hamilton et al, 'Public Health Interventions to Protect against Falsified Medicines: A Systematic Review of International, National and Local Policies' (2016) 31(10) *Health Policy and Planning* 1448, 1449.

[40] 'Pharmaceutical Crime: First INTERPOL-AFRIPOL Front-Line Operation sees Arrests and Seizures across Africa' *Interpol* (2 March 2022) https://www.interpol.int/en/News-and-Events/News/2022/Pharmaceutical-crime-first-INTERPOL-AFRIPOL-front-line-operation-sees-arrests-and-seizures-across-Africa.

[41] See also Olatunji (n 30).

[42] Laurence R Helfer and Graeme Austin (eds), *Human Rights and Intellectual Property: Mapping the Global Interface* (Cambridge University Press, 2011) 519–520.

[43] Estimates that 2.5% of world trade in 2019 was illicit: OECD/EUIPO (n 27) 52.

for 12 weeks.[44] Despite this sophistication, it was substandard, threatening the health of recipients.[45] Other counterfeit products such as masks bearing counterfeit trade marks seized worldwide in the Covid-19 pandemic can be ineffective because they are not of expected quality.[46]

Counterfeit cigarettes also pose complex challenges.[47] The plain packaging case study identified the human rights benefits of limiting the exercise of broad trade mark rights by tobacco companies. Yet the Uruguayan government recently cited counterfeit trade as a justification for reintroducing some branding on cigarettes.[48] Although it participates in multilateral cooperation to effect tracking and tracing of illicit tobacco, Uruguay argued that these systems lacked coordinated approaches between different suppliers and limited branding was needed.[49] The human rights arguments supporting removing branding from cigarettes outweighed this argument but the measures indicate the potential impact of illicit trade on the overall effectiveness of measures like tobacco plain packaging to protect the right to health.

In the United States Supreme Court decisions suspending the prohibition on registration of scandalous, disparaging and offensive marks considered in the contrary marks case study, entitlement to regulation for cross-border trade mark enforcement protection was identified as one of several benefits of trade mark registration.[50] However, because the prohibitions on contrary marks operate in other jurisdictions, these American registrations may be vulnerable to counterfeiting because states that implement *TRIPS* minimum standards for enforcement often rely on local registrations to support seizure of counterfeit goods by customs and border officials.

Recent reform proposals for stronger administrative, judicial and criminal measures to strengthen protection for intellectual property rights have not gained broad multilateral support.[51] Although the Kenyan case study suggests

---

[44] *Health Care Complaints Commission v Attia* [2016] NSWCATOD 167, [69].

[45] *Attia v Health Care Complaints Commission* [2017] NSWSC 1066, [111].

[46] Mariachiara Ippolito et al, 'Counterfeit Filtering Facepiece Respirators are Posing an Additional Risk to Healthcare Workers during COVID-19 Pandemic' (2020) 48(7) *American Journal of Infection Control* 853, 854.

[47] See Jonathan Liberman, 'Combating Counterfeit Medicines and Illicit Trade in Tobacco Products: Minefields in Global Governance' (2012) 40(2) *Journal of Law, Medicine and Ethics* 326.

[48] *Sociedad Uruguaya de Tabacología v Estado Poder Ejecutivo*, Juzgados Letrados de Familia [Family Court of Uruguay], IUE 2-54452/2022, 19 October 2022 [tr author].

[49] Ibid.

[50] *In re Tam,* 808 F 3d 1321, 1328 (Fed Cir, 2015).

[51] Kimberlee Weatherall, 'Safeguards for Defendant Rights and Interests in International Intellectual Property Enforcement Treaties' (2016) 32(1) *American Univ-*

that the effectiveness of a *TRIPS*-plus approach is highly problematic where limited resources are available for implementation, the Australian comparison demonstrates uncertainties about the effectiveness of existing approaches to enforcement even where countries are well-resourced.

Change is indicated by the impact of substandard counterfeit goods on rights to health and life, uncertainty about the extent of the problem and the way that counterfeit goods undermine the functional role of trade marks as an identifier. The instrument for change proposed in this chapter operationalises human rights standards,[52] building on the important considerations for assessing the relationship between trade marks and human rights that are identified in the HRATM framework developed and applied in this book. The rest of this chapter moves the focus of a human rights culture for trade marks from the assessment approach of the case studies to a transformative plan for reform of enforcement mechanisms for trade marks that refocuses trade mark protection on the core badge of origin function. The new approach focuses reform on an effective provenance assurance mechanism and greater data collection that is designed to realise human rights protection.

3 REFORM AND HUMAN RIGHTS

3.1 Failed Attempts at Reform

International trade frequently crosses borders and international coordination is important. In many countries, counterfeit goods primarily come from overseas. China is estimated to be the source of more than half of counterfeit goods, globally.[53] WTO Members must provide cross-border measures that permit seizure of imported counterfeit goods.[54] Customs officials often effect these measures and the World Customs Organization provides standards for state cooperation on a range of customs measures, including counterfeit activities.[55] Although the WHO regulates substandard and falsified medication, there is no treaty in this respect.[56] Other international institutions that are important

---

ersity International Law Review 211, 219 ('Safeguards for Defendant Rights and Interests in International Intellectual Property Enforcement Treaties').

52 Paul Hunt, 'Refreshing Human Rights for our Time and Place' (2021) 29 *Waikato Law Review* 60, 64.

53 OECD/EUIPO (n 27) 20.

54 *TRIPS* (n 1) pt III s 4.

55 Seuba (n 7) 31.

56 World Health Organization, *WHO Global Surveillance and Monitoring System for Substandard and Falsified Medical Products: Executive Summary*, WHO Doc WHO/EMP/RHT/SAV/2017.01 (4 February 2017) 6 https://apps.who.int/iris/handle/10665/339295.

for managing counterfeiting include the United Nations Office on Drugs and Crime and Interpol. These institutions do not work within a human rights framework, and although they can partner with the WHO, they are not bound by WHO principles.

Counterfeit products are characterised by 'deliberate mislabelling with respect to identity or source'.[57] Trade marks are used globally to regulate counterfeit products as *TRIPS* requires Members to establish mechanisms to restrict cross-border trade in counterfeit trade mark goods. WTO Members must implement minimum international standards for the protection of trade marks and the enforcement of intellectual property rights, found in *TRIPS*.[58] *TRIPS* requires states to provide measures for the private owners of intellectual property rights to enforce their rights.[59] *TRIPS* also requires states to provide criminal remedies where trade mark counterfeiting occurs on a commercial scale.[60] Although the state primarily funds expensive infrastructure to detect, seize and prohibit counterfeit goods, the emphasis of *TRIPS* obligations is on the private rights of intellectual property owners, often assuming owners will initiate private actions to enforce their rights.[61] Emphasis on the rights of private owners can limit the effectiveness of anti-counterfeiting measures. Cross-border detection of counterfeit goods often relies on owners to register their intellectual property rights with domestic customs authorities and provide a security or assurance when they register their rights: applicants may be charged for expenses such as storage of seized goods.[62] Where the seizure is contested and an applicant seeks to enforce their rights, they must indemnify the importer, owner and consignee of the goods for the wrongful detention of goods.[63] These mechanisms provide important safeguards against abuse of rights by intellectual property owners, but they may also deter registration of intellectual property rights with customs authorities.[64] *TRIPS* criminal enforcement processes rely less on involvement by intellectual property owners.[65] However, criminal enforcement rates can vary in practice.[66]

---

57 Seuba (n 7) 363.

58 *TRIPS* (n 1) pt II s 2; pt III.

59 Ibid pt III s 2.

60 Ibid pt III s 5.

61 Osei Tutu (n 25) 770.

62 *TRIPS* (n 1) art 53.

63 Ibid art 56.

64 See Olatunji (n 30) 603–604.

65 The MEDICRIME Convention explicitly separates itself from intellectual property rights protection: *Convention on Counterfeiting of Medical Products and Similar Crimes involving Threats to Public Health (MEDICRIME Convention)*, opened for signature 28 October 2011, CETS No 211 (entered into force 1 January 2016) Preamble.

66 Seuba notes significant diversity: Seuba (n 7) 371.

Increasingly, cross-border cooperation to share intelligence about counterfeit activities is important,[67] as the scope of counterfeiting appears to be expanding at a worrying rate.[68] The significant threats to health posed by falsified medicines are recognised by institutions such as the WHO, the United Nations Office of Drugs and Crime, and the Council of Europe.[69] Deterring counterfeit activities through cooperation on administrative, civil and criminal procedures has been a focus of attempts to address counterfeiting by developed countries,[70] which are often lobbied by rights owners to increase domestic penalties and push for international reforms.[71]

TRIPS was innovative in addressing enforcement, by implementing minimum standards for addressing cross-border transfer of counterfeit goods. However, developing countries contested many enforcement standards proposed during its negotiation.[72] Compromises introduced open-ended legal concepts such as 'fair and equitable' and 'commercial scale' into the enforcement section of the text.[73] Developing countries have subsequently resisted an ongoing emphasis on enforcement in TRIPS Council that focuses on protecting the private rights of intellectual property owners for the benefit of economies with strong technological and innovation sectors.[74] The interpretation of the enforcement provisions by the WTO Dispute Panel in the *China – Intellectual Property Rights* dispute indicated that states could expect reasonable domestic regulatory autonomy in their interpretation of cross-border enforcement provisions of *TRIPS* to take advantage of the flexibilities embedded in the agreement.[75] The decision also highlighted the fact that WTO Members are not

---

[67] *TRIPS* (n 1) art 69.

[68] OECD/EUIPO (n 27) 25.

[69] Stefania Negri, 'The Medicrime Convention: Combating Pharmaceutical Crimes through European Criminal Law and Beyond' (2016) 7(3) *New Journal of European Criminal Law* 350, 366–367.

[70] Seuba notes that cooperation provisions are usually drafted by developed countries: Seuba (n 7) 187.

[71] See Peter Drahos, 'Expanding Intellectual Property's Empire: The Role of FTAs' (2003) *Grain* 1, 2–6 https://www.grain.org/article/entries/3614-expanding-intellectual-property-s-empire-the-role-of-ftas.

[72] Yu, 'TRIPS and its Achilles Heel' (n 28) 495.

[73] Ibid.

[74] Seuba (n 7) 154.

[75] Daniel Gervais, 'China – Measures Affecting the Protection and Enforcement of Intellectual Property Rights' (2009) 103 *American Journal of International Law* 549, 555. See Rochelle C Dreyfuss and Susy Frankel, 'From Incentive to Commodity to Asset: How International Law is Reconceptualizing Intellectual Property' (2015) 36(4) *Michigan Journal of International Law* 557, 565–566.

obliged to monitor exports for counterfeiting.[76] The recognition of domestic regulatory autonomy in implementation of *TRIPS* enforcement standards in *China – Intellectual Property Rights* further encouraged states with strong intellectual property economies to push for more enforcement in bilateral and plurilateral agreements.[77]

One approach to concerns about enforcement was the unsuccessful attempt by a group of developed and developing countries to agree to stronger *TRIPS*-plus enforcement standards that included export regulation in 2011 in the Anti-Counterfeiting Trade Agreement ('ACTA').[78] Despite preambular rhetoric, the enshrined obligations failed to prioritise international cooperation and focused on civil procedure.[79] The negotiation of ACTA raised several concerns about the negative impact of *TRIPS*-plus enforcement mechanisms for human rights, particularly access to medicine and civil and political rights.[80] Arguments that mechanisms for in-transit seizures proposed during the negotiations were inconsistent with *TRIPS* standards were raised in parallel in a WTO dispute involving the seizure of generic medicines in-transit from India to South America in the Netherlands.[81] The narrow membership of the negotiating groups also influenced a narrow focus on penalties and civil procedures rather than the need for greater international assistance and cooperation to support all states to address counterfeiting in a manner that reflected their available resources. Domestic enforcement procedures including inspection, seizure and prosecution of alleged counterfeiters are resource-intensive and difficult to implement to effectively prevent trade in counterfeit goods, even in well-resourced countries.[82] The resource and time implications of embedding increased standards for enforcement can also constrain future implementation

---

[76] *Panel Report, China – Measures Affecting the Protection and Enforcement of Intellectual Property Rights,* WTO Doc WT/DS362/R (26 January 2009) [7.231]. See Seuba (n 7) 295.

[77] See Yu, 'TRIPS and its Achilles Heel' (n 28) 511.

[78] Ibid 508.

[79] Kimberlee Weatherall, 'Politics, Compromise, Text and the Failures of the Anti-Counterfeiting Trade Agreement' (2011) 33(2) *Sydney Law Review* 229, 239–240 ('Politics, Compromise, Text and the Failures of the Anti-Counterfeiting Trade Agreement').

[80] See Douwe Korff and Ian Brown, *Opinion on the Compatibility of the Anti-Counterfeiting Trade Agreement (ACTA) with the European Convention on Human Rights and the EU Charter of Fundamental Rights* (Greens/European Free Alliance, European Parliament, 8 October 2011) 6 https://www.greens-efa.eu/legacy/fileadmin/dam/Documents/Studies/Democracy/ACTA_fundamental_rights_assessment.pdf.

[81] Weatherall, 'Politics, Compromise, Text and the Failures of the Anti-Counterfeiting Trade Agreement' (n 79) 245.

[82] Peter K Yu, 'The Comparative Economics of International Intellectual Property Agreements' in Theodore Eisenberg and Giovanni B Ramello (eds), *Comparative Law*

of more effective approaches, such as the technological mechanisms proposed in this chapter.[83]

ACTA measures prompted widespread protests within the states that are signatories to the agreement; only Japan ratified it and it has not entered into force.[84] However, dissatisfaction with the effectiveness of enforcement standards in *TRIPS* has prompted additional attempts at reform. Key to these efforts are *TRIPS*-plus enforcement standards introduced through bilateral and plurilateral trade agreements[85] that can introduce beneficial changes such as increased data-sharing about counterfeiting activities between states[86] but also enshrine stronger penalties that rely on strong administrative and judicial systems to be effective.[87] The original proposals of the East African Community discussed in Chapter 5 exemplify this type of *TRIPS*-plus approach.[88] The next section assesses the human rights implications of unrealistic standards on states that have very limited resources to improve administrative and judicial machinery so that the system will be more effective.[89]

3.2 Human Rights Justifications for Change

Counterfeit goods engage states' individual and collective obligations to protect human rights to health[90] and life and to cooperate to address and solve international health problems.[91] A rights-based framework needs to complement the trade and public health response and recognise that non-medical counterfeit products also pose serious problems for individual health and safety.[92] *ICESCR* obliges states to protect individuals from threats to health posed by third par-

---

and Economics (Edward Elgar Publishing, 2016) 282, 291–295; Fink, Maskus and Qian (n 37) 3.

83 Kimberlee Weatherall, 'Intellectual Property in the TPP: Not "The New TRIPS"' (2016) 16 *Melbourne Journal of International Law* 257, 280–282, 285 ('Intellectual Property in the TPP: Not "The New TRIPS"').

84 Seuba (n 7) 404.

85 Yu, 'TRIPS and its Achilles Heel' (n 28) 511–514.

86 *Comprehensive and Progressive Agreement for Trans-Pacific Partnership*, signed 8 March 2018, [2018] ATS 23 (entered into force 30 December 2018).

87 Weatherall, 'Intellectual Property in the TPP: Not "The New TRIPS"' (n 83) 280–282.

88 See Olatunji (n 30) 597–600.

89 See Maskus (n 4) 226–228.

90 *International Covenant on Economic, Social and Cultural Rights*, opened for signature 16 December 1966, 993 UNTS 3 (entered into force 3 January 1976) art 12 ('*ICESCR*').

91 *Charter of the United Nations* arts 55, 56.

92 OECD/EUIPO (n 27) 22.

ties.[93] Not all counterfeit goods are of poor quality or harmful to health, but counterfeiters do not have the same incentive as trade mark owners to produce quality products and may not comply with health and safety standards.[94] States that fail to 'take all necessary measures to safeguard persons within their jurisdiction from infringements of the right to health by third parties' violate their obligations to protect the right to health.[95] Determining what measures are necessary to meet these obligations is difficult to assess when not all counterfeit goods are detected, not all seized goods are tested for health risks and not all counterfeit goods pose health threats.[96] Assessing the scope of this threat to health is also difficult because of insufficient publicly available data about seized goods. Although more transparent testing of seized goods should improve accurate assessments of the nature of the threat to health, resource constraints restrict this type of testing in many countries.[97] Without this data about counterfeit goods, it is also difficult to know whether the economic justifications for addressing counterfeiting are being met.[98]

Article 2 of *ICESCR* requires states to act individually and cooperatively to progressively realise economic, social and cultural rights, including through economic and technical assistance. Cooperative and effective solutions can include transferring counterfeit detection technology between states.[99] As counterfeit goods are frequently imported, aiding detection in other countries can reduce international distribution of counterfeit goods, complementing the domestic focus of a public health approach and acknowledging the finite nature of resources available to address counterfeiting.[100] A rights-based approach recognises protection obligations for states to regulate a range of actors, including third party counterfeiters and other actors in complex supply chains. The United Nations Guiding Principles on Business and Human Rights provide relevant standards of accountability for non-state actors, consistent with the emphasis of rights-based frameworks on transparency, monitoring

---

[93] *General Comment 14* (n 26) [35].

[94] See OECD/EUIPO, *Trade in Counterfeit Goods and Free Trade Zones: Evidence from Recent Trends* (OECD Publishing, 2018) 32 https://www.oecd-ilibrary.org/trade/trade-in-counterfeit-goods-and-free-trade-zones_9789264289550-en.

[95] *General Comment 14* (n 26) [51].

[96] *See* Osei Tutu (n 25) 804.

[97] See Fink, Maskus and Qian (n 37) 2–3.

[98] Ibid.

[99] See ETO Consortium, *Maastricht Principles on the Extraterritorial Obligations of States in the Area of Economic, Social and Cultural Rights* (28 September 2011) principle 31 https://www.fidh.org/IMG/pdf/maastricht-eto-principles-uk_web.pdf ('*M-aastricht Principles*').

[100] See also discussion of health resourcing in Hunt (n 13) 116.

and accountability.[101] The Maastricht Principles clarify that all states are required to 'take action, separately, and jointly through international cooperation, to protect economic, social and cultural rights of persons within their territories and extraterritorially'.[102]

The right to health is not the only relevant concern. If legal regimes cannot effectively deter counterfeit goods, industries may be unwilling to distribute intellectual property-protected products or invest in production infrastructure that can also support technology transfer.[103] This can limit progressive realisation of the human right to access applications of the benefits of science.[104] Additionally, CESCR interprets the right to health to oblige states to:

> respect the enjoyment of the right to health in other countries, and to prevent third parties from violating the right in other countries, if they are able to influence these third parties by way of legal or political means, in accordance with the Charter of the United Nations and applicable international law.[105]

Accordingly all *ICESCR* parties are obliged to implement effective multilateral solutions to problems posed by counterfeit goods. Current multilateral arrangements do not fulfil this obligation.

The enforcement provisions of *TRIPS* that structure the international regime for the detection of counterfeit goods primarily protect the private rights of intellectual property owners. Developing states that are net importers of products protected by trade marks and invest resources in anti-counterfeiting infrastructure are economically less well off than net exporters of intellectual property. Maskus recognises health benefits as one of the strongest incentives for poorer countries to invest in expensive machinery to implement effective anti-counterfeiting regimes, but calculates the cost to still exceed these health benefits over a 20-year period.[106] Osei Tutu has argued that the

---

[101] John Ruggie, *Report of the Special Representative of the Secretary-General on the Issue of Human Rights and Transnational Corporations and Other Business Enterprises: Guiding Principles on Business and Human Rights: Implementing the United Nations 'Protect, Respect and Remedy' Framework*, UN Doc A/HRC/17/31 (21 March 2011) ('*Ruggie Report*') annex, adopted by the Human Rights Council, *Human Rights and Transnational Corporations and Other Business Enterprises*, HRC Res 17/4, UN GAOR, 17th sess, 33rd mtg, Agenda Item 3, UN Doc A/HRC/RES/17/4 (6 July 2011, adopted 16 June 2011) ('*Guiding Principles Resolution*').

[102] See principle 27 of *Maastricht Principles* (n 99).

[103] See Maskus (n 4) 11. Fink, Maskus and Qian find that little is known about how counterfeiting and piracy impacts technology transfer: Fink, Maskus and Qian (n 37) 16.

[104] *ICESCR* (n 90) art 15(1)(b).

[105] *General Comment 14* (n 26) [39].

[106] Maskus (n 4) 226–228.

health and safety justification for policing counterfeit goods may not justify the resources committed by states in addressing counterfeiting activities.[107] Rather than emphasising intellectual property rights, Osei Tutu suggests that a public interest test should be applied to assessing the appropriateness of regulating counterfeit pharmaceutical goods, to address goods that are in fact dangerous to health.[108] This removes emphasis from intellectual property, but even these solutions require effective mechanisms for detection and deterrence. Rights-based principles of progressive realisation, maximum available resources, effectiveness and international assistance and cooperation should also shape the response to these concerns. Some states have limited resources to protect economic, social and cultural rights, parties to *ICESCR* have obligations to assist them to address human rights problems posed by counterfeit goods so that unequal, economic resources do not prevent effective solutions.

The alternative rights-based approach proposed in this chapter to deter counterfeiting by using technology to assure provenance is designed to protect rights but also to securely gather information that can create a better understanding of how negatively human rights are impacted by trade in counterfeits and the weight and focus that should be given to deterrence and protection. Making secure data about provenance more transparently available can make it possible to test the accuracy of existing data about counterfeit goods which has been criticised as coming from private actors with economic interests in intellectual property enforcement.[109] The opportunities for self-verification by different actors in the supply chain can also address separate structural problems for enforcement with corruption and institutional distrust of anti-counterfeiting authorities identified in Kenya in Chapter 5.[110]

Any protection a new mechanism provides for private rights must be governed by human rights principles such as progressive realisation and international cooperation and assistance. This is particularly relevant for less developed states with significant resource constraints. If regional and bilateral agreements use trade incentives to require poorly resourced countries to implement onerous and expensive enforcement machinery that is ineffective, this may divert resources that could be better spent on improving socio-economic standards that are essential to the realisation of the right to health in those countries and relevant to obligations for international cooperation to realise

---

[107] See J Janewa Osei Tutu, 'Corporate "Human Rights" to Intellectual Property Protection?' (2015) 55 *Santa Clara Law Review* 1. See also Maskus ibid.

[108] See Osei Tutu (n 25) 800–808.

[109] Seuba (n 7) 70–73; Fink, Maskus and Qian (n 37) 19–22.

[110] *National Baseline Survey* (n 29) 40. See also Schneider and Ferguson (n 33) 9–19.

core minimum standards of health in all states.[111] The current emphasis given to intellectual property-based mechanisms to implement anti-counterfeiting measures places little weight on the harms to health that counterfeit goods can pose.[112] Unrealistic standards will not prompt multilateral reforms that permit states to discharge their obligations to protect individuals against threats to their health posed by third party counterfeiters.

4 PROPOSALS FOR CHANGE

Human rights provide unifying principles for all of the institutions that are concerned with international trade in counterfeit goods. The majority of state actors in these institutions are bound to ensure that the policies and decisions of institutional organisations conform with *ICESCR*.[113] Human rights principles can underpin an inter-institutional approach to counterfeiting as they recognise intellectual property as a social product. Although protection of intellectual property can function to incentivise socially beneficial innovation, this function needs to be balanced against human rights to access the benefits of science and to the highest attainable standards of health in a human rights framework.[114] Human rights principles should guide United Nations

---

[111] *General Comment 14* (n 26) [38]–[42].

[112] There is some recognition in the requirement for penalty assessments to consider threats to health or safety in *Trans-Pacific Partnership Agreement between the Government of Australia and the Governments of: Brunei Darussalam, Canada, Chile, Japan, Malaysia, Mexico, New Zealand, Peru, Singapore, United States of America and Vietnam*, signed 4 February 2016 [2016] ATNIF 2 (not yet in force) art 18.77(6)(b) ('*TPP 2016*').

[113] Committee on Economic, Social and Cultural Rights, *General Comment No 17: The Right of Everyone to Benefit from the Protection of the Moral and Material Interests Resulting from Any Scientific, Literary or Artistic Production of Which He or She Is the Author (Art 15, Para 1(c) of the Covenant)*, UN ESCOR, 35th sess, UN Doc E/C.12/GC/17 (12 January 2006) [56] ('*General Comment 17*'); *General Comment 14* (n 26) [64], [39], [42], [50].

[114] Committee on Economic, Social and Cultural Rights, *General Comment No 25: On Science and Economic, Social and Cultural Rights (Article 15 (1) (b), (2), (3) and (4) of the International Covenant on Economic, Social and Cultural Rights)*, UN ESCOR, 67th sess, UN Doc E/C.12/GC/25 (20 April 2020) [62] ('*General Comment 25*') provides that 'A balance must be reached between intellectual property and the open access and sharing of scientific knowledge and its applications, especially those linked to the realization of other economic, social and cultural rights, such as the rights to health, education and food'; *General Comment 17* (n 113) [22]. See also Christophe Geiger, 'Implementing Intellectual Property Provisions in Human Rights Instruments: Towards a New Social Contract for the Protection of Intangibles' in Christophe Geiger (ed), *Research Handbook on Human Rights and Intellectual Property* (Edward Elgar Publishing, 2015) 661.

organisations such as the World Intellectual Property Organization ('WIPO'), which is concerned with intellectual property enforcement activities such as anti-counterfeiting. Trade marks can provide a useful basis for prosecuting counterfeiters, and their use, as required by *TRIPS*, remains practical and valuable. However, trade marks and technological mechanisms need to be part of a new approach to detection and deterrence that recognises the rights of a range of individual stakeholders.

A rights-based approach that supports intellectual property enforcement measures is more likely to be effective in ensuring adequate protection of both intellectual property rights and rights to health and life than an approach that focuses primarily on protection of intellectual property rights. This broader approach is better suited to ensure that the system is consistent with the following economic justifications identified by Fink, Maskus and Qian for systematically regulating anti-counterfeiting internationally.[115] First, infringements of intellectual property rights undermine trust in rules-based systems that underpin modern market-based economies.[116] Second, counterfeit products can confuse consumers and may be ineffective or even dangerous, as with adulterated medicines and foodstuffs or non-certified engine replacement parts.[117] Third, extensive counterfeiting can significantly deter the emergence of new products and firms, and piracy can block the development of creative industries, especially in poor countries where entry conditions are already weak.[118] These objectives are partially addressed by existing public health and intellectual property regimes. However, dealing with counterfeit products in multiple institutions that differently emphasise economic concerns of private actors, law enforcement and public health objectives without prioritising human rights is problematic. The identified economic justifications for addressing counterfeiting also engage human rights considerations, but these are rarely recognised. The anti-counterfeiting case study demonstrates how ineffective or dangerous counterfeit medical products threaten rights to health and life. A range of economic, social and cultural rights can be impacted where widespread counterfeiting becomes a disincentive for the importation of innovative products that can improve rights including health and access to food.

Ongoing problems with the effectiveness of existing measures indicate that economic imperatives and human rights obligations justify reform. Integrating rights-based principles into the mechanism that is used to build consensus on implementing detection technology multilaterally can encourage states with

---

115 See Fink, Maskus and Qian (n 37) 33–36.

116 Ibid 2.

117 Ibid.

118 Ibid 3.

diverse economic circumstances to participate in regimes that deter trade in substandard goods.[119] A transformative approach needs to address the failure of the premise underlying *TRIPS* that developed state parties to the agreement would support technology transfer to less developed states so that they can access and share the benefits of applications of science.[120] Previous attempts at reform of enforcement mechanisms in the international intellectual property system provide limited incentive for participation by less-developed countries that derive limited income from intellectual property protected exports.[121] Maskus has noted that protection of individuals from health threats may be critical in encouraging countries that do not benefit economically from high intellectual property standards to invest in anti-counterfeiting regimes.[122] A new approach that embeds requirements to provide technology transfer mechanisms to support participation in a rights-based framework can better support countries of varying economic development to adopt technological mechanisms to detect and deter counterfeiting more efficiently. Monitoring and accountability principles would support requirements that states address requests for technology transfer from other states.

Proposed approaches to expanding existing anti-counterfeiting protection should be scrutinised to ensure that they require states to use their resources effectively in progressive realisation of economic, social and cultural rights, consistent with human rights benchmarks.[123] Where the specific economic conditions in poorer states mean that investment in multilateral anti-counterfeiting reform is not justified but international cooperation benefits the global community, wealthier states may need to invest more in technical assistance, such as developing and distributing detection technology.[124] A critical aspect of this reform is ensuring participation across the broad range of stakeholders impacted by counterfeiting, including holders of intellectual property rights as well as all individuals, as they possess human rights entitlements to protection from threats to health posed by counterfeiting. Transparency is another critical feature of a rights-based framework. The FCGP should emphasise the collection and sharing of data that will enable states to understand better the scope

---

[119] See discussion of benefits and difficulties of global cooperation for cybersecurity in Martha Finnemore and Duncan B Hollis, 'Constructing Norms for Global Cybersecurity' (2016) 110 *American Journal of International Law* 425, 467.

[120] *General Comment 25* (n 114) [62].

[121] Yu, 'TRIPS and its Achilles Heel' (n 28) 514–515, 525.

[122] Maskus (n 4) 226–228.

[123] Committee on Economic, Social and Cultural Rights, *General Comment No 3: The Nature of States Parties' Obligations (Art 2, Para 1 of the Covenant)*, UN ESCOR, 5th sess, UN Doc E/1991/23 (14 December 1990) [9].

[124] *General Comment 14* (n 26) [38].

of the problem posed by counterfeiting and its human rights and economic implications. The following section considers technological approaches that are relevant to the measures an FCGP would enshrine.

4.1 Technological Features of a Framework Convention on Goods Provenance

Technology is increasingly critical to detecting and deterring counterfeiting. Numerous technological responses use mobile phone technology that permits consumers and other stakeholders to verify product provenance. These address the increasing sophistication of counterfeit products and the opportunities for broader distribution of counterfeits facilitated by the online marketplace.[125] Mobile phone applications such as image scanners, radio frequency identification and scratch barcodes have been used to make detection of counterfeit goods easier within certain supply chains.[126] One field where there has been broad use of technological measures to detect counterfeit products is pharmaceuticals. Mackey and Nayyar identify common characteristics of evolving designs and conceptualisation of anti-counterfeit solutions that are suitable for addressing pharmaceutical counterfeiting.[127] Critically for their suitability to address counterfeiting in all parts of the world, they are 'specifically designed to overcome existing barriers of adoption and implementation faced by traditional anticounterfeit technology'.[128] Solutions such as molecular fingerprinting and hand-held laboratories may have been justifiable for high-value pharmaceuticals, but the new approaches are scalable for lower-cost pharmaceuticals and other low-cost items.[129] Checking mechanisms, including scratch codes on pharmaceutical packaging, have developed to identify substandard and falsified medicines in countries like Nigeria and India that enable product verification using mobile phones.[130] The technological approach in Nigeria has been successful in reducing distribution of counterfeit pharmaceuticals.[131]

---

125 Dégardin, Roggo and Margo (n 38) 170.

126 Tim K Mackey and Gaurvika Nayyar, 'A Review of Existing and Emerging Digital Technologies to Combat the Global Trade in Fake Medicines' (2017) 16(5) *Expert Opinion on Drug Safety* 587, 591; Agustín Ciapponi et al, 'Mobile Apps for Detecting Falsified and Substandard Drugs: A Systematic Review' (2021) 16(2) *PloS One* 1, 4.

127 Mackey and Nayyar (n 126) 597.

128 Ibid.

129 Ibid.

130 Dégardin, Roggo and Margo (n 38) 171.

131 Schneider and Ferugson (n 33) 25.

The Kenya Revenue Authority has also successfully used technology to track tobacco, wine and spirits and address illicit trade.[132]

Scalable technological solutions can deter counterfeiting in many industries where substandard goods pose significant harm. Unfortunately, well-resourced counterfeiters in this 'new branch of organized crime'[133] can circumvent technological anti-counterfeiting solutions by reusing packaging, mimicking identification codes and producing products with identical appearances even though these products may not function to purpose or may include harmful ingredients.[134] However, these solutions do not necessarily operate in isolation. Mature technological measures for addressing counterfeiting such as mobile phones and radio frequency identification can be integrated with other forms of digital technology such as blockchain. Blockchain is a much newer technological approach but it 'represents a potentially revolutionizing mechanism [that enables stakeholders to share] supply chain information via a more trustworthy, secured, and accessible distributed and decentralised digital ledger'.[135] In combination with other solutions, blockchain can stymie counterfeit activities that attempt to exploit the security risks posed by digital technologies. Criminal organisations involved in counterfeiting will seek to attack these digital solutions. Blockchain can limit these cyber-security threats by enabling data authorisation and data cloning. Concerns about the ability of counterfeiters to mimic or undermine technology-based provenance mechanisms have prompted proposals for using blockchain technology to provide additional security for provenance identifiers. The importance of this for distribution of the Covid-19 vaccine has been recognised by UNICEF. UNICEF is developing a Global Trust Repository Project to implement blockchain-verified vaccine tracking as part of the COVAX initiative.[136]

Blockchain is an important vehicle for reliable data-sharing. A range of actors, including the United States Food and Drug Administration, are increasingly investigating the use of blockchain technology as a mechanism

---

132 Ibid.

133 Dégardin, Roggo and Margo (n 38) 167.

134 See Melanie Jose, 'Raising the Bar on Australia's Border Measures: Improvements to the Notice of Objection Scheme Resulting from the IP Laws Amendment (Raising the Bar) Act 2012' (2012) 90 *Intellectual Property Forum* 52; Rebecca Puddy, 'Smashing Solution to China's Imitation Game', *The Australian* (10 January 2016). See also Michael Smith, 'Chinese Police Seize 50,000 Bottles of Fake Penfolds', *Australian Financial Review* (online, 27 March 2018) https://www.afr.com/news/world/asia/chinese-police-seize-50000-bottles-of-fake-penfolds-20180327-h0y19c.

135 Mackey and Nayyar (n 126) 597.

136 United Nations Global Marketplace, 'UNICEF: Development of A Global Trust Repository – Solution, Implementation and Operation Services' (11 June 2021) https://www.ungm.org/Public/Notice/131648.

that can use a shared database with separately confirmed and encrypted entries to identify goods and communicate information about them.[137] Corporate actors such as Walmart are already successfully using blockchain technology to verify food supply chains, and pharmaceutical companies are piloting blockchain-based ledgers.[138] Rather than storing the relevant information on a central ledger, distributed ledger technology underlying blockchain shares data in multiple locations; this removes the single point of failure and reduces the likelihood of security breaches.[139] Cryptography underpinning distributed ledger technology 'enables an immutable and verifiable chain of custody that can be used to support product investigation' as well as independent verification of provenance.[140] The Internet of Things can provide unique identifiers for products that can be used to transfer data over a network, enabling many to access reliable information regarding the origin of goods and intellectual property rights associated with goods on devices and machines.[141] Currently, blockchain technology can use identifiers embedded onto packaging but in the future minute cryptographic anchors could be embedded into fabrics or onto pharmaceuticals.[142] A key feature of blockchain is that the decentralised ledger is tamper-evident, so it is possible to confirm the integrity of the information extracted from the ledger, making blockchain a highly trustworthy source. This can assist customs authorities to detect imported counterfeit goods but also enable end users to confirm the provenance of both imported and domestically produced goods.[143] A mechanism for end users to accurately identify counterfeits can significantly improve the effectiveness of detection as it does not solely rely on state authorities to identify counterfeit goods.

---

[137] IBM et al, *FDA DSCSA: Blockchain Interoperability Pilot Project Report* (February 2020) https://www.ibm.com/downloads/cas/9V2LRYG5.

[138] Frederick Mostert and Wang Jue, 'The Application and Challenges of Blockchain in Intellectual Property Driven Businesses in China' (2018) 11 *Tsinghua China Law Review* 13, 18–19.

[139] Mark Van Rijmenam and Philippa Ryan, *Blockchain: Transforming Your Business and Our World* (Routledge, 2018) 22.

[140] IBM et al (n 137) 15.

[141] Ibid 16–20.

[142] K R Balasubramanyam, 'Blockchain Technology can Help Weed Out Fakes, says IBM', *Economic Times* (online, 21 March 2018) https://economictimes.indiatimes.com/tech/internet/blockchain-technology-can-help-weed-out-fakes-says-ibm/articleshow/63389546.cms. See also Martin Holland, Josip Stjepandić and Christopher Nigischer, 'Intellectual Property Protection of 3D Print Supply Chain with Blockchain Technology' in Institute of Electrical and Electronics Engineers Inc (eds), *IEEE International Conference on Engineering, Technology and Innovation* (IEEE, 2018) 971.

[143] Van Rijmenam and Ryan (n 139) 121.

Investing in technology that integrates blockchain is also appealing because it can communicate additional important information, including identifying authorised licensees of intellectual property owners.[144] It could also communicate information about products that are generic or parallel imports. Further checks and balances are possible where it can provide secure information about ingredients for suppliers.[145] Blockchain could also add value by providing data records and enable authorities to collect and share intelligence about counterfeits between authorities across jurisdictions. Although it is not tamper-proof, information secured through blockchain technology is tamper-evident: all of the decentralised records will not match each other if they are changed after data about products is transferred on the blockchain. Consequently, if security mechanisms are penetrated, this can be detected when records are reviewed.

Coordination is needed to facilitate use of this information and balance transparency against the need for some intelligence-sharing to remain confidential in collaborative efforts to prosecute counterfeiters. Costs resulting from the infrastructure associated with widespread dissemination of technology means that cooperation incorporating decentralised technology such as blockchain is likely to require international assistance from wealthier states to others to enable more states to adopt the relevant technology. Where intellectual property rights attach to provenance technology, broad cooperation can facilitate collective bargaining through patent pools or encourage patent pledges,[146] which reduces the cost of technology transfer.[147] Effective detection technology requires widespread agreement about standards and interoperability protocols.[148] Standards that encourage uniform approaches to information-sharing can enable better coordination. Blockchain systems can be widely adopted and adapted, as blockchain is based on open source code that can be amended without payment of licensing fees to copyright owners.[149] However, intellectual property is likely to protect further technology that integrates blockchain

---

[144] See Mostert and Jue (n 138) 32–33.

[145] Ibid 18–19.

[146] Huang-Chih Sung, 'When Open Source Software Encounters Patents: Blockchain as an Example to Explore the Dilemma and Solutions' (2018) 18 *John Marshall Review of Intellectual Property Law* 55, 80.

[147] See Robert C Bird and Daniel R Cahoy, 'Human Rights, Technology, and Food: Coordinating Access and Innovation for 2050 and Beyond' (2015) 52 *American Business Law Journal* 435, 484–487.

[148] World Intellectual Property Organization ('WIPO'), *Committee on WIPO Standards, Seventh Session Report*, CWS/7/29 (3 September 2019) 8 https://www.wipo.int/edocs/mdocs/cws/en/cws_7/cws_7_29.pdf; Fran Casino et al, 'A Systematic Literature Review of Blockchain-Based Applications: Current Status, Classification and Open Issues' (2019) 36 *Telematics and Informatics* 55, 71.

[149] Sung (n 146) 57.

detection into supply chains for goods such as personal protective equipment ('PPE') and pharmaceuticals. Intellectual property-protectable innovation may valuably enable the development of highly effective, environmentally sustainable security protocols. The security protocol underlying bitcoin requires vast amounts of electricity so that the expanding chain continues to be verified, rather than relying on a centralised system.[150] Alternative protocols exist and should be assessed for their sustainability, as well as their ability to withstand breaches and other blockchain vulnerabilities.[151] Blockchain is an appealing safeguard but recent incursions of blockchain security suggest that even this mechanism is not completely immutable.[152]

The capacity for a range of actors who are stakeholders in supply chains to benefit from technology-based mechanisms to address counterfeiting[153] can build consensus towards reform that does not rely on widespread multilateral agreement. However, achieving common standards and cooperation would make secure, technologically-driven provenance assurance approaches more affordable, worldwide. Technological approaches are emerging in different jurisdictions, but a rights-based approach can help consolidate them so that they support a human rights culture for trade marks. In the United States, full traceability of drugs will be required from 2023.[154] In Europe, the European Union Intellectual Property Office ('EUIPO') is part of a plan to use blockchain and non-fungible tokens to authenticate physical products, which can permit stakeholders to trace provenance and intellectual property rights.[155] WIPO has already recognised that blockchain can play an important role in intellectual property protection and requires widespread cooperation regarding standards, but this needs to be part of a broader supply chain approach.[156] Significant further engagement between states and other stakeholders is required for technological measures to become viable solutions to detecting and deterring counterfeit activities. Cost-effective access to these types of technology will be crucial to blockchain being a viable widespread solution and providing an effective global response to counterfeiting. A technology-focused rights-based

---

150 Ahmed Farouk et al, 'Blockchain Platform for Industrial Healthcare: Vision and Future Opportunities' (2020) 154 *Computer Communications* 223, 228.

151 Ibid.

152 See Bishwas C Gupta et al, 'An Insecurity Study of Ethereum Smart Contract' in *International Conference on Security, Privacy, and Applied Cryptography Engineering* (Springer, 2020) 188.

153 See Mostert and Jue (n 138) 16–20.

154 *Drug Supply Chain Security Act* (DSCSA) (2013) (United States of America).

155 Ernesto Van Der Sar, 'EU Initiative Uses Blockchain and NFTs to Fight IP Infringement' *Torrent Freak* (6 September 2022) https://torrentfreak.com/eu-initiative-uses-blockchain-and-nfts-to-fight-ip-infringement-220906/.

156 See World Intellectual Property Organization (n 148) 8; Casino et al (n 148) 71.

institutional approach also needs to be flexible so that stakeholders can adopt new and more cost-effective technological approaches to detecting and deterring anti-counterfeiting which may present better opportunities for protection from counterfeits in the future.

4.2 Institutional Features of a Framework Convention on Goods Provenance ('FCGP')

This section explores how multilateral consensus could develop within the FCGP. The way that the Framework Convention on Tobacco Control ('FCTC') has been used to establish evolving multilateral consensus about tobacco control mechanisms was explored in the plain packaging case study. Within the FCTC, tobacco control has evolved through the collaborative mechanism of using protocols as guidance for the implementation of the core agreement. This aligns with the detailed guidance that treaty-making bodies provide about individual human rights or human rights principles.[157] Awareness of explicit engagement with human rights institutions is slowly evolving in the FCTC Conference of Parties.[158] An FCGP needs to be more explicit about embedding human rights principles from the outset. This section translates the concerns of the HRATM framework into guidance for embedding rights-based principles, including human rights accountability, into the new mechanism.

Adopting the approach of using evolving multilateral cooperation to revise and innovate institutional standards found in the FCTC and other framework conventions would enable parties to the FCGP mechanism to reach broader agreement on principles regarding enhanced enforcement and then more specific guidelines to be developed as consensus builds.[159] This can permit a sector-by-sector approach which prioritises secure provenance technology for the goods which pose the greatest concerns for human rights. Specific approaches for detection of certain counterfeit products such as PPE and pharmaceuticals can also be supported. A Protocol to Eliminate Illicit Trade in Tobacco Products has developed through the FCTC.[160] The development and implementation of this instrument provides lessons for the institutional development of the FCGP. The involvement of tobacco companies in the

---

[157] See, for example, *General Comment 14* (n 26).

[158] Conference of the Parties to the World Health Organization Framework Convention on Tobacco Control, *Report of the Eighth Session of the Conference of the Parties to the WHO Framework Convention on Tobacco Control* (October 2018) [111].

[159] See Lawrence O Gostin, *Global Health Law* (Harvard University Press, 2014) 435–439.

[160] *Protocol to Eliminate Illicit Trade in Tobacco Products*, WHO Doc FCTC/COP5(1) (12 November 2012).

protocol development process has been controversial because of their interest in enforcing their own private rights.[161] Not all FCTC parties have signed or ratified the agreement.[162] Despite its leading role in implementing tobacco plain packaging, Uruguay has recently attempted to reintroduce some cigarette branding, citing difficulties implementing obligations found within the protocol for tracking and tracing tobacco, including insufficient compatibility between tracing mechanisms used by different manufacturers.[163]

A framework convention structure permits states to be more agile in identifying and considering other technological solutions to deter counterfeiting within a rights-based framework, using conferences of parties to negotiate more detailed technology-specific guidance on an ongoing basis. Technology will support secure reporting about detection of substandard goods and goods that do not have tracing mechanisms attached: the way that this information is distributed should be agreed by the parties to discourage private actors from dominating the discourse about counterfeit goods.[164] Human rights considerations can shape the way that the FCGP aids protection of private rights. Guiding private actors who use tracking and tracing to cooperate and meet human rights obligations will be central to the success of the FCGP.

Change needs to engage a diverse range of actors and encourage active participation of states, civil society and intergovernmental organisations. It can also implement technological measures that encourage participation by key stakeholders in the supply chain and individuals who wish to confirm provenance themselves. Protocols can develop guidance on the reporting of health and safety concerns about all goods, which may help identify the prevalence of substandard goods that are not counterfeit. Uniform technological standards can also permit voluntary adoption of the technology in lower priority sectors, subject to cost-sharing arrangements. The agreement should embed cost-sharing while recognising concerns about institutional capture of the

---

[161] See Liberman (n 47) 340–341; See also Neil Boister, 'The European Anti-Fraud Office and the Protocol to Eliminate Illicit Trade in Tobacco Products' in Andrew D Mitchell and Tania Voon (eds), *The Global Tobacco Epidemic and the Law* (Edward Elgar Publishing, 2014) 64.

[162] United Nations Treaty Collection, '4. a Protocol to Eliminate Illicit Trade in Tobacco Products' 'https://treaties.un.org/Pages/ViewDetails.aspx?src=TREATY&mtdsg_no=IX-4-a&chapter=9&clang=_en.

[163] *Sociedad Uruguaya de Tabacología v Estado Poder Ejecutivo*, Juzgados Letrados de Familia [Family Court of Uruguay], IUE 2-54452/2022, 19 October 2022 [tr author].

[164] See approach taken within Framework Convention on Tobacco Control and concerns raised by Liberman (n 47) 340–342; see also Oscar A Cabrera and Lawrence O Gostin, 'Human Rights and the Framework Convention on Tobacco Control: Mutually Reinforcing Systems' (2011) 7(3) *International Journal of Law in Context* 285.

mechanism by self-interested private actors and encourage corporations to participate without passing costs on to the most vulnerable.[165] Secure provenance assurance will deter counterfeit trade and empower individuals to identify and reject counterfeit products. Consumers can knowingly purchase counterfeit goods for a range of reasons: this chapter does not resolve those issues but the FCGP will implement mechanisms that increase consumer awareness that goods are counterfeit.

Equitably distributing the cost of the technology and embedding technological tracing mechanisms on or into goods is critical. The FCGP should embed equitable sharing of the costs of implementing this new approach between states, aligned with principles of progressive realisation. Realisation of human rights should be recognised in the preamble and as an objective of the agreement. Specific reference should also be made to the rights that have been relevantly identified in this book, including rights to health, privacy, a fair trial and access to applications of the benefits of science. Recognition of the right to property should align with the approach taken in key human rights agreements and reflect the importance of a knowledge commons.[166]

Key principles of progressive realisation, effectiveness and international cooperation and assistance to ensure that all parties achieve the identified human rights objectives of the agreement should be included, along with the need to promote transparency and participation. The preamble should also recognise the importance of promoting the rights of those most impacted by the harmful effects of distribution of goods outside of traditional supply chains. Monitoring and accountability should be built into the agreement to ensure that it operates consistently with human rights principles, and an agreed transparency framework will support this.[167] Impact assessments should be part of the negotiation of the agreement and subsequent protocols that implement the measures agreed. Considerations of effectiveness will be supported by an emphasis in the agreement on transparently communicating secured information to assure provenance and communicate intellectual property ownership.

These measures should develop through ongoing international cooperation that is directed towards evolving multilateral consensus. General agreement will need to be reached on the features that technology will implement, key

---

[165] See Bird and Cahoy (n 147) 484–487.

[166] Peter K Yu, 'The Anatomy of the Human Rights Framework for Intellectual Property' (2016) 69(1) *SMU Law Review* 37, 94 ('The Anatomy of the Human Rights Framework for Intellectual Property').

[167] See OHCHR guidance on embedding human rights into FCCC: 'Integrating Human Rights at the UNFCCC', *United Nations Office of the High Commissioner for Human Rights* https://www.ohchr.org/en/climate-change/integrating-human-rights-unfccc.

principles related to implementation and then protocols can be agreed to implement the technology. Adapting the structure of the Framework Convention on Tobacco Control,[168] the general FCGP agreement should include the following:

- Measures relating to provenance identification:
  - Parties shall identify goods of concern and develop requirements for tracing of goods.
  - Individuals shall have access to information about the origin of these goods.
- Measures relating to secure tracing:
  - Parties shall develop security measures to protect tracing of goods.
  - Parties shall agree on standards that facilitate secure tracing of goods.
  - Parties shall agree on mechanisms to ensure individuals have access to reliable provenance information.
  - Parties shall agree on mechanisms to report detection of counterfeit goods and substandard goods.
- Measures relating to intellectual property identification:
  - Parties agree that tracing mechanisms shall communicate any trade mark and copyright recordation or registration related to goods. Parties shall agree on any additional types of information about intellectual property that should be communicated through tracing.
- Measures relating to collection and distribution of information:
  - Parties agree categories of information that may be collected during tracking and tracing.
  - Parties agree on approaches to distribution of information and any confidentiality protocols associated with this.
  - Parties agree other reporting mechanisms to report goods that do not have tracing mechanisms attached and other objectives that support detection of counterfeit goods, consistent with the principles of this agreement.

The FCGP should also include agreement to monitor and assess human rights through regular human rights assessments of the impact of the measures agreed in this convention. During development of protocols to implement measures, human rights assessment should be conducted and be a critical consideration. Obligations of international cooperation and assistance need to be explicitly recognised through provisions about scientific and technical cooperation; cooperation with industry and supply chains; technical assistance and technol-

[168] See *WHO Framework Convention on Tobacco Control*, opened for signature 21 May 2003, 2302 UNTS 166 (entered into force 27 February 2005) preamble ('*FCTC*').

ogy transfer; and financial resources that commit to equitable distribution of implementation costs between stakeholders.

Broad cooperation to deter counterfeiting and facilitate detection will benefit intellectual property rights holders and encourage their participation. Blockchain technology has already commercially benefited companies that use it to market that its products are part of secure supply chains that guarantee organic or fair trade origin.[169] Although the FCGP aims to complement the enforcement provisions of *TRIPS*, it is also intended to transform the current approach to negotiating *TRIPS*-plus agreements regarding trade mark enforcement. Copyright piracy is beyond the scope of this book, yet it could be addressed through the FCGP: many goods protected by copyright are also protected by trade marks.

A rights-based approach recognises that anti-counterfeiting measures engage obligations pursuant to the right to health as well as property rights. Protection of intellectual property rights is consistent with a rights-based approach if it is balanced against other relevant rights. Integrating information about trade mark ownership into technological tracing measures available to consumers strengthens the normatively justified function of trade marks to provide consumers with information about the origin of their products, incentivising owners to maintain associated quality standards.[170] There may also be human-rights-based benefits to providing information about other intellectual property rights through the tracing process. Clearly identifying a good as a generic product to customs may reduce inappropriate seizures. For example, border inspectors may be less likely to confuse international non-proprietary names on generic pharmaceutical products with similar trade marks registered for originator products.[171]

The FCGP recognises that problems with counterfeiting are not limited to the reliance on enforcement of trade mark rights to deter illicit trade and problems with the effectiveness of intellectual property-focused protection mechanisms. Features of the FCGP, such as permitting individuals to self-verify provenance, can address structural problems, including corruption. Making this technology cost-effective can also support consumer access to generic products and provide information that assures them that these are also good-quality products. The FCGP is designed to support enforcement activities in a manner consistent with realisation of human rights. Any human rights protection that supports individual intellectual property rights should

---

169 Van Rijmenam and Ryan (n 139) 120–124.

170 See Fink, Maskus and Qian (n 37) 5–6.

171 See Kappoori M Gopakumar and Nirmalya Syam, 'International Nonproprietary Names and Trademarks: A Public Health Perspective' (2008) 11(2) *Journal of World Intellectual Property* 63, 64.

be balanced against rights to participate in culture and access the benefits of science. This new approach to provenance tracing should strengthen human rights protection by deterring trade in substandard counterfeit goods, which will support the core function of trade marks by adopting an approach that is consistent with a human rights culture.

5 CONCLUSION

The international legal framework needs to adopt a rights-based framework to better facilitate public health and intellectual property protection using human rights benchmarks to ensure adequate protection for individuals from health threats posed by counterfeiting. It should also recognise the critical role of secure technology for effectively addressing threats posed by counterfeiting. There are many technological mechanisms currently in place to address counterfeiting, but international coordination should better harness these mechanisms so that they can be used consistently across supply chains. Secure data collection and transfer using mechanisms such as blockchain are critical features of this unified approach. Integrating sophisticated verification technology into a rights-based institutional approach should address the problems present in the existing system for detection and deterrence of counterfeit activities that pose health concerns.

This chapter uses principles from the HRATM framework to propose a transformative integration of trade mark protection, innovative detection technology and a rights-based approach into an institutional framework that will better address the serious threats to health that counterfeit products can pose worldwide. Blockchain and other technology-based innovations can improve supply chain security to better detect and deter counterfeiting. A rights-based approach to reforming anti-counterfeiting regimes strengthens a public health approach. The proposal builds on key findings from each of the case studies about the relationship between trade marks and human rights which are discussed in the first part of this chapter and analysed further in the following chapter.

Attention needs to be given to the role that both human rights and intellectual property can play in reform, ensuring that appropriate weight is given to the protection of economic, social and cultural rights.[172] There has long been an emphasis on the relationship between patent protection and the right to health.[173] This proposal addresses the concern explored in the previous chapter that trade marks can also be critically important mechanisms for ensuring quality

[172] See Okediji (n 11).
[173] Helfer and Austin (n 42) 90.

medical products are accessible and available in response to global health concerns. Modifying the role of trade marks in protecting against counterfeiting so that it is part of a broader approach to securing supply chains and protecting against third party threats to individual rights to health can not only address this but 'encourage creativity and innovation that benefits society as a whole'.[174] The approach proposed in this chapter provides a model for another element of a human rights culture for trade marks. The following chapter will consider the range of approaches considered and developed in this book that support the establishment and further development of that culture.

[174] Ibid 520.

7 Founding a global human rights culture for trade marks: planning for success

1 INTRODUCTION

A human rights culture for trade marks enables states to recognise their obligations to respect, protect, promote and fulfil human rights. This requires stakeholders to adjust trade mark rights to meet human rights objectives. This chapter identifies the foundations for a human rights culture and different mechanisms that help stakeholders to understand the relationship between human rights and trade mark law and the problems that fragmentation between the fields can pose. The value of different approaches to understanding the relationship between trade marks and human rights has been recognised in each of the case studies of plain packaging, contrary marks and anti-counterfeiting. Each case study analyses the human rights implications of trade mark protection and the local conditions which influence those implications. Local conditions influence the way in which prescriptive frameworks apply to the trade mark protection analysed in each case study, and their suitability for preventing and addressing conflicts at a domestic and international level. A human rights culture for trade marks has both domestic and international aspects, but diverse economic, legal and geo-political local conditions means that it may operate differently between states. Recognising this can support a transformative integration of human rights into trade mark law.[1] Ensuring that a human rights culture is pluralistic to the extent that it proposes solutions to human rights problems that are responsive to different local conditions reflects the inclusive and constructive approach of human rights institutions and the flexibility for domestic calibration that international intellectual property law permits.

Features of both fields support a pluralistic approach to a human rights culture. One of the reasons that human rights institutions are argued to be

[1] See Ruth Okediji, 'Does Intellectual Property Need Human Rights?' (2018) 50(1) *New York University Journal of International Law and Politics* 19.

toothless is that a human rights approach to compliance focuses on inclusion.[2] It is preferable to continue to include states that do not meet human rights standards, as this encourages continuing involvement in the institutions, increasing the likelihood of improvement. Resource constraints may impede implementation by states of economic, social and cultural rights, prompting the use of progressive realisation to measure compliance. Where resources impede realisation of a core obligation of the right, this engages the obligation of other states to provide international cooperation and assistance to support less-well-resourced states.[3] The approach taken in *TRIPS* recognises that there will be domestic differences in implementation of international intellectual property law.

The next section of this chapter identifies foundational features of a human rights culture for trade marks, drawing on findings from the case studies. The third section identifies lessons from the application of existing prescriptive models to the case studies to understand their value in a human rights culture for trade marks. The fourth section explores ways that these lessons apply to trade and investment agreements.

2 CULTURAL FOUNDATIONS

This section identifies features of a culture that harmonises trade marks and human rights. The normative and hierarchical claims considered in the first part of this book can be useful tools to justify the need to build a positive human rights culture for trade marks. The case studies and associated proposals for reform show how these tools can work in practice.

2.1 The Human Rights Assessment for Trade Marks ('HRATM') Framework

Chapter 2 explored the way that a human rights-based approach to health provides a valuable basis for an analytical framework that can be applied to trade marks. This Human Rights Assessment for Trade Marks ('HRATM') framework addresses human rights concerns that are directly relevant to trade marks and the need to ensure that models harmonising human rights and intellectual property recognise the critical importance of economic, social and cul-

---

2 Rhona K M Smith, 'Human Rights in International Law' in Michael Goodhart (ed), *Human Rights: Politics and Practice* (Oxford University Press, 3rd ed, 2016) 60, 72.

3 Committee on Economic, Social and Cultural Rights, *General Comment No 3: The Nature of States Parties' Obligations (Art 2, Para 1 of the Covenant)*, UN ESCOR, 5th sess, UN Doc E/1991/23 (14 December 1990) [13]–[14] ('*General Comment 3*').

tural rights. The application of the HRATM framework in the contrary marks case study demonstrates that the framework remains relevant when the rights engaged are primarily civil or political rights, such as freedom of expression, and the right to health is not engaged.

The HRATM framework adapts existing assessment tools so that they can be applied to intellectual property concerns and explores the following questions:

1. What human rights are implicated by the trade mark laws studied and how are they impacted by the operation of the legislation specifically (as opposed to other factors)?
2. What mechanisms for monitoring and accountability are in place to ensure that human rights standards are met?
3. Are principles of participation, empowerment and transparency met in the formulation and operation of the laws?
4. Are principles of international cooperation and assistance relevant to the realisation of human rights in relation to this law?
5. How can rights and interests be balanced against each other? Are any restrictions on human rights or their progressive realisation permissible? If the law restricts certain human rights, is this balanced against benefits for other human rights?

This assessment approach uses existing legal standards to assess the human rights implications of trade mark protection. Additional questions focus on strengthening a rights-based approach that emphasises operationalising human rights by implementing the standards found in human rights law.[4] An assessment tool is important because the first step to using human rights as a tool of transformation is to understand the complex interactions between intellectual property and human rights.

This book has identified examples where important human rights concerns for domestic and international trade mark protection are underexplored. Although the focus in the literature has previously been on the relationship between trade marks and freedom of expression,[5] a range of human rights are relevant to trade mark protection. Monitoring and accountability are important features of a human rights culture, which make it easier to identify and recognise conflict between the fields of intellectual property and human

---

[4] Paul Hunt, 'Refreshing Human Rights for our Time and Place' (2021) 29 *Waikato Law Review* 60, 64.

[5] See, for example, Laurence R Helfer and Graeme Austin (eds), *Human Rights and Intellectual Property: Mapping the Global Interface* (Cambridge University Press, 2011) 283–312.

rights. The case studies demonstrate the way in which the legislation studied engages multiple other human rights considerations, suggesting that an integrated assessment of relevant human rights implications of legislation is the best approach to analysis of intellectual property. Other important features of the human rights analytical approach used in this book are the interrelated and interdependent nature of rights; progressive realisation of economic, social and cultural rights; very limited permissible restrictions on rights; the importance of participation and transparency and obligations of international cooperation and assistance. Transparency and participation support diverse approaches to human rights advocacy and permit assessment of accountability with human rights standards.

2.2 Lessons From Applying the HRATM Framework

This book has used the HRATM framework to explore the relationship between trade marks and human rights in three case studies engaging questions of the nature of trade mark rights and their registration and enforcement. This analysis supported proposals for ensuring that the operation of trade mark law is consistent with human rights. The case studies demonstrate ways in which trade mark legislation can foster and restrict human rights. They include comparisons that explore the nature and impact of local conditions for states in relation to plain packaging that limits the use of trade marks, registrations for contrary marks and enforcement of trade marks to limit counterfeiting. The pluralistic approach of this book supports working within these conditions to improve the realisation of human rights in the jurisdiction in focus. However, an international approach to some of the problems identified could also meaningfully address some of the concerns that trade mark protection poses for human rights.

In practice, considerations of human rights are not central to the development of trade mark laws, although intellectual property rights, including trade marks, can function to both protect and restrict the integrated rights to access the benefits of science and culture that comprise *ICESCR* Article 15.[6] This reflects the separate development of human rights law and intellectual property law which has resulted in fragmentation between the fields.[7] Fragmentation increases the likelihood of conflict between trade marks and human rights concerns remaining unidentified or unaddressed, particularly where it does

---

[6] *International Covenant on Economic, Social and Cultural Rights*, opened for signature 16 December 1966, 993 UNTS 3 (entered into force 3 January 1976) art 15 ('*ICESCR*').

[7] See Chapter 1, section 2.

not result in the type of direct conflict that was evident in the plain packaging disputes. Yet greater monitoring and assessment could assist trade mark protection to function to better protect human rights. The case studies in this book show that the true human rights impacts of trade mark protection are much broader than the relationship between trade marks and freedom of expression, and include rights to health, life, protection from hate speech and discrimination, rights to benefit from science and culture, privacy and a fair trial.

Human rights concerns remaining unidentified or unaddressed may have a negative impact on the capacity of intellectual property frameworks to support realisation of human rights. The plain packaging case study in Chapter 3 finds that the Australian legislation disputed in the World Trade Organization ('WTO') by four other states was justified by human rights considerations. Yet these justifications were not argued in support of the measures nor considered.[8] Although the decisions suspending mechanisms to refuse trade mark registration for scandalous, disparaging and offensive marks relied on American First Amendment free speech justifications,[9] the contrary marks case study analysed in Chapter 4 shows that this does not align with human rights to freedom of expression and protection from discrimination and hate speech. Once human rights considerations are recognised, these examples evidence fragmentation between states about the extent to which their human rights obligations should restrict the scope of rights available to trade mark owners. Flexibility for states to implement intellectual property obligations permits some regulatory autonomy to develop domestically sensitive intellectual property laws. However, states are also bound by international law to recognise their human rights obligations that are relevant to domestic implementation of international intellectual property standards.

An important feature of a human rights culture for trade mark protection is the development of an appropriate forum for resolving serious conflicts between human rights and intellectual property. Objectives of systemic integration between intellectual property and human rights can be realised if states use interpretive tools in international law and argue the relevance of human rights to intellectual property. Systemic integration is also relevant to understanding which dispute resolution mechanisms might be most appropriate for

---

[8] See Panel Report, *Australia – Certain Measures Concerning Trademarks, Geographical Indications and Other Plain Packaging Requirements Applicable to Tobacco Products and Packaging*, WTO Doc WT/DS435/R, WT/DS441/R, WT/DS458/R, WT/DS467/R (28 June 2018).

[9] *Matal v Tam*, 137 S Ct 1744, 1747 (2017); *Iancu v Brunetti,* 139 S Ct 2294, 2297 (2019).

permitting recognition of both human rights and intellectual property.[10] Dual recognition is less likely in the human rights institutions as they are presently structured: their focus is on human rights. Although the *Australia – Tobacco Plain Packaging* decision provides a basis for arguing that human rights considerations are relevant to justification of policies that restrict trade mark rights in the WTO dispute mechanisms, human rights have not yet been successfully used in the small number of decided cases involving *TRIPS*. The extremely protracted tobacco plain packaging disputes also intensified regulatory chill for plain packaging policies. Although it has never been used, the judicial mechanism for the *Paris Convention* is the International Court of Justice.[11] This could be an appropriate mechanism for systemic integration as it has jurisdiction to consider human rights obligations. There is already evidence of a human rights culture in the World Intellectual Property Organization ('WIPO'), so this may be an area for future consideration.[12]

Problematically, the structure of bilateral, regional and multilateral trade and investment agreements encourages compliance more strongly than relevant human rights mechanisms can, when conflicts between the two fields crystallise in disputes. Analysis of the plain packaging case study identifies the chilling regulatory impact of disputes about plain packaging legislation at domestic, bilateral and international levels on plain packaging policies that are important for the realisation of the right to health. As this chilling effect has restrained other states from implementing similar legislation, despite their stated desire to do so, the actions of the disputing tobacco companies have indirectly restricted states from progressively realising their right to health protection obligations in international law.[13] An emphasis on human rights scrutiny is important in order to recognise and address the impact of regulatory chill of this nature. Regime shifts away from the WTO towards regional and bilateral mechanisms suggest a need for greater human rights scrutiny of the

---

[10] Henning Grosse Ruse-Khan, 'A Conflict-of-Laws Approach to Competing Rationalities in International Law: The Case of Plain Packaging between Intellectual Property, Trade, Investment and Health' (2013) 9(2) *Journal of Private International Law* 308, 331.

[11] Sam Ricketson, *The Paris Convention for the Protection of Industrial Property: A Commentary* (Oxford University Press, 2015) 323.

[12] For example, the *Marrakesh Treaty* is the first treaty in international law that explicitly focuses on intellectual property and human rights. *Marrakesh Treaty to Facilitate Access to Published Works for Persons Who Are Blind, Visually Impaired, or Otherwise Print Disabled*, opened for signature 27 June 2013 [2014] ATNIF 1 (entered into force 30 September 2016).

[13] See Benjamin Hawkins, Chris Holden and Sophie Mackinder, 'A Multi-Level, Multi-Jurisdictional Strategy: Transnational Tobacco Companies' Attempts to Obstruct Tobacco Packaging Restrictions' (2019) 14(4) *Global Public Health* 570.

obligations and dispute resolution mechanisms than currently exists. States need to continue to recognise the importance of human rights in the negotiation of bilateral, plurilateral and multilateral agreements and also in WTO disputes.

Detailed human rights scrutiny of international agreements containing intellectual property provisions, as well as existing and prospective domestic intellectual property legislation, is necessary. Some jurisdictions have greatly expanded protection available for trade mark owners and required other states to implement *TRIPS*-plus provisions in trade and investment agreements.[14]

Positive recognition of human rights is strengthened by transparent assessment of policy content and design and proposed bilateral, plurilateral and multilateral agreements, while they are being negotiated. This proactive approach is preferable to reliance on human rights as a corrective.[15] Murumba explains that using human rights as a 'weapon of last resort' is problematic for balancing interests in the international legal system.[16] Currently, intellectual property laws embed order consistent with a command–sanction approach that states more readily implement than the considerations of justice that are more closely aligned with human rights.[17] Many of the human rights concerns identified in this book are amplified by a trend towards expanding the rights of trade mark owners beyond the normative justifications for trade mark law, primarily found in economic theory that is linked to utilitarian justifications for intellectual property protection.[18] The key function of trade marks supported by this normative justification is the role that trade marks play in reducing consumer search costs by protecting the goodwill of trade mark owners who are incentivised to use their marks to indicate origin and provide consistent quality. The anti-counterfeiting case study in Chapter 5 uses the threats posed by counterfeit medical products in the Covid-19 pandemic to argue that more attention should be given to preventing counterfeiting so that trade marks function as a reliable badge of origin. Where counterfeit trade marks facilitate trade in substandard goods there can be very serious implications for human rights to health and life.

---

[14] See Burton Ong, 'The Trademark Law Provisions of Bilateral Free Trade Agreements' in Graeme B Dinwoodie and Marc D Janis (eds), *Trademark Law and Theory: A Handbook of Contemporary Research* (Edward Elgar Publishing, 2008) 229.

[15] Samuel Murumba, 'Foxes and Hedgehogs at the Intersection of Human Rights and Intellectual Property' (2012) 38(1) *Monash University Law Review* 119, 135.

[16] Ibid 134.

[17] Ibid 133.

[18] William Fisher, 'Theories of Intellectual Property' in Stephen R Munzer (ed), *New Essays in the Legal and Political Theory of Property* (Cambridge University Press, 2001) 168, 169; William M Landes and Richard A Posner, *The Economic Structure of Intellectual Property Law* (Harvard University Press, 2003) 173.

2.3 Transformative Application of the HRATM Framework

Trade marks can support human rights when they function effectively to prevent trade in substandard goods. Chapter 6 has proposed an approach that embeds rights-based principles into the design of a new multilateral agreement that can strengthen protection for trade mark owners by empowering consumers and other actors in the supply chain to reject and report substandard and counterfeit goods. This approach addresses human rights concerns related to trade mark enforcement not being effective vehicles to prevent trade in substandard goods produced outside of normal trade channels that can threaten the right to health. The Framework Convention on Goods Provenance ('FCGP') proposal builds on application of the HRATM framework and other prescriptive models in the case studies. The focus of the agreement is on preventing the dissemination of substandard goods, as these pose the most serious human rights concerns. There is a correlation between substandard goods that engage human rights to health and life and goods that bear counterfeit marks, but there is also a lack of reliable data for states to understand this relationship. The FCGP addresses this problem by using technology to track and trace goods to assure provenance without relying on trade marks. This is designed to deter counterfeiting operations as it will be easier for supply chain actors to detect counterfeit products more accurately. The instrument also facilitates better reporting of substandard goods and counterfeit goods. This can enable states to assess the extent to which strengthening other trade mark enforcement machinery will protect human rights. Effective trade mark enforcement can also encourage access to applications of the benefits of science. The rights-based principles in the HRATM framework guide institutional design of the FCGP.

The FCGP proposed in Chapter 6 uses rights-based principles to strengthen secure tracing of goods provenance that could also communicate trade mark rights. Investment in this mechanism would support the private rights of trade mark owners but it would also strengthen the public interest in trade marks providing an accurate indication of origin and quality. This badge of origin function is critical to the social welfare benefits provided by trade mark protection. A new technological approach to detection of counterfeit goods that is secured by blockchain could transform transparency of information about goods provenance that individuals can readily access, providing greater opportunities for understanding the impact of counterfeit goods on human rights. The proposal for an FCGP reflects a need for transformation of the existing reliance on intellectual property enforcement to address human rights problems associated with counterfeiting. It emphasises human rights assessment, monitoring and accountability, and international cooperation and assistance. This new approach could also support secure collection of information about counterfeit goods that will enable a better understanding of what resource investments are needed from stakeholders and how they should be deployed to build a system that supports equitable participation and also recognises the important human rights concerns posed by counterfeit goods.

The HRATM analysis tool can also support treaty analysis and parliamentary scrutiny. It will be useful for civil society to highlight the human rights implications of trade marks, where relevant, and for national human rights institutions who wish to address these implications. Human rights scrutiny is an important tool for understanding both protective and restrictive relationships between human rights and trade marks. The human rights-based approach to scrutiny of intellectual property legislation and international agreements, which this book develops in the HRATM framework, permits recognition of important features of economic, social and cultural rights grounded in the legislative analysis of each case study. The approach provides standards of analysis that should be useful for a range of actors. Advocates may use these analytical approaches to contest corporate attempts to expand human rights protection for intellectual property beyond appropriate boundaries.[19] Forman characterises rights as 'drivers of social change' that permit social actors and policymakers to collect evidence about human rights impacts that could influence adjustments to law, policy and programmes.[20] Helfer and Austin's welfare preservation considerations can also recognise state obligations to protect intellectual property. The anti-counterfeiting case study demonstrates that, where a range of structural issues contribute to human rights concerns, change may be necessary, but this may need to be broader than modification of intellectual property rights. These assessments can also be difficult without sufficient data to understand the true nature of the problem.

Different mechanisms that assess human rights compliance can support a human rights culture for trade marks. This book has identified analytical approaches found in prescriptive harmonising models that seek to address conflict between human rights and intellectual property. Appropriate mechanisms for promoting and fostering a human rights culture for trade marks have been tested, particularly by applying principles and mechanisms from conceptual

---

[19] See Susan K Sell, *Private Power, Public Law: The Globalization of Intellectual Property Rights* (Cambridge University Press, 2003); Peter K Yu, 'Ten Common Questions about Intellectual Property and Human Rights' (2007) 23(4) *Georgia State University Law Review* 709, 730.

[20] Lisa Forman, 'From TRIPS-Plus to Rights-Plus? Exploring Right to Health Impact Assessment of Trade-Related Intellectual Property Rights through the Thai Experience' (2012) 7(2) *Asian Journal of WTO and International Health Law and Policy* 347, 355. See also Prawase Wasi, '"Triangle That Moves the Mountain" and Health Systems Reform Movement in Thailand' (2000) 4(2) *WHO Human Resources for Health Development Journal* 106.

models to the case study analysis. These foundations for a human rights culture for trade marks can be tailored to divergent local conditions within states. The next section considers how specific models have been useful to understanding the relationship between trade marks and human rights in the case studies.

3 LESSONS FROM APPLYING THE MODELS

The analytical approaches used and applied in this book to understand the relationship between human rights and trade marks can support a human rights culture for trade marks that acknowledges both the protective and restrictive dimensions of the relationship between human rights and trade marks. Chapter 2 assessed the way that different models conceptualising the relationship between human rights and intellectual property applied to trade marks. Prescriptive models that proposed different approaches to harmonising the relationship were preferable to models that emphasised either conflict or coexistence. Three different types of prescriptive models developed by Yu, Geiger, and Helfer and Austin can be useful in understanding the human rights implications of trade marks, strengthening harmonisation between the two fields and recognising considerations of both justice and order.[21]

3.1 The Value of Prescriptive Models

Analysing concrete domestic examples of trade mark protection shows that prescriptive models can have different value, depending on the local conditions. Geiger's incorporation of the right to benefit from science and culture into constitutional human rights protection may not be directly applicable to a state like Australia that lacks analogous constitutional protection for human rights.[22] However, a growing international recognition of the right to benefit from science and culture in other jurisdictions, which do incorporate this protection, may be indirectly relevant if it influences parliamentary scrutiny in countries that use this, like Australia. Similarly, principles from Yu's models can influence policy analysis, civil society activity, and scrutiny of legislation and international agreements that engage human rights protection for creators of scientific, literary and artistic productions.[23] Yu interprets the right to prop-

---

21 Murumba (n 15) 140–141.

22 See Christophe Geiger, 'Implementing Intellectual Property Provisions in Human Rights Instruments: Towards a New Social Contract for the Protection of Intangibles' in Christophe Geiger (ed), *Research Handbook on Human Rights and Intellectual Property* (Edward Elgar Publishing, 2015) 661.

23 Peter K Yu, 'The Anatomy of the Human Rights Framework for Intellectual Property' (2016) 69(1) *SMU Law Review* 37.

erty from the perspective of the public as well as the individual, arguing that it can support the development of a creative commons.[24] Helfer and Austin provide a model that can harmonise the relationship in diverse local conditions but embed protection for the individual right to property that may not be recognised in all jurisdictions.[25]

Geiger and Yu's approaches help to define what protections human rights might offer in relation to trade marks. Geiger's suggestion of three alternative approaches might also be adapted to recognise domestic differences. Yu identifies that trade marks can play a functional role in relation to the protection of scientific productions. Yu's model might be expanded to recognise protection for some trade marks that qualify as literary and artistic productions in order to encourage the production of culturally significant trade marks. Implementing one of Geiger's approaches into domestic and regional constitutions, and using Yu's model of analysis to understand what intellectual property protections might qualify for human rights protection, can support policymakers to integrate human rights protection into intellectual property regimes. Practice and recognition of a human rights-based approach to intellectual property protection could influence the inclusion of human rights considerations in the interpretation of *TRIPS* in the WTO.[26] The plain packaging case study supports the relevance of human rights considerations to WTO disputes. The anti-counterfeiting legislation case study also finds that if trade marks do not function as accurate badges of origin, this can negatively impact rights to health and life.

Not all of the jurisdictions studied in this book provide comprehensive constitutional protection for human rights. This limits the value of Geiger's approach in those jurisdictions as it relies on the mature system of regional human rights protection. Nonetheless, constitutional recognition in Europe and other jurisdictions that provide comprehensive protection for human rights may generate decisions that are beneficial tools to aid understanding of the nature of relevant human rights[27] and support domestic advocacy in states where human rights concerns are identified. The Kenyan government failed to change anti-counterfeiting legislation to respond to the finding of the Kenyan Supreme

---

[24] Ibid 94.

[25] See Helfer and Austin (n 5) 513–516.

[26] See Christophe Geiger and Luc Desaunettes-Barbero, 'The Revitalisation of the Object and Purpose of the TRIPS Agreement: The Plain Packaging Reports and the Awakening of the TRIPS Flexibility Clauses' in Jonathan Griffiths and Tuomas Mylly (eds), *Global Intellectual Property Protection and New Constitutionalism: Hedging Exclusive Rights* (Oxford University Press, 2021) 267.

[27] Ernst-Ulrich Petersmann, 'Human Rights and International Economic Law' (2012) 4(2) *Trade Law and Development* 283, 297. See also Geiger (n 22).

Court that the operation of the *Anti-Counterfeit Act 2008* could restrict access to generic medicines and engage serious concerns for human rights to life and health.[28] This is an important reminder that monitoring must be accompanied by accountability. However, judicial recognition that trade mark protection engages human rights concerns is important. Adopting Geiger's proposal to integrate expanded protection for *ICESCR* Article 15 in European human rights frameworks provides opportunities for further interpretation of how trade mark rights can be balanced with human rights concerns. Yu's analytical approach also provides useful interpretive assistance for actors advocating a human rights culture for intellectual property.

Helfer and Austin focus on protecting human rights ends but argue that restrictions on intellectual property should be focused to preserve its social benefits. This approach can address the following welfare preservation considerations:[29]

1. Is intellectual property actually restrictive of the relevant human right or freedom or are other factors, such as structural limitations, causing the restriction?
2. What is the positive impact of intellectual property?
3. What is the negative impact of intellectual property?
4. What is the relative causal contribution of intellectual property in comparison with other factors?
5. What legal and policy measures can facilitate human rights outcomes?

These welfare preservation considerations can be part of an approach that recognises the social welfare benefits of intellectual property. However, the scope of protection Helfer and Austin offer for economic, social and cultural rights is limited, as is the protection available in Geiger's fundamental rights approach. This important limitation needs to be addressed.

3.2 The Importance of Addressing Economic, Social and Cultural Rights in an Integrated Human Rights Assessment

Chapter 2 identified limits of the prescriptive models analysed in their application to trade marks and recognition that human rights protection must be holistic and integrated. This requires recognition of civil and political rights as well as economic, social and cultural rights. Okediji identifies important

[28] Wilfrid O Lusi, 'Effective Anti-Counterfeiting Legal System: A Key Enabler for Growth of Kenya's Pharmaceutical Industry' (Doctoral dissertation, Strathmore University, 2020) 52.

[29] Helfer and Austin (n 5) 519–520.

concerns about the current function of human rights frameworks for intellectual property.[30] She argues that the most serious problem is the failure to effectively recognise economic, social and cultural rights in the intellectual property and human rights discourse.[31] The extent to which Helfer and Austin permit modification of intellectual property rights to protect economic, social and cultural rights is also important for recognising that different local conditions will influence progressive realisation of rights. In states with limited resources, the acceptable standard of economic, social and cultural rights may need to be adjusted to include the expectation that other states should provide aid for realisation of these rights. If their model doesn't support progressive realisation and changes to intellectual property rights that are consistent with progressive realisation, it may be vulnerable to the limitations of human rights frameworks for intellectual property that Okediji identifies: she argues that they are generally only useful in developed states and fail to effect distributive justice.[32] The HRATM framework and the way that it supports the proposal for an FCGP in Chapter 6 recognises the importance of balancing economic, social and cultural rights concerns posed by trade marks, as well as civil and political rights. It also draws attention to rights-based principles, such as international assistance and cooperation, that can strengthen the realisation of economic, social and cultural rights.

A range of human rights interests has been identified in each case study, and these interests need to be balanced against each other while considering the most effective way to preserve the social welfare benefits of intellectual property when modification is necessary to realise human rights. Each model supports recognition of a level of human rights primacy. This level depends on the relevant threshold for human rights protection. In the models of Helfer and Austin, and Yu, civil and political rights are subject to little restriction. In relation to economic, social and cultural rights, Yu relevantly considers both a core minimum approach to protection and a progressive realisation model. He suggests, but does not prescribe, how the approaches can be used together. The relevance of economic, social and cultural rights to each of the cases identified in this book suggests that progressive realisation is the appropriate threshold to be considered in assessing human rights protection. This corresponds to recognising that a positive approach to fostering and promoting human rights forms part of states' binding human rights obligations. These thresholds should also be recognised in the constitutional regimes that Geiger's model addresses.[33]

---

[30] Okediji (n 1) 3.

[31] Ibid 4.

[32] See ibid 37–38.

[33] Ducoloumbier questions this in Europe: Peggy Ducoulombier, 'Interaction between Human Rights: Are All Human Rights Equal?' in Christophe Geiger (ed),

The HRATM framework focuses attention on economic, social and cultural rights by conducting integrated rights analysis and recognising principles of progressive realisation, maximum available resources and international cooperation and assistance in that analysis. These principles also underpin the FCGP proposal. This translates standards from assessment tools into unifying mechanisms for strengthening trade mark rights, consistent with human rights.

3.3 Principles Underlying a Human Rights Culture for Trade Marks

The foundations of a human rights culture for trade marks developed in this book are designed to be immediately useful for policymakers to understand human rights concerns associated with trade marks. The HRATM framework and the other prescriptive models support this approach. Chapter 6 explores a more transformative approach which places less emphasis on existing intellectual property structures in addressing human rights concerns related to trade mark enforcement. It shows how transformation might occur, but this comprehensive approach will not always be necessary to support a human rights culture for trade marks. Careful assessment and implementation of rights-based principles are critical tools for policymakers in a human rights culture. Together the HRATM framework and the prescriptive models support the following principles underlying a human rights culture for trade marks.

Trade marks can function to support realisation of *ICESCR* Article 15(1)(c), but other human rights considerations will limit this. It is important to balance other human rights against this protection: any moral interests that can be claimed by authors of artistic productions underlying tobacco trade marks are likely to be outweighed by the human right to health interests of regulating tobacco consumption. The other rights integrated into Article 15 protection are relevant to trade mark protection. The contrary marks case study identified examples where Article 15(1)(c) protection was likely to be outweighed by rights to participation in culture in Article 15(1)(a). The anti-counterfeiting case study identified the way that trade marks can function to increase access to applications of the benefits of scientific progress in Article 15(1)(b).

Trade marks provide social welfare benefits. They are not of the same status as human rights, but normative justifications for protection of trade marks can align with human rights protection. The contrary marks case study showed how trade mark protection can justify some limits of freedom of expression, consistent with structured exceptions provided in international human rights

---

Research Handbook on Human Rights and Intellectual Property (Edward Elgar Publishing, 2015) 39.

law.[34] Where broad protection for trade marks does not further these core functions, it is more likely to align with order rather than justice.

Close human rights scrutiny of broad trade mark protection is important to protect human rights. Yet, where possible, social welfare benefits should be recognised.[35] Where trade marks function as a reliable badge of origin, they provide information that can empower individuals to protect themselves from third party threats to health and life posed by substandard and falsified goods. However, individuals rely on multilateral standards and institutions associated with trade mark enforcement. States are responsible for ensuring that these institutions operate to support realisation of economic, social and cultural rights.[36] They are also responsible for international cooperation to ensure realisation of all human rights.[37]

In circumstances of conflict between competing rights, it is important to protect economic, social and cultural rights as well as civil and political rights. Protecting economic, social and cultural rights associated with trade marks and other forms of intellectual property can be a complex exercise which requires ongoing assessment, reflecting the expectation that economic, social and cultural rights will be progressively realised.

4 TRANSFORMING TRADE AND INVESTMENT AGREEMENTS

Several features of the HRATM framework and the proposal for an FCGP in Chapter 6 are useful for developing a new approach to trade and investment agreements that recognises human rights protection and embeds the rights-based principles that are prioritised in the proposed analytical framework. The rights-based principles are relevant to human rights concerns associated with a broad scope of intellectual property protection. The framework is useful for broader assessments of the relationship between intellectual property and human rights because it focuses attention on the protection of economic, social and cultural rights by including considerations of progressive realisation and international cooperation and assistance.[38] The other analytical approaches that have been applied in this book can also guide awareness of issues that are relevant to protection of copyright, patents or other forms of

[34] *International Covenant on Civil and Political Rights*, opened for signature 16 December 1966, 999 UNTS 171 (entered into force 23 March 1976) art 19 ('*ICCPR*').

[35] Helfer and Austin (n 5) 520.

[36] *General Comment 3* (n 3) [13]–[14].

[37] *Charter of the United Nations* arts 55, 56.

[38] See Paul Hunt, 'Interpreting the International Right to Health in a Human Rights-Based Approach to Health' (2016) 18(2) *Health and Human Rights* 109.

intellectual property but have not been the focus of this book. For example, patent protection engages the right to access applications of the benefits of scientific progress, and Geiger's approach is useful for ensuring that domestic and regional constitutions recognise this right when they consider mechanisms in trade and investment agreements that provide further protection for patent holders.[39]

Any proposal for further protection of intellectual property within a trade and investment agreement needs to be closely and transparently scrutinised. There are numerous examples in this book where the exercise of broad trade mark protection poses human rights concerns, particularly in the contrary marks and plain packaging case studies. Transparency is particularly important for human rights concerns that engage the rights of vulnerable peoples, as they often depend on civil society organisations to advocate on their behalf.[40] Transparency in the process of agreement is also important to preserve the utility of trade and investment agreements so that, unlike *ACTA*, they enter into force.[41]

Considering human rights in both the design and implementation of trade and investment agreements is critical, but this is only useful if there is political will to engage with that process and states commit to implementing the changes suggested by impact assessments or to revising agreements and seeking further assessment if alternatives are preferred. The sustainability impact assessments undertaken by the European Union have included human rights assessments in combination with economic, social and environmental assessments since 2012.[42] This provides important guidance for developing assessments in this context, but it is unclear how much influence this process has on negotiations.[43]

Recognising the protection and realisation of human rights in the objectives of the agreement is also important. If monitoring detects negative human rights outcomes resulting from the implementation of intellectual property protection provisions in the agreement, an objective of protection and reali-

---

[39] See Christophe Geiger, 'Building an Ethical Framework for Intellectual Property in the EU: Time to Revise the Charter of Fundamental Rights' in Gustavo Ghidini (ed), *Reforming Intellectual Property* (Edward Elgar Publishing, 2022) 77.

[40] For example, Beth Goldblatt, 'Claiming Women's Social and Economic Rights in Australia' (2017) 23(2) *Australian Journal of Human Rights* 261, 269.

[41] Susan K Sell, 'The Dynamics of International IP Policymaking' in Daniel J Gervais (ed), *Intellectual Property, Trade and Development: Strategies to Optimize Economic Development in a TRIPS-Plus Era* (Oxford University Press, 2nd ed, 2014) 76.

[42] European Commission – Trade, *Handbook for Trade Sustainability Impact Assessment* (Publications Office of the European Union, 2nd ed, April 2016) 4–5 http://trade.ec.europa.eu/doclib/docs/2016/april/tradoc_154464.PDF.

[43] Ibid 21–22.

sation of human rights can support arguments that the protection should be implemented differently. Proactive recognition of specific human rights is also valuable for regulation of trade and investment agreements. The wording of the European Trade Mark Directive discussed in Chapter 4 recognised the relevance of freedom of expression to trade marks and provides a useful example: '[f]urthermore, this Directive should be applied in a way that ensures full respect for fundamental rights and freedoms, and in particular the freedom of expression.'[44] Recognising these rights increases the likelihood of accountability following monitoring through human rights impact assessments and other means. The European Union incorporates an essential elements clause into bilateral trade and investment agreements that requires parties to protect human rights and democracy.[45] This is important, but the nature of economic, social and cultural rights may mean that realisation of human rights requires more explicit integration of human rights accountability mechanisms into trade and investment agreements. This is particularly relevant for areas such as trade marks where the human rights implications are not widely recognised. For example, international cooperation and assistance obligations may operate differently depending on local conditions in relevant trade partners. Sharing of specific technology or know-how that supports trade mark enforcement procedures and mechanisms may be relevant to specific countries and be specifically included in technical assistance and cooperation provisions of a trade and investment agreement. More specific human rights assessments that address these issues are an important part of agreement design and ongoing monitoring of the implementation of these agreements.

Attention also needs to be given to mechanisms that provide additional protection for intellectual property owners generally, such as investor–state dispute mechanisms. The Uruguay comparison in the plain packaging case study recognised that investor–state dispute mechanisms could protect investors against arbitrary expropriation of property and require states to ensure that the operation of judicial processes does not result in a denial of justice, which is relevant to the protection of civil rights.[46] However, the use of these mechanisms can also be problematic. The interlocutory judgment in the Philip Morris–Australia dispute recognised the complainant's bad faith in bringing

---

[44] *Directive (EU) 2015/2436 of the European Parliament and of the Council of 16 December 2015 to Approximate the Laws of the Member States Relating to Trade Marks* [2015] OJ L 336/1.

[45] Jia-Jhen Liao, 'Strengthening Global Governance for Human Rights through New-Era FTAs: Beyond Trade-Related Aspects?' (2020) 15 *Asian Journal of WTO & International Health Law & Policy* 653, 664.

[46] See *Philip Morris Brands Sàrl v Uruguay* (Award, ICSID Arbitral Tribunal, Case No ARB/10/7, 8 July 2016) [499]–[500].

the action, but even defending the interlocutory proceedings was an expensive exercise for Australia.[47] Problematically, the use of investor–state disputes by tobacco companies to contest plain packaging legislation in Australia and Uruguay was part of a systematic approach to disrupting tobacco control.[48]

As United Nations Independent Expert on the Promotion of a Democratic and Equitable International Order, Alfred-Maurice de Zayas listed numerous cases of disputes impacting negatively on human rights, including the *Philip Morris–Australia* investor–state arbitration.[49] He has recommended the abolition of the investor–state dispute settlement system and its replacement with potential alternatives, including an international investment court, state-to-state settlement before the International Court of Justice, and adjudication by domestic courts bound by the protections for civil rights contained in the *International Covenant on Civil and Political Rights*.[50] These recommendations are aimed at enhancing uniformity and reducing the ability of investor businesses to use these actions, or the threat of them, to directly change policies made by democratic governments in accordance with their international obligations.[51] This is an important objective, but other approaches are useful.

To avoid misuse of protections for intellectual property owners found in trade and investment agreements, exceptions mechanisms should be closely scrutinised. The *Comprehensive and Progressive Agreement for Trans-Pacific Partnership* ('CPTPP') includes mechanisms for addressing frivolous claims, waiver of rights to bring other legal proceedings, shorter limitation periods for claims, requirements for greater transparency and a code of conduct for arbitrators.[52] A provision in the *China–Australia Free Trade Agreement* that permits state-to-state negotiations once investor–state disputes are initiated

---

[47] *Philip Morris Asia Ltd v Australia* (Final Award regarding Costs, Permanent Court of Arbitration, Case No 2012-12, 8 March 2017).

[48] See Benjamin Hawkins, Chris Holden and Sophie Mackinder, 'A Multi-Level, Multi-Jurisdictional Strategy: Transnational Tobacco Companies' Attempts to Obstruct Tobacco Packaging Restrictions' (2019) 14(4) *Global Public Health* 570.

[49] Alfred-Maurice de Zayas, *Report of the Independent Expert on the Promotion of a Democratic and Equitable International Order*, UN GAOR, 70th sess, Agenda Item 73(b), UN Doc A/70/285 (5 August 2015) [27]–[37] ('*Report of the Independent Expert on the Promotion of a Democratic and Equitable International Order* (2015)').

[50] Ibid [55]. But see later concerns about an investment court: Alfred-Maurice de Zayas, *Report of the Independent Expert on the Promotion of a Democratic and Equitable International Order*, UN GAOR, 33rd sess, Agenda Item 3, UN Doc A/HRC/33/40 (12 July 2016) [2], [43]–[54].

[51] de Zayas, *Report of the Independent Expert on the Promotion of a Democratic and Equitable International Order* (2015) (n 49) [23]–[24].

[52] See *Comprehensive and Progressive Agreement for Trans-Pacific Partnership*, signed 8 March 2018, [2018] ATS 23 (entered into force 30 December 2018) ch 9 ('*CPTPP*').

may permit greater protection for state policies that protect human rights.[53] However, even these approaches may not be sufficient safeguards, so ongoing monitoring of the use of investor–state dispute mechanisms remains important.

Human rights problems for trade and investment agreements are not limited to new agreements. There are already over 3,000 investment agreements in operation worldwide.[54] States need to consider how to address potential claims in those agreements. Chapter 3 argued that explicit consideration of human rights obligations in the development of intellectual property policies limiting owner rights was important. Explicit consideration could strengthen defences when limitations of intellectual property rights need to be justified in the development of intellectual property policies that can engage investor–state disputes or the WTO Dispute Settlement Mechanisms. *Amicus curiae* briefs that support human rights justifications are also useful.[55]

Agreements can be renegotiated: the agreement between Australia and Hong Kong that was used by Philip Morris to bring its complaint against plain packaging has been renegotiated.[56] The new expropriation clause does not apply:

> to the issuance of compulsory licences granted in relation to intellectual property rights in accordance with the TRIPS Agreement, or to the revocation, limitation or creation of intellectual property rights, to the extent that the issuance, revocation, limitation or creation is consistent with Chapter 14 (Intellectual Property) of the FTA and the TRIPS Agreement.

Given the potential explored in the plain packaging case study for the objectives and principles provisions of *TRIPS* to be useful mechanisms for states who wish to rely on human rights obligations, direct reference to those *TRIPS* provisions in intellectual property sections of trade agreements may also be useful to promote a human rights culture.[57] However, the plain packaging case study also finds that the current approach to both arguing and interpreting these provisions does not focus on human rights, so important human rights

---

[53] *Free Trade Agreement between the Government of Australia and the Government of the People's Republic of China*, signed 17 June 2015, [2015] ATS 15 (entered into force 20 December 2015).

[54] Cynthia Ho, 'A Collision Course Between TRIPS Flexibilities and Investor-State Proceedings' (2016) 6 *UC Irvine Law Review* 395, 407.

[55] See *Philip Morris Brands Sàrl v Uruguay* (Award, ICSID Arbitral Tribunal, Case No ARB/10/7, 8 July 2016) [304].

[56] *Investment Agreement between the Government of Australia and the Government of the Hong Kong Special Administrative Region of the People's Republic of China*, signed 26 March 2019, [2020] ATS 5 (entered into force 17 January 2020) art 10.5. See also *CPTPP* Article 9.8(5).

[57] See *CPTPP* (n 52) ch 18.

obligations may continue to be excluded, even if other trade agreements were interpreted consistently with *TRIPS*.

These recommendations can be another valuable foundation for a human rights culture for trade marks. However, human rights protection is dynamic. Useful tools and mechanisms for building a human rights culture must be flexible, drawing on the principles identified in this chapter and throughout the book

5 CONCLUSION

A human rights culture for trade marks fosters and protects human rights. The case studies in this book highlight the complex relationship between trade marks and human rights. The human rights implications of each case study are significant. They support greater emphasis on understanding the human rights implications of trade marks. The case studies also show that there are further, interrelated human rights that human rights-based analysis of trade marks should consider. The HRATM framework used in the case studies provides a mechanism for human rights analysis of intellectual property mechanisms that supports the progressive realisation of economic, social and cultural rights and encourages international cooperation and assistance to achieve this. Importantly, this HRATM framework should be only one component of a broader human rights culture influencing the protection of trade marks. The framework was adapted to propose the FCGP, a new international framework that supports the social welfare benefits of trade mark protection by using technology to securely assure provenance. This chapter also adapted the principles to encourage stronger human rights protection in trade and investment agreements that protect intellectual property rights. In many circumstances, additional questions that emphasise the benefits of intellectual property should supplement the analytical approach. Recognition of the right to benefit from science and culture in domestic and regional frameworks is strengthened by approaches that guide understanding of what those rights protect and how they should be balanced against other rights. Domestic application of these mechanisms should also influence international progress towards recognising the relevance of human rights in existing international intellectual property structures. A culture of human rights to support trade marks will need to be adapted to recognise local differences. A flourishing human rights culture for trade marks and intellectual property is a longer-term goal, but all steps, no matter how small, are important in progressing towards this outcome.

Index